Creative Homeowner Press

62-72 Myrtle Avenue
Passaic, NJ 07055
800 631-7795

CUSTOMER INFORMATION SERVICE

(PLEASE PRINT)

Name _____

Address _____ Apt. # _____

City _____ State _____ Zip _____

Book(s) Purchased: _____

I bought the book(s) for:
☐ General Repairs   ☐ Minor Remodeling   ☐ Major Renovations

My interests are:
☐ Woodworking   ☐ Plumbing   ☐ Other _____
☐ Project Building   ☐ Electrical   _____

I bought the book(s) in: ☐ Home Center   ☐ Book Store
☐ Discount Store   ☐ Direct Mail   ☐ Catalog Showroom

What specific tools have you purchased to complete your projects?

_____

☐ *PLEASE SEND ME YOUR CATALOG.*   *Thank You*

WALKS, WALLS AND FENCES

Plus Projects for Steps, Ramps, Gates, Retaining Walls, Privacy Screens

JAMES E. RUSSEL

CREATIVE HOMEOWNER PRESS™ A DIVISION OF FEDERAL MARKETING CORPORATION, PASSAIC, NJ

Manufactured in United States of America

Current Printing (last digit)
10 9 8 7 6 5 4 3 2

Editorial Director: Shirley M. Horowitz
Editor: Marilyn Auer
Art Director: Léone Lewensohn
Designer: Paul Sochacki
Additional drawings: Norman Nuding

Cover photograph: Wayne Eslyn, Lied's Nursery

ISBN: 0–932944–36–1 (paperback)
ISBN: 0–932944–35–3 (hardcover)
LC. 81–65752

CREATIVE HOMEOWNER PRESS™
BOOK SERIES
A DIVISION OF FEDERAL
MARKETING CORPORATION
62–72 MYRTLE AVENUE, PASSAIC, NJ 07055

FOREWORD

When you buy or build a home, you are also buying the space around it—a yard. Whether lots are large or small, most homeowners never get beyond thinking of landscaping as a few bushes and a tree "to balance the house".

Walks, Walls and Fences urges the reader and his family to consider the space available in the yard as an extension of the space in the home: an attractive area that will provide the family with the maximum use of and pleasure from the home.

The reader will find how to plan, create and finish a yard that will be appropriate to the home and terrain, as well as a special and personal family project.

PROJECTS LIST

CONTENTS

1 PLANNING THE TOTAL SETTING

The best plans for landscaping are created keeping the house interior in mind. Your landscape should be considered an extension of the interior of your house and in mild climates, the reverse may be a more appropriate thought. Always consider the relationship between the inside and outside spaces of your home. It does not take much planning to realize that you do not want a high-activity play area for children beneath a study window. Nor would you place a swimming pool so that users would have to enter the house through a living or formal area with expensive carpets. Going a step beyond such basic considerations, you will soon understand the potential relationship between interior

and exterior materials. Some materials—slate, brick, and tile, for example—can be extended from the interior to the exterior to become walks, terraces, steps and ramps.

An odd and pleasant thing happens when you use materials in this manner; you notice an increased sense of space. Perhaps this is because so many houses have become little more than a group of small cubicles. When this is the case, you have only a limited sense of space beyond the cubicle you find yourself in. When design and function of interior spaces relate clearly to each other and to the outside spaces, and when this relationship is reinforced with the same or similar materials, all the spaces become tied

together. Wherever a person is, there is a sense of the whole, a kind of continuous space with subtle distinctions of usage. Thus, an enlarged sense of space and improved quality of the space is achieved.

An improved view may very well give an entirely new focus to your rooms. You may change your furniture arrangement or interior color scheme to be more compatible with the view. Your window treatment may very well show off rather than mask the outside area.

GETTING STARTED
The planning process is not something reserved for landscape architects. Planning is a way of thinking and working that

Low brick retaining walls disguise and support differences in grade, as well as provide decorative borders for concrete walks.

keeps you from wasting valuable time and making expensive mistakes. Changes are inevitable as families change; if you do not plan, you will end up "managing by crisis". Planning simply helps you get the most out of your time.

However, it seems to be a human trait to assume that an outdoor project can be done with less care than an indoor one. Many amateurs consider planning detrimental to the fun of doing a job. Some professional landscaping people also consider planning a "bother". Perhaps this is because the physical work appears to be the "real work" of outdoor projects. The result of this misconception may be garden walls and fences that bulge and lean or cut a yard in two, walks filled with cracks, all leading to an eventual reluctance to spend time around the completed projects.

Your exterior work, even if you have had little or no landscaping or building experience, need not become a white elephant. You can make any garden project pleasant to look at and to use. You can do this because many garden projects are very simple, if you think your way through them beforehand, break the work into manageable proportions in terms of available work time and labor, and get professional advice on problems that require special expertise.

You do not have to be a landscape architect to plan your lawn, but you do have to have a plan. Study the sun, wind, and drainage patterns of your lawn. Sun and drainage have a lot to do with the type of soil you have and what plants will prosper on it. Sun and wind influence the positioning of fences, walls, and activity areas.

Studying Your Yard

First, draw a plan of your lot as it exists. The plan should show trees, shrubs, and any landmarks. You may have a set of plans your builder or architect left behind. If not, check the legal documents you received when you bought the house—you may find a survey that locates your house on the lot. This survey will save measuring time and will confirm your property lines. If you do not have a survey, and you are planning work at or near the property lines or the city setback line, a survey is not a luxury; it is a necessity. Most surveyors have done suburban work for so long that they have become very fast and competitive. It should not cost a great deal to have a survey made of a typical suburban lot. If you do hire a surveyor, you might want him to stake out your project area for you while he is there.

Drawing a plan of the existing lot. From the survey or from measuring your lot, draw the existing plan at a scale of at least ¼ inch equals 1 foot. This is a convenient scale for visualizing improvements. To draw your plan you should have a drafting board, a T-square, a triangle, vellum or other good quality tracing paper, and an architect's scale.

Place a sheet of vellum or tracing paper in the center of the drawing board. Position the long edge of the sheet parallel to the bottom of the board and the long piece of the T-square. Either a vinyl or paper protective mat should already be attached to the board. Using a standard twelve inch rule, measure the width of the paper (top to bottom) and put a light mark at the center. Draw a very light horizontal line through the mark, from border to border, on the sheet using the T-square and a 2H pencil. Hold the pencil against the T-square so the tip of the lead is pointed slightly away from the edge. Draw a barely visible line using minimum pressure. It should be just dark enough to be seen but not dark enough to be part of the drawing.

Next measure the sheet from side to side and draw a very light vertical line through the center. Lay the triangle along the upper edge of the T-square and draw the pencil down from the top toward the T-square. Since the triangle is not as wide as the paper, drop the T-square once or twice to make the line continuous from top to bottom.

Compute the maximum length and width of your lot from the survey. Since the plan is usually drawn with the front of the house toward the bottom of the sheet, start with the dimension that represents the maximum size of the lot from side to side. If your lot is considerably deeper than it is wide, you may want to orient the plan so that the front of the house faces toward the right side of the sheet instead of the bottom. If so, use the maximum dimension from front to back to begin your drawing.

Assuming that your lot is deeper than it is wide, measure from the center of the sheet, where the lines you have drawn intersect, half the length of your lot along the horizontal line in both directions using the ¼ scale (all measurements on the plan will be done with the ¼ scale). If the dimension is in even feet, place the zero on the architect's scale at the center and place a light mark at the proper number of feet (half the total) on the horizontal line. Repeat in the opposite direction. If the dimension is in feet and inches, count back from the zero the distance of the number of inches and place the scale so that this inch line is on the center. Then

Landscaping walls of treated timbers or cross ties can be covered with any of a variety of materials, such as this weather-resistant, scalloped shingle.

place a light mark on the horizontal line at the foot mark. Repeat in the opposite direction. Using the triangle, draw a very light vertical line through each mark. Now, mark the width of the lot in the same manner along the vertical line. Draw very light horizontal lines through each mark using the T-square. The resulting box represents the maximum limits of your lot. If your lot is a rectangle, then the box will represent the actual outside boundries.

If you do not have the time or equipment to do the drawings yourself, everything except finding the property lines is an easy job for a junior draftsman in an architectural office or for a drafting student. Check with your area extension service or technical school placement office to find a capable drafting student who can work from your sketches. If you have considerable landscaping to do, include the floor plan of your house on the lot plan, too. The plan you draw will serve you in time to come: when you improve kitchens or bathrooms; when you expand or add rooms. The drawn plan is a tool of the planning process.

Even if most of your landscaping has been done and you are just making a few changes or additions, it would still be wise to sketch out your plan to scale on graph paper. The art supply centers and blueprint shops have graph paper in a variety of scales. The ¼ inch equals 1 foot is the smallest you would want to use.

When you have drawn your house and landscape as it exists, have enough blueprints made (several dollars each at the blueprint shop) so that everyone in the household can have one. People of all ages are more easily involved and take projects more seriously when they each have their own prints.

CHARACTERISTICS OF YOUR PROPERTY

Each area of the country is different from other areas. In some cases every few feet ground may contain major differences in the soil surface and substrata that may affect the planning and execution of even simple landscaping.

Drainage Patterns and Soil Qualities

Drainage patterns are relatively simple to determine—simply watch what happens

A stepped brick retaining wall adjusts to the increasing grade. Retaining walls of this height often should be designed by an engineer.

A fence made of lengths of rustic-looking preservative-treated timbers can visually set off and physically separate a gardening plot.

to water during a heavy rain. If you live in a subdivision, you are unlikely to have any real drainage problem. Developers are required to shape and grade the lots for good drainage, but what is "good drainage"? Generally, good drainage means that your lot will shed water after a heavy rain and not retain puddles in low spots.

Variables. The type of soil, as well as the shape of your lawn surface, influences how your lawn drains. Sandy soils drain well; they soak up water well. The water table (the natural water level in the soil)

also influences drainage. Therefore, when you think of drainage, beyond the assurance your lot does not stand in water, you have to consider how your project—your walk, wall, fence, plants—will affect the drainage pattern. Then ask yourself what kind of drainage the project requires. For example, some groundcovers require good drainage and rich soils to prosper; others require almost the opposite. Clays (fine-grained soils) are difficult to handle in areas of extreme cold; hard freezes tend to cause destructive frost heave in water-laden clay.

Walks can be laid on a bed of gravel (a "good" drainage material) separating them from the fine-grained soils that cause heave. Walls and fences with deeper foundations can sometimes be drained by similar methods. Laying the foundation footings on gravel and bringing the gravel up around the foundation wall will drain off the water and help prevent frost heave. Another, sometimes necessary, and much more expensive method is to remove the fine-grained soil down to where your foundation footings will be and replace it with sandy soil or gravel. In areas where you think the problem is this severe, you should consult your building department or a civil engineer.

Soil types. Since the type of soil in your yard is so important to drainage and landscaping, one of the first things you should do before planning is to find out what type of soil you have. To do this you need a soil analysis. Inexpensive soil test kits are available at most garden centers. The centers can show you how to do the test, or for a small service fee, they may do it for you. You also can check with your local agricultural extension agency; they sometimes do the testing free. No matter how it is done, take as many samples as reasonable from areas all over the lawn. The more samples you take, the more you will know about the soil and about what can be built on it or planted in it.

Solutions: catch basins, swales, walls and contouring. If you live in a subdivision, you probably do not have any particular drainage problems. However, if you do, there are many ways to deal with them. Low areas that frequently stand in water can be drained by building a catch basin at the lowest point. Catch basins appear to be miniature "man holes", like those in city streets. A drain line at the bottom of the basin takes the water to a disposal point, usually a storm drain. Care must be taken in locating catch basins or they would flood the house if there were a stoppage or a backup in the drain line. Catch basins are expensive projects and should be planned by a civil engineer or landscape architect.

Another method of handling problem drainage areas is to create a swale. A swale can be visualized as a type of shallow ditch. Swales are cheap and frequently used in residential construction. If the sides are not too steep, swales

Brick combines easily with insets of metal fencing to give an open line of sight while still providing needed boundaries and privacy.

Catch basins look like tiny manholes. They must be carefully planned and should be designed by a civil engineer or landscape architect.

can usually be grass-covered or planted with some other ground cover. If the swale is steep enough so that water running over it would wear or tear free the grass or other ground covers, you may line it with any type of heavy stone or masonry rubble. Stones 4 to 6 inches in diameter should withstand runoff that is just short of a river. If the swale is out of sight, you can use broken concrete or ceramic tiles. You may have seen swales with concrete surfaces along expressways where the slope of the sides of the expressway rises steeply. Concrete swales are not handsome to look at but they last a long time. They are laid much like concrete walks.

Another way of dealing with problem drainage areas is with retaining walls. Retaining wall construction varies widely in expense and difficulty. These walls are discussed in detail in Chapter 9. Generally, what retaining walls do is separate an area into terraces that can be drained more easily than one large area. A series of retaining walls will control both drainage and erosion problems.

In your plan you must consider surface drainage first and shape your lawn so that water drains away from the house and other structures and does not stand in pools and puddles. You must keep the soil and your overall plans in mind when you ultimately devise your grading plan. It will be a process of compromise. For example, if you have your mind set on a certain kind of plant or groundcover that requires loose, sandy soil, you cannot expect to keep that soil in place on a steep slope; therefore, you would need to consider a way to level the slope enough to have the plants you want. Sometimes the expense will be greater than your budget allows. Problems like this are what make the services of a landscape architect sometimes cheaper (because of time, materials and labor saved) than planning it all yourself. Always remember that nurseries and landscape contractors who do plant installation will put their ''products'' where you tell them to, and people often pressure contractors to do poor planting. Remember that suppliers usually do not guarantee a tree or shrub beyond a year. If it dies after that—it is yours.

Plants and Planting

When you get your soil analysis, you will

Steep swales need to be lined with large, heavy pieces of stone or masonry rubble in order to withstand fast water runoff and creeping erosion.

Tall stone retaining walls must be constructed to withstand high pressure loads. This is not a job for the homeowner; consult a professional for the design.

be able to discuss your ideas more intelligently with a landscape architect, landscape contractor or nursery, or garden center. Every plant needs a certain combination of shade, climate, and soil conditions for best growth and survival. You need to consider the activities of each area in your lawn before you select plants.

Ground cover. Grass is just ground cover. For heavy foot traffic, sports, outdoor cooking, and so forth, it is the best live ground cover you can buy.

If you do not spend much time using the lawn, consider other ground covers that require much less attention but have as much ornamental value as grass. Any garden center should sell ground covers suitable for your area. Sandwort, for instance (Arenaria and Minuartia) will prosper in many areas of the country. Sandwort grows to a height of about 2 inches, then stops. Therefore you do not have to mow it. It prospers in either full sun or light shade. It requires good drainage and sandy, moist, and slightly acid soil. It looks a little like grass, but in the spring it produces a tiny, white bloom. It is always green, but in very cold areas it will turn a kind of silver.

Juniper will withstand some foot traffic, but not as much as Sandwort. There are many varieties of Juniper; they grow from about 4 inches to 2 feet and may be yellow-green, bright green, greenish blue, or silver-blue. There are even more

For a low-cost, easy-to-build walk, lay concrete blocks in bark or other soft materials. The loose materials also make a good base for many types of ground cover.

Brick is a traditional favorite for planter boxes because it is easy to use and it enhances nearly any shrub or flower planting.

colors and sizes in the many varieties of the species. Weather will influence the color somewhat. Juniper is an excellent low-maintenance ground cover for slopes, borders, and in areas where the soil is poor—Juniper prospers in poor soil. It will grow in a variety of light conditions.

Landscaping is a matching game; you must match the elements of lawn form (graded slopes, terraces, retaining walls and/or berms) with what nature requires plants to have. It is a good, challenging game to learn.

Trees. Your lot, in town or country, will probably have some trees or other plants that you will want to move. Shrubs are not much of a problem. You need to check their soil and light requirements and be sure the shrubs have the same when the plants are moved. A garden center may do the actual moving for you, for a service fee. Moving trees is another and more difficult matter. The best rule is: do not move trees. Almost any plan, any material, any activity, can be worked around a tree without moving it. Trees are very sensitive to being moved. They are even sensitive to any changes in drainage; they can be killed by removing soil close by, or by adding soil.

If you absolutely must move a tree, or alter the earth around it in any way, consult a landscape architect. He will advise you about the particular tree and your plan, and he can refer you to a tree service. It takes heavy equipment to move trees.

Utilities

An important detail of landscape planning is checking out the location of all utility and telephone lines and easements before you do any digging, paving or building. If your house is not too old, the utility and phone companies probably have plans of their respective equipment on your property. If they do not have the plans, ask them to come out and inspect your lot and help you find any underground lines. It is a good idea to back up such visits with a letter to the appropriate department at the utility or phone company, recapping what was said at the inspection. If there is a conflict about placement of paving over gas or other lines and you feel the utilities are being over-protective of their equipment, call your building official. He may be able to

give you a more objective opinion. However, locating the lines is a serious matter, because breaking water lines is expensive and cutting electrical and gas lines is, at the very least, dangerous.

Weather and Climate Influences

Your planning should be in harmony with the climate. Know the weather extremes, wind conditions, sun and shade in your area. Unless you undertake a major remodeling, you inherit whatever building

orientation the developer used. However, you can design a new landscape and new outdoor structures that will make the most of your climate. To do this, study your project plans the same way you did for drainage. That is, take each element of the design and ask yourself: what do I want out of this project? Where, within the possible locations, will the project work best for what I want it to do? What material will best meet the functional requirements and blend with my existing

Retaining walls of preservative-treated lumber or cross ties (railroad ties) can double as planters for a pleasing landscaping effect.

English ivy and periwinkle plants act as ground cover under a tree. Ground cover serves a variety of purposes. It is especially useful in areas that do not receive much light.

house and landscape? For example, study a fence. Ask yourself what you want *most* from the fence, because the game of matching design and planning with nature and the existing surroundings is always a compromise. This is especially true in a city. Is privacy most important? Then you may want the tallest board fence your area building code will allow. If you also want to maximize the lawn size for activities, you will want your fence as near the lot lines as possible. You may prefer to pull the fence closer to the house for more intimate, informal areas, and plant the rest of the lawn in a ground cover that requires very little time to maintain.

Light and wind. After thinking about the fence awhile, you may decide that a board fence will cut out the light that you value. In this case you might elect to use a lath fence that offers some privacy but lets in a maximum of light and wind (treasured in the summertime South; not so treasured in coastal areas, where the steady drive of it may be a nuisance if not restrained with a fence or screen).

If the visual aspect of the fence is most important to you, you may decide on a brick fence. There is some question about when a brick fence becomes a wall, of course. Generally, if the brick structure has many perforations, it functions as a fence or screen. If it is solid, it is a wall. Many think of brick as the most beautiful of building materials for any structure.

Sound control. If the acoustical value of the fence is most important to you, then brick is one of the better materials. However, the fact is most materials are far inferior to earth for dampening sound. Even a solid brick wall will not dampen sound very effectively. The best way to stop sound is to build up tall earth berms, or mounds—the higher the better; and this is usually impossible on city and suburban lots. You will, however, experience a psychological relief by building a fence between you and the noise source. Perhaps removing the noise source (streets, playgrounds or swimming pools) from sight causes this, just as seeing water—such as a fountain—makes you feel cooler. All this is not to say that you do not achieve some relief from noise by building walls and fences. It is to say that brick walls are very expensive structures and if your prime purpose in building one is to shut out the droning roar of an expressway or something similar, you will be wasting your money. The study of sound is a relatively new field in housing and there are not many standards or studies to call on for advice.

Alternating segments of natural materials combine well, as seen in this brick and wood arrangement that uses the brick columns as piers and the wood as infill.

An alternative to the solid wood fence can be created with a series of vertical boards fastened to opposite sides of the frame's horizontal stringers. This system lets in some light and allows breezes into the yard.

Wood fences offer a number of benefits to the home landscaper, including sound and wind control as well as visual privacy.

Protection

If your most important goal for the fence is security, you may be perfectly happy with a tall, chain-link fence. This fence is cheap, fast and easy to install, and it will not offer an intruder a hiding place inside. Some of the newer chain-link fences have square posts which seem to look better than the old utilitarian round ones. The fence material can be bought with vinyl coatings in earth colors and other colors.

You can see that planning and design is a matching game that is played best when you have thought out your desires careful-ly and know what you want and why. Add to that knowledge the ability to compromise and the patience to restudy your plan when it needs modifying to meet your budget. If you do these things, you will be pleased with the results of your work.

The wooden stockade fence not only has a long and honorable history, but is relatively easy, fast, and inexpensive to build.

A brick wall with recessed panels and decorative screens can create a relatively formal, traditional design.

This brick wall has a more open screen than the one shown to the left, permitting additional air and light into the yard.

Stone posts, built with openings to hold wooden rails that span the posts, set off boundaries but offer no privacy.

You can choose among a variety of wrought iron fence designs. The fencing material may be used alone or set on a low base.

Plastic panels can be used as infill for wood-frame fences. The panels fit into grooves cut into the wooden frame.

The stucco wall texture can be created by applying a parging (coating) of plaster over a solid wall of concrete block.

Stone walls give acoustical and visual privacy, but rarely give the homeowner a feeling of being isolated or enclosed.

Wire fencing is not only the most economical choice for a high wall, but is the easiest to install for security.

YOUR PERSONAL PLAN
Designing Your Landscape

The first part of your active planning process is very personal. Let everyone in the family draw up personal plans without restrictions. Give each person a plan, a lot of tracing paper and several pencils. Now retire separately to decide individually on what is wanted in the yard and where each thing should be located.

The method. Lay a sheet of tracing paper over the blueprint drawing of your lot. Forget that anyone ever said "no" or "you can't do that." Sketch any design that comes to mind, any form that interests you. Think about how the shapes you draw relate to the interior spaces of the house. Do not worry about how you are going to build what you draw at this stage. You are designing space; lay out the areas in forms you like. Do not become committed to anything you draw. There are many ways to do any project. The paper is cheap and if the idea does not hold up, throw it away.

As you work, you will have some ideas you like and some you do not. Almost every sketch, however, will include some features you like. Leave the tracing paper on the blueprint and put another piece over it. Trace the part you like and throw the rest away. Using this process of addition and subtraction, you will finally come to a total plan that you think (at the moment) is perfect. Leave it alone for a day or two and then look at it again. Sometimes you will not like it at all after you have been away from it. Then you will have to adjust and rework the design. When you have the plan you like, start thinking more about materials and how to build the project. When each person has created a design, it is time to compare.

The Family Conference

When you compare sketches, some of the ideas will be similar, some wildly different. All designs should be attempts to solve the same problems of area usage, traffic definition, and control. Now is the time to decide which ideas address the same problem and which one design handles the problem best. There may be entirely too many ideas to incorporate into one plan, and you will have to edit your designs. Compromises will be needed; everyone should agree that the goal is to create the best plan. Sometimes the best ideas come from the children, al-though this may not be apparent at first. Try to free your thinking from other designs you have seen; children are often better at this than adults. This may be a troublesome process, but the alternative is for some one person in the family to dictate the design and then conscript the others as unenthusiastic, if willing, labor.

At this point, budget considerations and limitations will have to be incorporated in the design. The budget will be affected by how much work you will undertake and how much will be hired out. Assign a "desirable" cost figure to the plan, and an "outside limit" figure. Keep these figures in mind when costing out materials, labor, and other expenses.

Completing the plan. When the plan is complete, you may want to "draw" it on the lot with stakes and string, with bricks, or even with a garden hose if it is a free-form design. Many people have trouble visualizing two-dimensional drawings.

Complete the preliminary sketch of the plan, showing any major areas such as terraces, the walks that connect them, and the fences and/or walls that may enclose them. You should have checked building set-back lines, fence height limitations, and code restrictions before you drew anything. Ask your community building code official for advice when you need it. These officers are not used enough for this, and most will be happy to offer advice on building, kinds of contractors, and materials suppliers—as well as telling you what you cannot do. Use them positively.

Neighborhood Public Relations

When you finish the preliminary plan, talk to the neighbors about it. You are not asking for their approval when you do this, but they will be more comfortable if they believe you know what you are doing, are not going to flood them, or give them an ugly fence to look at. You even may get some volunteer labor.

Preparing for the Work

After the preliminary plan is complete, (although it need not be precise in dimensioning of the layout or contain many construction details), do a materials take-off. That is, break the work into increments and determine how much of each kind of material you need for each phase of the plan.

With your plan and materials take-off, you can shop for everything efficiently and save money as contractors do. You will get better cooperation if you call a lime and cement dealer and ask him what he charges to deliver four cubic yards of gravel, giving him the size and color, than if you tell him you are building a walkway and you need some kind of gravel, but you are not sure what kind or size or color or how much. Building suppliers sell materials; their advice on design matters is unpredictable—

This design contrasts the smooth texture, vertical lines, and bright white of the picket fencing with the horizontal movement and rich color of the brick base.

sometimes good, sometimes not. The most efficient approach for buying material, for hiring labor, and for selecting contractors or other professionals is to use each one for only his (or her) expertise.

Professional Consultation

If you decide on extensive work, you will do well to consult with a landscape architect. For example, if you are building a retaining wall against a considerable slope (see Chapter 9), the forces pressing against such a wall will be enormous. Regardless of the solutions you see in landscaping books, you need the help of a professional to get the most efficient engineering solution to your particular problem and soil conditions. Many professionals will work on an hourly consultation basis. You might, for example, employ a landscape architect to check out your plan for as little as $25 an hour, and an hour may be all you need. Your planning and effort will not have been wasted because landscaping professionals prefer to work with someone who knows what he wants and how much the job will cost. It is easier for the professional to help after you have worked out a basic plan, and it is cheaper for you. Shop for professionals just as you do for any of the other services, and as you will shop for the materials.

REEVALUATING THE PLAN

When you have checked the costs of the materials and services needed for your design, you may find that you cannot afford it. Do not be discouraged. This happens to professionals, too; it is part of the process. The design of spaces is the most important thing you accomplished with your plan. Go back to the drawing board and look for ways to cut costs. You will find ways, always. A pea gravel walkway may serve you just as well as a brick one, at least until you are able to add the brick walk. You may not be able to build a masonry wall but, on second thought, the privacy may have been the most important factor to you and a pressure-treated wood fence may work just as well. A good plan, one that designs space, will not be dependent on one set of materials. The cost-cutting process also can be a valuable experience; many people (probably most) never go through this part of the planning process. Instead, they lose patience; they may call

a contractor, walk around the lot with him and give him vague ideas of what is wanted. Then they tell the contractor what they have to spend, hoping by some magic of the trade that the contractor will make everything all right. The alternative reaction is to go ahead with the high-priced project and later regret it.

When the plan is complete, do any construction detailing necessary and very accurately dimension the plan. This will

be your "working drawing". Now you can set priorities and distribute work—another job that requires sportsmanship and compromise. Ordinarily, grading and paving and walks come first. Then planting and grass sowing and/or sodding. Finally, the walls and fences, when you are sure they will not block access to any remaining work.

Now you are ready to begin the next phase of your project.

Loose walks require raised edgings to hold the material in place. The walks must be raked and replaced frequently.

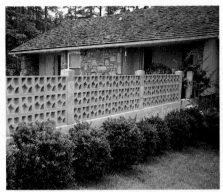

Concrete block walls need not be dull. You can design your own screen patterns, but keep structural requirements in mind.

Concrete walls are not as easy to construct as most of the other materials described in this chapter, but do offer unusual effects. The shape must be created with a wooden form.

2 WORKING WITH LANDSCAPING PROFESSIONALS

When you are unable to do your own design or landscaping work, you can still save considerable money by acting as your own general contractor. The plan, however, is still important. It is the reference point for all the work and it helps define the sequence of work and the payments schedules.

Well-developed plantings can disguise a wall's concrete base. Complementary natural wall materials emphasize the shrubbery.

If you have a handmade wrought-iron fence, like this one, preserve it! Today's precast versions may not be as durable.

TYPES OF LANDSCAPE PROFESSIONALS
The Landscape Architect

Ideally, a potential client goes to a landscape architect who has been recommended by someone satisfied with the architect's services. The landscape architect and the client—you—after discussing your desires and budget, sign the American Society of Landscape Architects Standard Form of Agreement Between Owner and Landscape Architect. This sounds weightier than it is. The contract simply spells out what is to be done, what the fee will be, and how the payments will be made. The range of services and fees possible varies widely from architect to architect.

Once the client has approved the architect's plan, the architect aids the client in selecting a landscape contractor, who will in turn acquire the plants and materials to carry out the plan. The contractor implements the plan according to the landscape architect's specifications. The landscape architect, if he has been authorized to do so, will inspect the job while in progress and authorize payments to the contractor when work indicates payment is appropriate.

This is a synopsis of the ideal arrangement. In practice, many of the landscaping professions have merged and crossed over until it is sometimes difficult for the consumer to tell which professional, or combination of professionals, he is talking to and which of them he really needs.

In most states, only a person licensed by the state may use the term or title "landscape architect". In these states, a landscape architect has passed a rigorous state examination and has probably completed four or five years at an accredited institution offering landscape architecture. The intensity of the training is similar to that of the profession of building architecture or of engineering. The landscape architect is trained for total landscape design of home sites, apartment complexes, office buildings, parks, city planning—anything.

Many people have the mistaken idea that they cannot afford a landscape architect. In fact, if you are undertaking a major project or are unfamiliar with landscaping theories, you often cannot afford *not* to have one. Since landscape architects tend to "graduate" from residential work for individuals to more lucrative commercial and institutional work, they are not much in the public eye. There are many reasonably priced architects, especially the younger ones, who do residential work. Many of these will work on an hourly basis. A rate of $25 per hour is common in some parts of the country.

The Landscape Designer

The landscape designer may perform part or all of the functions of the landscape architect. However, most designers are employed by landscape contractors to provide design services to clients. If hired by the contractor, the first loyalty will be to the employer, not to the homeowner. Most designers are able to do everything they claim to do, and do it well, but their title carries no legal requirements, and anyone may call himself a "landscape designer".

The Landscape Contractor

The landscape contractor traditionally does for the landscape architect what the general contractor does for the building architect; he executes the architect's plan for the client. The landscape contractor may do all work preparatory to planting—dig drainage and irrigation lines, build retaining walls and terraces, build fences and walks, and sometimes build storage facilities.

There are no educational requirements mandated by law for landscape contractors. Their skill comes from experience. Nowadays, however, the landscape contractor who has flourished may employ a landscape architect—a reverse on the old tradition—to complete his range of services. This may work well for you and be the service it is intended to be, or you may find you do not get as much service from the architect as you want. There is still another switch—the case of the landscape architect adding a contracting service to his business. This is the "design-build concept", which means that

Walkways and steps can be used to unify a backyard patio and recreation center.

The low lines of a rail fence define backyard space without visual disruption.

one organization will take the project from the design stage all the way to completion.

Nurserymen and Landscape Nurserymen

Nurserymen and landscape nurserymen traditionally grow plants for wholesale use by landscape contractors and/or retail sales. Today nurseries are often "warehouses" for plants bought from some distant regional growing center. This is fine if the owner knows his plants and is not just a marketing man. An individual's reputation will be an important guide in this area. In addition to being nurserymen, these men and women may also be architects or landscape contractors, or both. There are no legally required professional or educational standards as such for these professionals. Experience is the main teacher, and you should rely on references, jobs completed, and a carefully written agreement or bill of sale. With your plan in hand, go out and discover what is available. Visit local garden centers and nurseries to see what they stock and what various types of plants cost. Note the quality of the plants in each place and how well the plants are cared for.

WHICH EXPERTS TO USE?

There is no single best answer to this question. Your job, your skills, and your budget will determine your choice. Each of the professionals has a basic area of knowledge they excell in, and you must choose the one or combination that best serves your needs. The above information will be useful in evaluating them in light of the job you want done.

Talk with landscape architects and ask them which contractors and nurseries they recommend and why they recommend each one. Large contracting companies are often not suitable for small jobs. Conversely, small contractors may not have the equipment to do a big job. Enthusiasm is perhaps as important a measurement as any. Do not use a contractor for any job for which he has a visible lack of enthusiasm. For example, if a contractor employs a landscape architect or designer, but he is reluctant to make the architect directly accesible to you, or makes you feel rushed or uncomfortable when you ask design questions, do not use him for help in designing and planning your job. On the other hand do not expect design-oriented firms to do work that get their hands dirty—they probably will not do a good job on it. As implied earlier, to get a good job from any contractor, prepare yourself—know what you want, who will do what, how much each item—either service or material—will cost, and how much each job or project is worth to you.

Use your plan, whether designed yourself or designed for you, to shop for the plants and materials, act as your own general contractor, or hire subcontractors to carry out the plan. If you do not feel comfortable judging their work, hire a landscape architect on an hourly basis to come and check the work of the subcontractors before you pay for the work. This can be money well spent. Your plan and specifications are important. You will avoid misunderstandings about what work is to be done and what quality work is expected. Of course, if circumstances make it necessary, turn the entire job over to a landscape architect; if so, let him provide the plan, check the job during the work, and make the final inspection.

HOW MUCH TO SPEND
Project Investment Value

From a purely return-investment standpoint, say the experts, it is wise not to over-landscape, just as it is wise not to over-build. However, good landscaping creates what realtors call curb appeal, and it will help get prospects to stop and look and want to see the inside—important considerations to anyone subject to routine job transfers. There is a seasonal aspect to landscape value. In the winter, landscaping is not as important to value as it is in spring, when it becomes a visible asset.

A rule of thumb some landscape architects use to establish landscape budgets is that landscaping costs can be about 10 percent of the cost of the overall development. Applied to a house and lot designed to sell for $60,000, you could justify spending about $6,000 on landscaping, including planting and hard items like

When brick steps and walks are set in a mortar bed, with the correct gravel base for drainage, they will survive many winters.

In areas of frost heave, brick walks buckle if laid without a mortar bed and drainage.

terraces and drives, walls, walks, fences and installation costs. This is however, only a rough guide—particularly if housing costs in your area are quite high.

Contracts

Before any actual work begins, an owner should sign a standard contract with his architect, general contractor, or subcontractors. The contract is dated and specifies all the work to be done—by referencing other documents, drawings, and specifications—time of commencement, contract sum (this may be a stipulated amount, or cost of the work plus a fee, or any other agreed upon financial arrangement) and date of completion. The architect is often retained to inspect the work before payments are made, to offer general administration of the contract as the owner's representative, to interpret the contract documents (the plans and specifications) and other duties as—and if—specified.

In this scheme of things, the general contractor is responsible for all subcontractors. Any questions or complaints you had would be directed to the architect, who would talk to the general contractor, who would in turn talk to his subcontractors. This is the traditional chain of command.

Since your goal is to eliminate as much expense as possible by doing as much of the work as you can yourself, you may not have a standard contract, in the sense of the one described above. However, you still need to be aware of normal contractual obligations, responsibilities, and liabilities, so that when you insert yourself into one of these functions, you know what you are in for and expect to do.

If you eliminate the architect, you must provide whatever plans and specifications required by the general contractor and the subcontractors. If you eliminate the general contractor, you are architect and general contractor, and you must deal with the subcontractors directly. A general contractor usually employs a relatively small crew, largely supervisory people, who administer the work of the trades.

Insurance

The general contractor is normally required to provide liability insurance to protect himself and his employees under workmen's compensation acts, employees benefit acts, against claims for damages of bodily injury (including death), and property damage due to the work. The amount of the insurance is at least that required by law. The owner should be provided with proof of that insurance.

The owner, in turn, normally provides liability insurance protecting him from claims that arise from carrying out the work of the contract. The owner must also provide property insurance on the entire work site to its full insurable value. This includes the interests of the owner, any lender, and all contractors and insurance against fire, and extended coverage for vandalism and malicious mischief.

If you have friends or neighbors helping with the work, check with your homeowner's policy or your insurance agent to determine the limit of your liability coverage and for coverage against providing "an attractive nuisance". Children like to play on piles of dirt, stacks of boards or bricks, and in wet cement. Keep the working area off-limits and make sure you are insured against suits for injury if someone is hurt while in or around your project construction area.

Performance and Bonds

The general contractor and subcontractors may or may not have performance bonds. Bonds insure the owner sufficient funds with which to hire other contractors to finish the job in case the contracted contractor does not, for whatever reason, perform.

An ornamental wrought-iron fence in prefabricated units offers fast installation, open views, and personalized design.

Steps built from cross ties probably are the easiest kind you can construct. They are often combined with asphalt walks.

A board fence uses brick piers to tie the fence to a landscaping theme that incorporates brick, wood, and exposed aggregate.

Closed board infill set above ground level permits air circulation.

Cleanup duties. The general contractor is responsible for cleaning up the work. Not only before he leaves the job site, but all along. So you should not have to tolerate unreasonable debris on the site, such as loose paper or materials that block access to the house. The general contractor passes this responsibility along to his subcontractors. So each subcontractor should keep the site reasonably clean as the job progresses. Any debris left on the site by the subcontractors is the responsibility of the general contractor. That is you if you are acting as your own general contractor. Do not pay your subcontractors and let them leave before they do the cleanup. In contracting, the power of the purse is vast. In your contracts, spell out carefully what is to be done and how the payments are to be made; do not pay until the specified work is done. This should be agreed on with all the contractors you deal with, in the first place. The reverse is true too—when each step of the work is done, have the money ready, immediately.

Financing

Landscaping falls within the home-improvement loan programs of most banks. These programs lend money on any permanent improvement to a house or grounds—planting, fencing, terracing, walks, fences. For small loans, good credit usually will be sufficient to borrow money to landscape the property any way you choose. For larger loans, where the house will be called on for security, the lender will likely require a set of plans and specifications executed by a landscape architect and require a signed contract with a landscape contractor before he will disperse any money. The lender will tie the loan to the specified improvements and require they be executed to comply with the plans and specifications.

Shopping for money. It is usually wise to shop for money. At times it is a necessity. Before signing your contract, take your plans, the contract, and material giving your credit history and assets to several banks, savings and loans, your credit union, or mortgage company. The loan officers will be able to tell you if they have any money to lend, how much they will lend to you personally and how much they will lend on security. You may find that they will lend much more if the work is to be done professionally than if you are going to do all the work yourself.

When you have found the financial package that is best for you and meets your needs, you can go ahead with the contract signing. If you find that you will not be able to get the money you expected, you can go back to the architect or contractors and modify your plans or schedules. Be sure that the money is available as you need it. If the loan is substantial, sometimes a bank will schedule payouts to you in increments so that you are paying interest on only the portion disbursed and not on the entire amount from the first day of the loan. Investigate financing as carefully as you investigated the architects, contractors and nurserymen during the planning stages of the project.

Value

For the do-it-yourselfer, who often looks on the work as pleasure, the best rule of thumb about how much to spend is not some percentage of the total value of the home, but the amount he can afford to spend to do a job he will use and enjoy. A well-thought-out plan, carefully executed by the homeowner, will certainly improve property. A really good plan can be executed over a period of time. The resulting improvements will be enjoyed by the homeowner, and the improved view appreciated by neighbors and prospective buyers.

Brick surface walks benefit from edgings of brick or other materials—in this case, brick of a contrasting color.

3 GRADING AND DRAINAGE

Drainage affects walks, walls, fences, patios, retaining walls—anything we build that lays on the earth or penetrates it, including anything we plant. Before you start changing anything in your yard, you must understand all the variables involved in good drainage.

Most people think of good drainage only as shaping a lawn so that rain water runs off to the street and gutters and disappears. That is part of drainage, but not all of it. To study drainage, you need to know at least a little about soil.

THE GROUND
The earth is made up of many types of soil; the ground can vary a great deal in a very short distance. For example, your house may be built on clay or rock strata while a neighbor down the street may have a house on sandy soil. Rain soaks into these different soils at different rates, depending on how loose or compact they are. Clays are tight, fine-grained soils; sandy soils are loose. The differences between these nearly opposite soil types is something like the difference between coffee grinds. Water runs through a coarse, loosely packed grind quicker than through a fine, tightly packed grind. Anyone who has ever made drip coffee knows this. Therefore, drainage is not just directing water off the surface, it also involves the ability of the soil to let water soak down through it.

Plants
During the different seasons the amount of rainfall will vary as will, of course, the temperature. Plants, left to natural methods of procreation and travel, will go where they need to go—where the soil, water, and temperature suit them. Unless you are willing to import soil to match the needs of the plant—remembering that trees are plants—select plants that flourish naturally in your area. This kind of importing will work with small plants more easily than with trees because of

their deep root systems. This is not to say you should not tamper with nature, as a purist might say. In fact, there is no way to avoid altering nature in some way and living. However, your landscaping will work better if you know enough about your soil to match the plants to the soil. Avoid fad plants sold to create exotic effects.

Natural boulders and cut stone combine for an unusual retaining wall.

Long, fairly steep slopes call for wide stepped ramps that are easy to navigate. Step locations are dictated by the grade.

Water
Drainage affects all our structures, especially in extreme cold. Everyone knows that water expands when it freezes. You must take care to keep water from building up under walks, other paving, foundations, along the earth side of retaining walls, and so forth. The general rule is to keep the ground under structures as dry as

A foot bridge may be flat, but most often is built with a slight arch to span gullies, creeks, and other shallow depressions.

Stepped ramps can be constructed of cross ties and concrete. The curve of the ramp helps reduce the steepness of the incline.

possible. The obvious part of drainage, surface drainage, can be handled by assuring that you always grade so that water runs away from your structures and is not allowed to build up around them. In addition, underground drainage is usually controlled by using materials that drain well. You protect walks, paving, floor slabs, foundation footings and other elements in contact with the earth by laying a bed of gravel or sand underneath them. Assuming the surface drainage is adequate, the gravel or sand directs water away and keeps the structures from being

A retaining wall is backed up by a concrete and rubble rise that directs water runoff over the adjacent wooden walk.

Brick steps retains traction when wet, lowering the risk of falls and injury.

A drainage pipe under an asphalt drive feeds into this rubble and concrete swale.

damaged by freezing water. Retaining walls and other vertical surfaces can be protected by laying a vertical bed of gravel up along them and by providing drainage weep holes to allow water to escape through them. Drainage standards are available from HUD or your building department for nearly any structure you might build either above or below ground.

Frost heave. Cold weather creates special problems for most structures—especially for structures on clay soil. Water that freezes in any soil will cause it to expand and will likely move or damage structures within that soil. Clayey soils are the worst. A Minnesota fence post, dropped into moist spring clay, may be squirted out the following January as if the earth resents its being there. This natural process is called frost heave.

There is no cure for frost heave, but there are a few ways to deal with it and to minimize its effects. One way, as indicated, is to improve drainage beneath and around underground structural elements so that water cannot build up. You do this with sand or gravel. When you do this, you are modifying—by removing—some of the clayey soil next to the underground element. At times it is necessary to use this method in a wholesale manner. For example, the clayey soil under a building slab might be removed completely down to the frost line and replaced with a soil less susceptible to frost heave. However, this solution may be impractical in some areas where the frost line may be almost as deep as the above-ground height of the building or wall. Another way of protecting structures beneath the ground is to extend the footings beneath the frost line; the frost line is the depth to which the earth freezes. This method can be expensive in areas of extreme cold. For protec-

tion against frost heave in areas where it is a serious problem, you need to consult either a local civil engineer or your building department for advise about your particular project.

If drainage is beginning to sound complicated, then you have understood what you have read. It is complicated. Fortunately, professionals, laymen, and others associated with building and landscaping have developed standards for building and planting in all parts of the country. Often a phone call to the right person—and your building department or agricultural extension service is often the place to start—can give you all the information you need in a few minutes. They will usually do this as a courtesy; you should not hesitate to call on these people. They are most often eager to help, as they should be—you pay their salaries.

Grading Your Lot

As indicated earlier, most of us inherited the soil and drainage accommodations the developer left us. Although the grading was done to efficiently get the water off each lot and to some disposal point, it probably was done the cheapest way possible. This usually means no retaining walls or catch basins—drainage devices that allow you more freedom to create interesting and useful spaces like terraces, walks and walls. This is not meant as a criticism of developers. A developer of speculative housing is required to provide drainage so that each house is protected from flooding. To do more—to spend money on custom landscaping—is asking him to gamble his investment on what an unknown buyer might want. However, in new developments it is not uncommon for a developer to extract his landscaping allowance and give it directly to the purchaser. The new owner then may contract separately for the landscaping plan he wishes. The developer may prefer to modify the plan to suit the buyer, applying the landscaping allowance toward the plan the buyer wishes built.

Grading Theory

To understand basic grading, it might help you to think of your rough lot as an aluminum foil pie pan. Assume the pan is dented and warped. If you place a small quantity of water at one side, and then tilt the pan, the water will take a certain course around the warps and into the dents, some of the water reaching the other side and some remaining in the dents. If you smooth out the pan with your hands, leveling the dents and straightening out the warps, you can influence the way the water reaches the other side of the pan.

Now, if you add, say, a child's building block, representing your house, you can reshape the surface of the pan so that the water runs around the block to the other side of the pan without touching the block. But, as you begin to complicate the problem, by adding a block representing a garage and another representing a terrace and another a play area for the children, you will begin to run into conflicts. When you get the water away from the house, you notice it runs against the garage. Clear that problem and perhaps the play area stands in water.

The cheapest way to handle surface drainage like this is to manipulate the surface of the lot until water runs to the street without disturbing any of the structures, walls, walks, or patios on the lot. One of the simplest ways to accomplish this is to create a swale—a simple, shallow depression—to guide away water that the surface configuration otherwise would not shed. If the arrangement of structures on your lot has created a depression, it may be necessary to construct a catch basin to collect the water and an underground line to carry off the water. Developers avoid this solution, if possible, because it is expensive. Catch basins and drainage lines usually require planning by an engineer or architect.

Making Changes

When you begin to make additions to your lot—patios, drives, walks, walls, steps, raised flower beds or gardens—you need to study the existing drainage pattern. This can be done easily by observing a heavy rain. (The heavier the rain the better.) If you are adding only an item or two—a new garage and drive, for example—and you think that is all you will be adding, you should conform to existing drainage patterns as much as possible. If, however, you know that over the years you will be altering your lawn radically, it is better to plan the whole development in advance and then add the new elements in accordance with the total plan. You may need a landscape architect for this.

Often the drainage pattern you inherit-

ed is far from adequate for the landscaping plan you have in mind. Then utilize some of the landscaping aids in this book: retaining walls of varying height, material, and design; steps of all kinds; dry wells; walls, walks, and fences. Retaining walls allow you to raise or lower areas. Steps allow you to move from one level to another comfortably. Dry wells may keep trouble spots dry. Walls and fences can offer you privacy, security, a wind break, and a degree of noise protection. They may also cut down on direct sunlight. Walks protect your feet and guide visitors through your outdoor living spaces. All these elements can be beautiful as well as functional, and all these elements require attention to drainage.

While your goals in landscaping may be purely aesthetic—to make your lawn a beautiful setting to live and relax in—it is difficult to separate beauty from function. Do not try to force a physical form on your lawn that it was not meant to have. For example, an almost perfectly flat lawn in Kansas is not likely to be en-

hanced by building unnatural earth terraces, retaining walls, or other unexpected structures. However, decks could give the lawn a variation in height, and, combined with compatible planting, the lawn could be very interesting and still appear natural for the terrain, climate, and soil.

Terraced beds can also serve as steps in which the ground cover planting enhances and becomes part of the brick design.

Wood retaining walls require less construction time than do masonry retaining walls. For instructions, see Chapter 9.

Two intersecting concrete block retaining walls, which support varying elevations, require two different structural designs.

High retaining walls require professional design. Previous masonry experience is necessary for building this wall.

Grading Practice

If you are not making extreme changes, you can do most residential grading with a few hand tools, some stakes, and a line level. Grading, for the typical suburban lot, is usually a matter of flattening, smoothing, and sloping the soil to drain away from the house and other structures to lower disposal points. If you have an uneven lot and you want a variety of space uses on it, the planning and execution may give you some trouble. A good grading plan will divert water away from your house and all your projects in a functional and aesthetically pleasing manner without drainage conflicts between the different areas. This can be rather complicated to work out on paper. You may need a landscape architect to help you recognize and plan the contours, but you can still do the project yourself.

Reshaping the ground slope. In an undeveloped lot, you would want to slope your front yard to drain toward the street.

Step one: loosening the soil. First loosen the soil with a double-ended pick—one with a pick at one end and a blade at the other. You then can use a long-handled, pointed shovel to fill the obvious depressions and level any mounds. If it is necessary to use a wheelbarrow to move the dirt, rent one with a pneumatic tire and sturdy framing. Work with the lot until it looks flat. Next use a rotary tiller and break up the soil until the clods are a convenient size for raking with a garden rake. Till back and forth in a tight grid pattern. Then rake the lot as smooth as you can with the rake.

Step two: determining the slope. Now you are ready to determine the existing slope and plan your new one. Place a stake at one corner of the foundation wall of your house. Place another stake at the

edge of the sidewalk, aligned and even with the first stake. Attach a string to the foundation wall stake at a point at least 8 inches down from the level of the first floor inside. Stretch the string to the stake at the sidewalk and attach it, leveling it with a line level. Make sure the string is not touching the ground anywhere. If it is, dig a trench under the string so it does not touch the ground. Measure up from the sidewalk to the string, and you will have the vertical rise. Measure the distance between the stakes, and you will have the horizontal run. Repeat this staking process at the opposite corner of the house.

To figure the slope, divide the inches of rise by the inches of run. The result will be the degree (percentage of) slope. For example, if the difference between the house and sidewalk is five inches and the distance from the house is 20 feet (240 inches), the slope is 2%.

Step three: making a gridwork guide. Stretch a line between the stakes at the sidewalk edge and attach where the first strings are tied. Now you have described a string boundary around the lot to be sloped. Drive stakes at six foot intervals around the string boundary and connect them with strings, forming a string gridwork over the lot. Check the strings for level with a line level.

Now you can move around the lot within the grid, shoveling and raking the soil so that it slopes down to the sidewalk at the desired rate. The string grid provides you with a handy slope check at many points on the lot. Use a yardstick regularly to check the distance between the string and the soil.

Repeat the process around the house, establishing the grade you want on each side. The rate of the slope away from the

house, drive, and different use areas varies according to the particular lay of your lot. If you employ a landscape architect, his plan will provide for adequate drainage of all areas. If you do not use an architect, and have questions about appropriate slope rates, call your building department or local HUD office. Either one can advise you on solving your particular problem.

When you have graded the soil as you want it, tamp it lightly to minimize uneven settlement.

EROSION CONTROL

Sloping the lot away from the house as just described is one of the typical methods of surface drainage. The purpose of such drainage is to protect some object, such as the house, or to keep areas from standing in water. On lots where there are steep natural grades, you must take steps to protect the soil itself—that is, prevent erosion.

Controlling Runoff

To stop erosion, you must control—slow down—the runoff of surface water. Often you can do this by planting groundcover. Sandwort, Thrift, Dianthus, Juniper, Pachysandra, and Taxus are good ground

What was originally just a rubble swale received such heavy water runoff that a bed of concrete was added to prevent erosion.

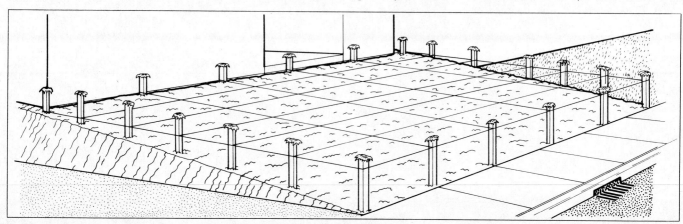

To calculate the ground slope, divide the height of the rise by the length of the horizontal run.

covers that will prosper in many parts of the country. These covers grow thickly, squeezing out most weeds and becoming a neat, uniform cover.

However, ground covers may not be enough for some steep slopes. If not, you may have to modify the slope itself. If your intent is only to stop erosion, then the method you choose should simply slow down the flow of water over the slope. You probably will want to choose the cheapest and simplest method.

Durable protection: stones. One of the easiest ways to stop erosion on steep slopes is with stones. All you have to do is line the slope with stones large enough to stay in place when water runs over them. Most stones have one flat side, so laying them is usually not a problem. Use a pointed shovel to scoop out enough earth so that the stones are in a secure position. The number and sizes of stone you use depends on the steepness of the slope and the amount of water that will run over it. A 4 to 6 inch layer of stones set approximately 2 inches or more in the ground should take care of most problem situations. You may want the entire surface covered with stone; however, you could space the stones somewhat and plant a ground cover between them. This will soften the appearance of the slope. A ground cover and stone combination is a good-looking solution to the problem of erosion.

Adding baffles. A second acceptable method is to slow the surface water and prevent soil erosion with the use of baffles. A baffle is any structure that will slow the flow of surface water by slight diversion. A baffle may be built of any appropriate material: pressure-treated wood cross ties, stone, masonry—or some combination of these and other materials. To use a cross tie baffle, lay the tie on the slope perpendicular to the flow of water. Deciding how deep to secure the tie in the earth is a matter of judgment; usually burying the tie halfway should be enough. Appearance now enters into the judgment. If the ties are unsightly, you may want to bury them a little deeper, but remember, their purpose is to slow water. How many you need is another matter of judgment; it depends on the steepness of the slope and the amount of water that flows over it. You can experiment with fewer cross ties than the slope appears to need and add more after you observe the

water action during a rain. You may prefer to use the garden hose to test how they slow the water. The cross ties are laid end to end across the slope.

You could, of course, combine cross ties, stones, and ground cover(s) to slow down surface water and prevent erosion. This might be one of the better looking solutions.

Terraces. Another way to slow down surface water on steep slopes is to build terraces. You do this by digging and manipulating the surface. Unless you have problem soil, a pick, pointed shovel, garden rake, and wheelbarrow are the only tools you will need. The terraces resemble a set of giant steps. These steps, when planted with grass or a ground cover, should slow down the flow of the surface water (see Chapter 9).

A long asphalt walkway on a hillside uses wooden baffles to slow down the water runoff that develops during heavy rainfalls.

Creating swales. Swales will help you to deal with water on steep slopes. The size and number of swales you need depend—as do all the other solutions—on the steepness of the slope and the amount of water that comes over it. For example, a mild slope might be handled by digging a swale two inches deep and about 18 inches wide. Round off the edges. Take the dirt you scoop out and lay it along the down side of the swale, patting it with the shovel to form a lip along the swale. This helps keep the water from running over the swale. The swales should be laid almost perpendicular to the direction of the water flow so that the water runs along the swale in the direction you choose.

Dry wells. There are cases where areas are difficult or impossible to grade

Stone retaining walls can follow the shape of the land; however, curves often call for the advice of a professional.

This gentle slope has a rubble swale that hugs the contours of the lot, in keeping with the rustic landscape impression.

for drainage economically. For example, where several natural swales formed by the intersection of two or more planes of land come together and form a low spot. In this case, you may be able to eliminate the standing water by digging a dry well. A dry well is simply a pit filled with coarse gravel or masonry rubble that allows water to run down through it quickly. The size of the dry well depends on the amount of water that it will have to absorb and on the depth of the water table. The building department can tell you how deep the water table is in your area. It is advisable to have an engineer or your building inspector check your plan before you go very far in working on this solution. The bottom of the well must be above the seasonal height of the water table.

Mud Jacking

Even when very carefully planned and built, some projects run into problems caused by uneven, and often unexplainable, settling or unusual ground frost heave. If your walk or drive has developed severe low spots or a lean in the wrong direction, you may have to resort to mud jacking.

Mud jacking, or under-sealing, is a method of raising concrete or other surfaces that have sunk due to poor soil compaction or the after-effects of frost heave. Holes are drilled in the pavement and a fluid concrete is pumped in under pressure. As the concrete is pumped in, the only place for the pavement to go is up. This process has some drawbacks for the homeowner. First, it is rather expensive, applied to small jobs. Second, it

requires considerable skill to perform—it is more art than science. Third, once you make a mistake in raising the slab or other pavement so that it is too high—that is it. It is not a forgiving process and you may have to dig out what you hoped to save.

The people most experienced with mud jacking are highway engineers and maintenance crews. They often use it on highways and at the ends of bridges, where the adjoining pavement sometimes drops. In areas subject to extreme changes of weather during the seasons, you will usually find several companies involved in mud jacking. However, in milder climate areas, this process is rarely applied.

Do-it-yourself? For some walk areas that have sunk, it may be a better course to simply jack-hammer the concrete out and replace the offending soil with gravel and properly-compacted soil.

If there is a small area near the edge of your walk or drive that has sunk, it is possible to raise it yourself. You will need a strong helper, because part of the job takes pure physical strength. You must dig out the ground under the sunken area, as well as a small space next to the walk. Remove enough material from underneath the walk so that you can insert a 2x4 (or heavier) board as a pry. Place a brick, stone or piece of 2x4 beneath the 2x4 pry. Push down on the pry and lift the walk or drive. Then force gravel into the hole. If the sunken area is very small, you may have leveled the area by this one action. However, you may find that it takes several tries to get the area filled and leveled. Force the gravel into the hole under as much pressure as possible and backfill the area next to the walk. Otherwise, the gravel will settle and spread, causing your repaired area to sink again.

POINTS TO REMEMBER

The following are some design considerations that may help you in planning both grading and drainage.

Purposes of Drainage

The first consideration in drainage is to keep the house and the access routes to it safe from flooding or excessive water. To accomplish this, a protective slope is draped around the house like an apron; protective swales may be used in combination with the slopes. The design of these protective measures varies with

Use a pry bar or 2x4 to lift up the slab so you can force gravel underneath it.

A long piece of 2x4 or 2x6 gives the best leverage; use a brick to brace the lumber.

Asphalt need not be black—in this case, stone aggregate was embedded for a rough, slip-resistant finish and a brighter surface.

your particular lot. If you do not use a landscape architect for planning your contours, have the building department or HUD check your plans.

Protect Your Property

Avoid grades that allow water to reach the foundation walls of new buildings or become trapped against new garden walls. This water can seep into basements and crawl spaces and cause mildew problems. A water buildup also exerts a great deal of pressure that can crack and weaken foundations of both houses and walls.

Respect Your Neighbor's Property

When planning or executing grading for drainage, study the grading of the houses on each side of your house and behind it. You can end up in a law suit if you divert runoff onto a neighbor's property. If a new house is built on a vacant lot next to you and causes you a drainage problem, call your building department. This is not unfriendly to your new neighbor; the building department can tell what the problem is and isolate responsibility quickly. In typical subdivision layout, the drainage may be all to the street, draining from a ridge along the back property lines of adjoining lots of all the houses. Perhaps part of the water may go to a swale along the back property lines, or a combination of these two, or more drainage plans may be used. In other words, your property is part of an overall drainage plan. It is your responsibility to make any changes in your drainage plan fit the overall plan and not disturb it or your

neighbors. Extensive changes in drainage often require consultation with a landscape architect or civil engineer.

Slope new paving toward existing drainage aid such as swales, ditches, catch basins, and dry wells.

Climate Extremes

In areas subject to frost heave, drainage becomes more critical because buildings, walls, paving, and fencing can be damaged or destroyed by it. If you live in an area that gets extremely cold, check with an architect or your building department for specific advice on drainage for projects you have in mind and for drainage problems you may be experiencing with a finished lot.

Preventing Excess Erosion

Sharp corners erode quicker than smooth ones. So round off the edges of swales you dig with a shovel. Take the earth you removed for the swale and form a lip, or slight berm, at the lower edge of the swale. Pat the berm smooth and compact with your shovel.

Drainage ditches and swales often run almost perpendicular to the flow of water down slopes they help drain. This way, they catch the most water and change its direction. Sometimes it is necessary to run swales or ditches in the direction of the water flow. When this is the case, line the bottom of the swale with stone or rubble—set deep enough so the water does not pull it out—to prevent erosion of the swale or ditch. A pointed shovel is all you need to set the stones or rubble in place.

Catch Basins and Dry Wells

When catch basins must be used, they should be installed where they will never overflow toward the house if they should become stopped up and overflow. The overall drainage and grading plan should be contoured so that if the basin should overflow, any water would flow away from the house.

If you use a dry well to drain problem areas, check with the building department to determine the depth of the ground water table. The bottom of the dry well should be above the water table at its seasonal height. Keep dry wells as far as possible from buildings and foundations of other structures. It should also be noted that the bottom of the dry well must project into a strata of porous soil capable of absorbing the water from the well. If you are unsure about the character of your subsoil, check with local experts—a landscape architect, civil engineer, the building department, or HUD—before proceeding with this project.

Protection of Utilities

Check with the utility and phone companies for location of existing underground lines before you dig. In addition, install any underground lines or equipment you may want before you begin paving.

Finally, it must be said that in dealing with the problems of drainage and grading, it is impossible to cover all possible situations. No one can give anything but example solutions to typical problems. So, if you are in doubt about which expert you need to help and guide you, refer again to Chapter 2.

Behind a retaining wall, the high berm provides a gently sloped earthfill.

The colorful rubble masonry used on these retaining walls and steps becomes an integral part of the yard design.

Patterns are a part of the complete effect of any landscaping project. Patterns are created by the way materials are installed. Brick accepts curves to create a pattern of movement and may be laid in a variety of bond patterns. Patterns can be emphasized by combining materials. Concrete will accept the pattern of the wood form—both the shape and texture.

4 WALK PATTERNS, FINISHES & EDGINGS

There is no such thing as a purely "decorative" wall, walk or fence. All these elements of your total outdoor living design have specific purposes (functions) and this is true of the patterns and finishes you choose for the materials. This chapter will discuss specific materials and help you decide what patterns and finishes you need for your project.

The first consideration in any project is its function: what is it going to do for you? Keep in mind the function of even the smallest details and your installation will be easier and the final product more desirable.

CHOOSING WALK MATERIALS
Cobblestone

Cobblestone has long been used as a building material for roads and surfaces that would receive heavy wear. Unfortunately, cobblestone also induces heavy wear on everything that crosses it. It is irregular, like the stones in ordinary rubble walls. It is difficult to walk on cobblestone in most shoes; it is nearly impossible to walk on cobblestone in high heels. In addition, this surface is more difficult to drain than is a smoother one. The cobblestone can be slippery to walk on, especially after a rain, and it is an awkward supporting surface for tables and chairs.

In moderate climates, cobblestone surfaces may be laid by simply scooping away the soil down to firm level and setting the stone directly on the ground. In colder climates, drainage becomes more important because of frost heave and the stone must be laid on a bed of gravel—usually a minimum of 4 inches thick. You should check with your building official for the exact local practice.

In some cities where a large number of the streets were once cobblestone, the material sometimes may be obtained at no cost other than hauling it away.

Flagstone

Flagstone, like cobblestone, has a long history as a paving material. It comes in distinctive, relatively bright colors and, used to excess in small, intimate areas—like patios—can be overwhelming. Sizes of flagstone also affect design and construction.

Because of its prominent coloring and the strong, irregular shapes, care must be taken in mixing flagstone with other materials. It works well with concrete where some variety or color is needed. Flagstone would not work as well with other stones in other patterns. Adjacent to rubble or ashlar walls—or other distinctly shaped and colored materials—the flagstone would make the design too busy and disturbing for the eye.

Flagstone is an excellent choice for walks, terraces, and steps in spacious natural surroundings. It seems to look especially good with planted joints of a hardy groundcover; however, it often works well in urban settings, offering a natural, warm contrast to common materials like asphalt and concrete. The things to watch in design are relative scale, and the combination of color and irregular shapes.

Flagstone is laid like the other paving materials. In moderate climates it may be laid directly on the earth. The more severe the climate, the greater the attention that must be paid to drainage and the base preparation. It is easiest to set other pavers or any cobblestone level in a base of sand. A sand base may be laid over tamped earth, or over tamped earth and tamped gravel. In areas of severe frost, lay the flagstone on a mortar base using the same techniques used in laying a smooth brick walk. It can be laid on a mortar bed with any kind of joint—a flush joint is best for most paving uses. For the most durable construction, use the narrowest joints possible.

Concrete Patio Blocks and Interlocking Pavers

Patio blocks. Concrete patio blocks come in a variety of sizes. Like other concrete blocks, patio blocks are relatively inexpensive. The blocks may be laid in a basketweave, ashlar, grid, running bond, or any pattern you may want. You can lay them like any other stone, de-

Granite provides a sturdier longer lasting wearing surface than flagstone, but is heavier and more difficult to cut.

There are many types of patio paving materials. Shown are the most common types: (from left), common block, interlocking concrete paving block, flagstone (quarried limestone), and patio block (1 x 2 feet, but can be split every 6 inches).

pending on their use. They can be utilized for rough walks through natural surroundings or smooth finish walks and terraces close to the house. Your purpose and your climate will determine the type joint and the method of installation.

Pavers. Interlocking pavers are another concrete product, with a wide variety of shapes, such as double hex units, curvilinear units, and other patterns. All of them interlock or interconnect naturally because of their shape. Most interlocking units are solid, but some have a perforated, waffle-like design to let grass or other ground covers grow through the units. The interlocking pavers require the same installation techniques as regular concrete pavers.

Brick

Brick is one of the most widely used building materials in the world. It can be used in a vast array of patterns in walls and walking surfaces. This is because of the many desirable characteristics offered. Brick is both a structural and finish material suitable for interior and exterior bearing walls—those that hold up a building—without addition of any other material. It has one of the most naturally beautiful surfaces of any building material. Brick is appropriate for patios, walks, fences, garden walls, balcony and deck columns, interior and exterior floors, steps, ramps, barbecue pits, retaining walls, and many other projects—and it will last many lifetimes.

Brick is available in a wide range of textures and colors with or without glazes or ceramic coatings. The ceramic coatings make brick easy to clean and water resistant. This type of brick is a good choice for the wainscots (lower portions) of walls in areas where there may be a lot of traffic, resulting in scuffing and abrasion of the brick. Another beneficial application of ceramic brick is on low patio walls which enclose or define an outdoor cooking area. Ceramic brick also can be used to add courses of color to walls; a few colored bricks may be set throughout a wall or other surface in a random design.

In spite of its many attributes, brick is essentially an inexpensive material, compared to other materials that do the same job. The only main drawback for an amateur builder is the skill required to use brick properly. However, if patient and careful—and always following the instructions for each project—you should be able to achieve sturdy, attractive results with brick.

Brick patterns. Brick lends itself to geometric patterns. Patterns in walls—running bond, offset bond, ashlar, stack, diagonal bond, diagonal stack—can be adapted for use in walks. These are all classic brick patterns. Some patterns, such as basketweave (square and diagonal) are suitable for walks only.

All patterns can be varied in appearance by your selection of joints between bricks. Standard masonry wall joints are

about ⅜ to ½ inch, but with walks you have more freedom than is possible for walls. For a hard-edge, formal walk appearance, maintain the standard joints, neatly finished with the appropriate joint tool (see the section on wall joints in Chapter 9). For a less formal appearance, the joints can be made somewhat irregular.

Inset patterns. Patterns can be created by weaving one material through another. For example, you can build a grid of cross ties and fill the spaces with brick (in any pattern that you like, as long as it seems appropriate to the total design). The cross ties would be the main visual interest in such a design and the brick would be the background. The main idea is similar to a plaid fabric, where you have one or two major brightly colored grids and the other colors are muted. Cross ties can be used in this fashion with other materials instead of just brick—concrete, asphalt, soil cement, stone, tile, or any of the wood or other "soft" walk materials.

Concrete pavers firmly interlock when sand is swept into the joints.

Paving bricks, which come in many other patterns as well as the one illustrated, are durable and can be used for patios, walkways and driveways. The units interlock for a smooth surface.

A brick walk can be extended using the same bond pattern to form steps.

(A) RUNNING BOND

(B) OFFSET BOND

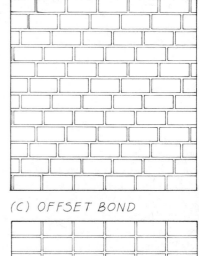

(C) OFFSET BOND

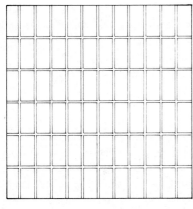

(D) COURSED ASHLAR

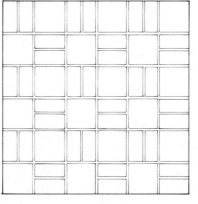

(E) PATTERNED ASHLAR

(F) HORIZONTAL STACK

(G) VERTICAL STACK

(H) BASKET WEAVE

(I) BASKET WEAVE

(J) DIAGONAL BOND

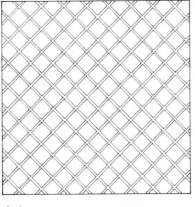

(K) DIAGONAL STACK

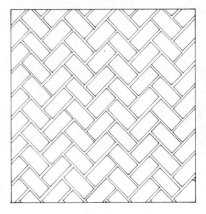

(L) DIAGONAL BASKET

Brick and other masonry can be laid in a variety of walkway patterns for a wide range of effects.

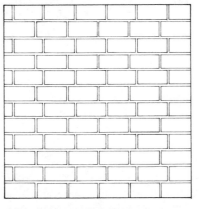

Soft Walks—Bark and Shells

While these materials involve maintenance problems, they have certain qualities that may make them very attractive. These natural materials create their own surface textures. The textures will appear different in different light situations. Generally, gravel, bark and shells provide good drainage and will also help build the soil if you are planning to install solid surface walks at a later date. They are quick and inexpensive to install—a major benefit to many cash-strapped homeowners.

All loose materials require sturdy edgings, of course, or the material will spread. Concrete, wood, or metal can be used. Design of edgings offers enormous

Timber pavers offer a firm foot path when similar to precast concrete blocks. They are placed over soft materials such as bark.

Gravel patios or walks need a raised border to keep the gravel from spilling out of the boundaries. Railroad ties set in trenches provide a suitable edging.

flexibility in a walk. Provided that your edging has reasonable flex/curvability, your walk can curve, or change shape and be the width you desire.

Warning. Children tend to look at these loose fill materials as a limitless sandpile substitute. You may find that, having carefully laid out your walk, installed the edgings, and raked the material smooth, your efforts are rewarded by a child (yours or your neighbor's) who has pushed whole areas into a giant "road building" project with a toy truck.

Maintenance. These walks require annual, or more frequent, renewal. Once your landscaping has been completed, there may be no way for a truck to get near your path in order to replenish the walk. You may face the prospect of pushing many wheelbarrow loads of gravel, bark, or shells to your walk and then raking the surface smooth.

Gravel

Gravel is an inexpensive walk material. It comes in many sizes and colors. There are two types: pea gravel, a natural rounded gravel, and crushed stone or rock. Pea gravel is relatively expensive and is sometimes difficult to find.

Gravel looks attractive with either concrete, wood or metal edgings. It can be placed easily and contained in a variety of shapes. The natural textures of gravel and gravel walks are visually interesting. However, it is difficult to walk on gravel in high heels.

Gravel is attractive when used under shrubs, evergreens, and in flower beds. It helps control weed growth and creates a finished look.

When used as a walk, gravel needs raking almost daily. Gravel scatters easily and tends to be carried away in heavy rains. It may also sink into the earth and require frequent—or at least annual—replenishment.

Asphalt

While it is seldom considered a decorative material, and does require permanent edgings and regular maintenance, asphalt has many fine qualities that make it attractive as a walk material. The surface is relatively smooth and reasonably durable. Asphalt can be combined with other materials to create a good looking and effective walk.

The surface of asphalt may be slippery

when wet, but surface treatment and good drainage can take care of that problem; decide this in the planning stage.

Timber Pavers

Landscaping timbers or cross ties also may be cut to form pavers. A thickness of approximately 4 inches works well; thinner pavers are likely to crack. The 2x6 pressure-treated timber edging combines well with the wood paver walk.

Lay the pavers with ½ inch joints on a 2 to 4 inch bed of sand. Pour sand over the surface of the pavers (a bucket at a time) and sweep it into the joints. Water the sand down with a light spray from the garden hose and repeat the addition of sand until the sand joints are flush with the top of the walk.

Concrete

Although the most solid of materials, concrete is extraordinarily versatile. It lends itself to impressions on its surface, to coloring, and to insets of other materials.

Joints for design and durability. In any considerable expanse of concrete, there will be control joints—the shallow "cuts" that prevent cracks where they are not wanted. As you will learn, concrete always cracks; the control joints just systematize where the cracks will be. Every so often you will have isolation joints also, to allow expansion where the concrete meets a dissimilar material. So any pattern you work out with concrete must consider the location of control and isolation joints. This is not difficult to handle. The control joints are simply shallow grooves in the concrete. They are not difficult or expensive to make. Instead of the mandatory number of control joints needed to protect your concrete, you may choose to use more, working them into

Masking the tops of the form grids will prevent their becoming stained or abraded during concrete placement.

the design. Permanent forms of redwood can also serve as control joints.

The isolation joints are a little more difficult to work into the design, but not much. They go all the way through the concrete and are ½ inch wide. They are more visible than control joints. But if you position the control joints between the isolation joints, as a design or pattern, it will look fine. You may have to add a few extra joints for design purposes.

Surface finishes. Finishes should be considered for their functional uses before one is selected arbitrarily, or simply because it looks good. Concrete can be finished so smoothly that it may be colored and waxed like enamel. Such a finish is perfect for some interior uses but usually inappropriate, and often dangerous, for outdoor use, where it would be slippery to walk on and present a constant maintenance problem. The choice of a surface pattern often brings with it the question of surface texture. Exposed aggregate, for example is not only attractive but nonslippery, making it a suitable choice for outdoor walks, steps, or pool surrounds.

Exposed aggregate. This is a popular concrete finish. An exposed aggregate—especially if the stone is inherently attractive—may be combined with a redwood or pressure-treated lumber grid for a dramatic walk. Smooth, water-worn stones can be especially pleasing to the eye when incorporated in this finish.

Pitted designs. A light concrete, pitted by the application of rock salt may, if carefully prepared, look rather like a travertine marble. Marble is not an appropriate choice for walks because it is very slippery when wet; the pitted concrete will have a slightly roughened surface and is safer.

Broomed texture. A broom finish may be anything from patterns of swirls or circles, a basketweave design or straight, light furrowing. A broom finish provides a safe nonskid surface.

PATTERNS, FORMS, FINISHES
Designing the Wood Forms

When you install the form work for a concrete walk, your first consideration is that the form work will hold the concrete or other material in place and in the desired shape. This ''shape'' may simply be a straight concrete drive with no elaboration. In the case of a wall or walk,

however, you may instead lay a more elaborate form system (a grid) to remain permanently. You may use redwood and leave the redwood in place because you like the way it looks set in the concrete. The first and most important task the redwood must perform is to hold the concrete in place and in the shape you want while it sets. The redwood joints serve another function, as control joints that keep the conccrete from cracking.

Surface Patterns

Of lesser functional importance may be the particular pattern you choose when you lay out stone pavers on a sand base or flagstone on a concrete base. This is a less formal material, some people call it rustic, and you have wide latitude in the way you may put the units down as a walk surface.

Finishes

Finishes have functions too. A broom-finished concrete slab is safer to walk on in the rain than a finely troweled surface. With any given material, you will usually be able to combine the pattern you want with the finish and function you need. For example, you might need a concrete surface and like the appearance of a very smooth finish. To keep it from being too slippery, you could ''etch'' or scribe a design you like onto the smooth surface. The etched design should look good, but it will also give traction—while the cuts may serve as control joints.

Creating patterns for random flagstone. For a concrete surface resembling

random flagstone you need to create patterns that resemble the appearance of joints found in a flagstone walk. Wood strips approximately ¼x1½ inches, 15 pound roofing felt, or a similar material can be used to form the patterns. Cut the strips in irregular lengths to simulate the edges of flagstone. If you use wood, undercut the edges a bit so the wood does not stick in the concrete when it dries. The strips should be cut to match the flagstone you would have selected had the surface really been built of that material.

The size of the area to be paved should be considered when selecting the size of the patterns. In large areas, for example, you can simulate large-sized simulated stone. In smaller areas, reduce the size until it looks right. The lengths of the strips for a typical project might run from a few inches to three feet.

Pretreated strips can be stained to match and left in place to serve as control joints.

Railroad ties set into concrete as permanent interior forms add a rustic texture and will also serve as control joints.

In all cases, give the slab the finish you intend the simulated flagstone to have; remember that flagstone comes in a variety of finishes. A broom finish is a good choice because it has an attractive texture and is safe underfoot.

Step-by-step instructions. Here are the basic procedures for producing a flagstone pattern in concrete.

(1) After screeding and darbying, let the concrete set until moisture is no longer on the surface.

(2) Before positioning the wood strips, soak them well, in water, to prevent their warping and popping out of the concrete.

(3) Carefully lay out the strips on the concrete in the design you want. Do not press them in yet.

(4) Rearrange the strips until you have the design you want. You can change their positions as long as they only sit lightly on the concrete.

(5) When you have the design you want (make it look as much like flagstone as you can but avoid peculiar shapes) press the strips in.

(6) Float the surface. Keep the strips flush with the top of the concrete.

(7) Clean excess concrete off the surfaces of the strips, using a trowel or putty knife.

(8) If you want a surface on the "flagstone" other than what you have—such as a trowel-smooth or broom-brush finish—add it now.

(9) Remove the wood strips the next day or, if felt strips were used, remove them after the concrete has cured.

Joints. You may leave the joints open or fill them with mortar in the appropriate style joint. If you use mortar in the joints, first flood the joints with water and let it sit long enough to soak in. It is best to do this the night before you apply the mortar. Brush the joints with a paste of portland cement and water before placing the mortar. Keep the paste off the concrete; have a sponge handy for wiping off any mistakes.

Using crazy concrete. An inexpensive alternative to stone, "crazy" concrete is concrete rubble, broken up from old walks, driveways, and the like. If you have some concrete work you are planning to remove, you can use that for crazy paving. Other sources of concrete rubble include contractors, wrecking companies, and the city public works department. They may sell the rubble and charge for delivering it to you especially if the material is popular in your area. However, it is sometimes possible to get the material free, including delivery. If you have a fixed time period in which to do your project, you should line up your material sources well in advance because the availability of concrete rubble often is unpredictable.

Making your own rubble. You can make your own concrete rubble to an exact, desired size. Build a form over sand or polyethelene so it is the same size as your walk. Pour in the concrete. The thickness of the concrete and the amount of reinforcement, if any, depends upon use, and the desired size of the concrete rubble, or pavers. For ordinary lawn and garden use, where the materials will only carry foot traffic, the concrete can be as thin as 2½ inches, but this should be the minimum thickness. Before the concrete hardens, cut the desired shapes with a steel trowel. After curing, the concrete work may still be whole, but a few taps with a heavy mallet or sledge hammer will easily break the units apart.

The practice of making your own rubble may be of questionable practicability. It is similar to laying a fake stone slab in concrete, but is tiresome because you have to haul the material into place. If the rustic appearance is what you are after, you can produce the same effect by scooping out the earth, forming the walk or slab shapes you want right in place. This is simpler than forming it, breaking it up, and then carrying it to where it is to be used.

Installation techniques. The main appeal of broken concrete lies in its low cost. It is probably more difficult to work with than concrete pavers, brick, or even irregular stones like flagstone, which generally are fairly thin. Concrete rubble often varies considerably in thickness, making a sand bed necessary in order to achieve a smooth surface.

However, if the material is readily available to you and appeals to you, use it as you would the other masonry paving materials. Lay it over a bed of sand about 2 inches thick to keep the pavers level. If frost heave is a problem, you will need about 4 inches of gravel under the sand to aid drainage. The joints are similar to those used for other masonry pavers. You may use mortar joints or sand joints. For the smoothest appearance, lay the rubble in a mortar bed and then mortar the joints flush, or rake them out a little. The rubble pavers will not lend themselves to tight joints because of the irregularity of the edges. Because of these irregular edges,

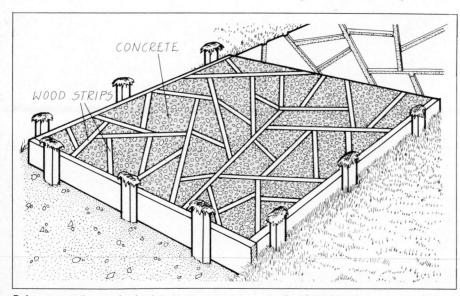

Before you set the wood strips into the concrete, be sure the final finish has already been achieved. In this case the aggregate was exposed before strips were placed.

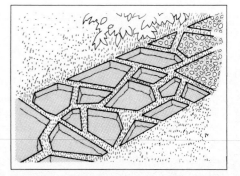

Flagsone shapes cut into stable soil are both base and form for the concrete.

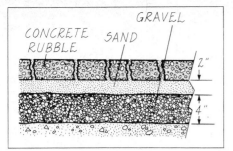

Concrete rubble requires a base of sand and gravel to prevent settling and erosion.

Do not stand on concrete when using stamper; stand on the pattern maker if necessary.

you may want to consider using a ground cover between the pavers.

The broken edges also will expose the aggregate texture under the surface. You may find this even more suitable for use in a rubble wall than as a paving material.

Producing stamped patterns. Any masonry materials such as brick, block, stone, cobbles, or tile, can be simulated in concrete. Any designs in these materials can be duplicated. You may create basketweave, stack bond, running bond, other patterns. However, to get the precision look of some of these materials, for example, tile or brick, you need special platform stamping tools.

Using stamping tools. The concrete is prepared as usual and finished to the desired texture. Then the platform pads are placed one next to the other in a row; at least two pads are required. Step on the pads, pushing them down until the desired depth of joint is achieved. Once the design is pressed in, a special jointer tool is used to smooth out any imperfections. Since the platform pads stamp several "courses" at a time, you should check the size of the platforms before you lay out your project. Design the walk to a multiple of the platform size, if possible. If not, hand stamps are available to finish out the odd dimensions. Also check the availability of platform pads before you plan a project based on them—they may not be available in your area. There are commercial contractors who will handle this type of work.

Adding hand-pressed impressions. There are still other patterns you can use on concrete: leaves, wood grain, circles made with different sized cans used like cookie cutters, sea shells, almost anything. These "forms" are simply pressed into the concrete to the desired depth, using a wood float or your hand. These designs can be fun, but they should be thought out carefully to avoid a pattern that makes you wonder, six months after you put it down, what you could have been thinking when you did it.

Using Colored Concrete

If you wish to add color, there is no reason why a plain concrete surface—or a flagstone or brick design—cannot be any color that works well with the total color scheme of your house and grounds. Concrete in a flagstone pattern might be colored yellow, gray, blue, black, burgundy, or other suitable choice. You will need to be more careful in the selection of a walk color than for a house paint color. Once you have colored the concrete, the only way to change it is to pour a new layer of concrete.

There are several ways to color concrete. You can choose among these methods:

(1) painting the concrete;
(2) blending a dry mix in with the concrete;
(3) blending the dry mix into only a portion of the concrete, pouring the colored concrete on last as a topping;
(4) using a "dry shake", which you sprinkle over the surface of wet concrete;
(5) using colored or tinted cement powder in the concrete.

Preparing the surface. Some paints are made to be applied to damp concrete, but most paints are for fully cured and dry concrete. Before you paint, make sure the surface is free of dirt, dust or grease. First wash the concrete with a stiff-bristled broom and household detergent. Then use a solvent to remove any stains that remain. Apply the paint according to the manufacturer's instruction; you can usually use a roller, brush or sprayer.

Applying portland-cement paints. Portland-cement paint is applied to wet concrete. You may need to sprinkle or spray water on the paint after it has hardened enough so it will not be washed off. Portland-cement paint is applied with a whitewash brush or similar brush.

Coloring the concrete mix. Integral mix color formulas are worked into the concrete before it is poured. There is a fairly wide range of integral mix concrete colors available and some manufacturers will custom-mix colors for you to match an existing color you may have. Integral mix colorants are one of the easiest ways to color concrete. Use white portland cement for your concrete and work the mix into the concrete until the color is uniform. Add water and mix until in concrete is of any even consistency and the color is the same throughout.

If you want to save a little money with integral colorants, you can mix a separate batch of concrete following the directions above and lay it over plain concrete as a topping. Lay the colored topping when the slab has hardened slightly and the surface water is gone. This is extra work for you and you save little money, but it can be done.

Applying dry shake color. The dry shake, like the integral colorant, is available in a fairly wide range of colors. Dry shakes are sprinkled over the concrete as the surface is being finished. The steps are:

(1) float the slab;
(2) sprinkle dry shake over the entire surface, as evenly as you can;
(3) float the surface again;
(4) sprinkle another coat of dry shake evenly over the entire surface;
(5) finish the concrete.

To finish the concrete, you can use a steel trowel for a very smooth surface, or you can just float it, or you may float the concrete and then broom finish it. Broom finishing tends to give more even-looking color than do the smoother finishes.

Curing colored concrete. It is more difficult to cure colored concrete than plain concrete. Curing usually requires the use of water. When you add water to the surface of colored concrete, the color may become splotched. You must be very careful to keep a fine and even spray. Burlap and other water-laden materials, sometimes laid over plain concrete to aid curing, also result in splotching problems with colored concrete.

The application procedures for dry shake and integral colorants are very similar, varying only a little from manufacturer to manufacturer. However, any variation in the application instructions should be noted and followed. Always follow the manufacturer's instructions for the particular colorant you use.

Colored cement powder. The advantage of choosing this last method of coloring cement is that other than paint, this may be the most effective way to color a concrete surface. The colors come already blended into the white cement powder. There also is cement produced especially for adding color; you also may buy portland cements in light tints.

BUILDING EDGINGS
Why Use Edgings?
The main requirement of any edging scheme is that it contain the material of the walk or drive. Concrete walks and drives need no special edging unless a concentrated load is likely to be placed at the edge. For example, if the drive or walk is placed so that an automobile will

Raised edgings with hard walks define the yard space and add visual interest. Interesting effects can be created by combining concrete block or stone with cross ties.

be driven frequently over the edge, perpendicular to the length of the drive, then it would be a good idea to thicken the slab where the auto will cross. Make the thickened area at the edges approximately a foot wide.

The need for edging is less apparent with a material like asphalt or concrete than it is for loose materials such as shells, bark, or gravel. Any asphalt surface, however, will last longer and look better if you protect its edges, which would gradually crumble off otherwise. The methods discussed here can be used to contain the loose walk and drive materials as well as asphalt or concrete.

How to Add Edgings to Asphalt
Thickening. Asphalt walks and drives can be protected by thickening the edges and turning them down beneath the ground surface. A 4 inch asphalt walk, drive, or patio could be protected by thickening the edges to 8 inches and making the edges about a foot wide all around. The thickening gives extra strength to the edges and turning them under the soil surface prevents their crumbling off.

Railroad ties. Another way to protect asphalt surfaces is to add a continuous edge of railroad ties. Both the asphalt and the ties rest on a 4 inch base of gravel or sand. The cross tie edging should be installed first, giving you a firm object against which you can tamp the cold asphalt. Hold the cross ties firmly in place with pressure-treated 2x4 stakes. Drive the stakes flush against the cross ties to a depth of about 2 feet. Then nail them to the cross ties with galvanized nails. For 8

foot railroad ties, use a stake at each end and one in the middle of each tie.

Concrete curb. Asphalt surfaces also can be protected with a concrete curb. The curb requires form work. All form work is laid out and leveled as discussed in Chapter 5. A concrete curb 8 inches wide and a foot deep should be adequate for most localities, but check local building codes. You will lay a concrete curb on 4 inches of gravel. After the concrete has cured, the asphalt can be tamped over 4 inches of gravel or coarse sand. The curb will make the tamping easier and allow you to build a denser walk or drive.

Landscaping timbers. Still another way of protecting asphalt is to use a pressure-treated 2x6 landscaping timber as a curb. The 2x6 is staked like the cross tie curb described above. The curb and asphalt rest on a 4-inch bed of sand. This is probably the least effective of the asphalt curbs described here. But, where it is desirable to have a less prominent edge for aesthetic reasons, or where your budget does not allow a more substantial method, this is an adequate curb.

Using Edgings on Other Materials
Loose walkway materials. In addition, all these curbing methods can be used to contain loose walk and drive materials such as shells, bark or gravel. The latter, for example, needs a raised edging such as brick, railroad ties, or granite rocks.

Hard walks. Brick walks and drives can be curbed with railroad ties, landscaping timber edges, or a concrete block foundation and brick trim as described above for asphalt surfaces.

Railroad ties used as edgings can be set flush to the wearing surface of the walk, but always must be at least 3 inches deep in a trench with the widest side face down.

Set ties in trench before installing pavers. Length of tie below ground should equal its length above ground level.

Edgings of cut-off, vertically placed railroad ties can be used to create a planter that also serves as a walkway border.

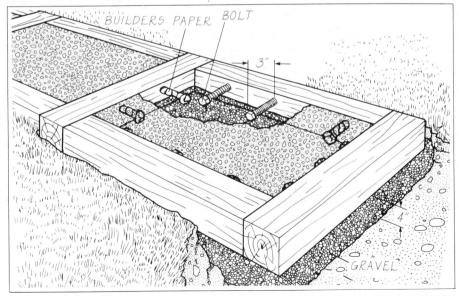

To hold cross ties permanently to concrete, install three bolts per tie before pouring the concrete. Wrap the bolts in builder's paper.

Cross ties. Cross ties of redwood or railroad ties may be used as a design element in walks or drives. In long walks, they can be laid perpendicular to the direction of the walk, as often as you like, to visually break up and de-emphasize the length of the walk. They can be used for similar reasons (as well as serving as a permanent form) to add interest to and visually break up large expanses of otherwise dull concrete. This is accomplished by laying the cross ties in a grid. Cross ties may be used as an edging material for concrete walks (or any concrete surface). They also may be used as permanent form work for the sides and treads of concrete steps. They are installed, in this case, in the same manner as ordinary forms.

Adding a support base. When cross ties are used as a gridwork, an edging material for concrete walks, or as a permanent form for the sides and tread edges of steps, they need a support base to keep them level and dry. They are heavy and they will lay level if you merely smooth the earth beneath them, but they may gradually settle if the soil has not been compacted. To prevent settling, you must compact the soil with a hand tamper and then lay down a 4-inch bed of gravel. The gravel will aid drainage and help combat frost heave.

Attaching the ties. You must provide a way to keep the concrete and ties on the same horizontal plane, while allowing space for the concrete to expand and contract. To do this, attach ½-inch diameter bolts that are 6 inches or longer to the side of the tie that will be in contact with the concrete. These bolts should be sunk into the tie, leaving 3 inches protruding from the tie. Space the bolts between 2 and 4 feet on center and place them continuously along the tie.

A section of 4-foot-wide walk will require three bolts evenly spaced along the length of the tie. Wrap the bolts in building paper, completely covering the bolts.

Mask the top of the grid with tape before pouring the concrete. This will prevent stains or debris from marring the wood surface.

Installing Concrete Block and Brick Edgings

Concrete block can be used as a curb base or ''mini-foundation'', allowing you to put a variety of masonry material on the base as a trim. Brick is a good trim to combine with the block.

First set the concrete block on a 4-inch bed of gravel or sand, mortaring the vertical joints as you set the individual blocks. Let the mortar set and then fill the block cores with concrete, leveling it with the top of the blocks. Before the concrete sets, put down a layer of mortar, and lay the bricks just as you would if you were building a brick wall. (Refer to Chapter 9 on building a brick wall.) You could build a concrete curb base (similar to the concrete curb described above) for asphalt surfaces and lay brick trim along it. Bricks may be set on edge instead of laid flat.

Adding Edgings to Wooden Walks

Creating the walk.   You may create a wood walk with 4x6 landscaping timbers which, when laid lengthways in the direction of the walk, can be tied together by nailing 1x3 spacers (approximately 1 foot long) at approximately 4 feet on center. Lay the timbers on a 4-inch gravel base. All the individual members are tied together, forming a whole.

Using a landscaping timber edging. Set a cross tie perpendicular to—and underneath—the walk, where the ends of landscaping timbers meet. The cross ties in this case are used just like cross ties under a railroad track (the landscaping timbers being the "railroad track"). Nail the landscaping timbers securely to the cross ties.

When 4x6 landscaping timbers used to create a walk are laid perpendicular to the direction of the walk, you can build a good edging by laying a continuous row of landscaping timbers on their 6-inch sides. The walk surface timbers will have been laid about an inch apart to facilitate

drainage. Nail the curb timbers to the walk timbers. Nail a 1-inch wide spacer, 6 inches long, between the walk timbers over the curb timber to provide extra strength by tying all the walk timbers together. This is optional, but recommended. The curb timbers rest on 4 inches of gravel, which extends under the walk but does not reach to the bottoms of the walk timbers.

Modular wood walks with edgings. For various reasons you may choose a modular wood walkway. The recurring pattern may be varied and the edging is integral with the construction of each modular section. Wood modules may be used with many other materials—gravel, brick, concrete, or asphalt—to create an integrated but varied visual pattern. A single wood module set on a bed of gravel may be an answer to small problems of drainage.

Choosing Cobblestone Edgings

This material is almost indestructable and requires relatively little base preparation. It can be used as swale material—to avoid erosion—or for any number of border uses around the lawn or garden. It is a handsome material and provides an attractive, rough contrast with a flat material such as concrete. It is an acceptable curbing for most walk materials: concrete, wood, brick, gravel (when the cobblestone joints are mortared), bark or wood chips, or other materials.

Creating Metal Edgings

There are various metal edgings that can be installed around walks. In an area where your primary concern is to keep grass out of a lightly used gravel or bark walk, you may use the lightweight aluminum edging sold as a garden edging. Use

a garden spade or lawn edger to cut a narrow, shallow trench for the edging; if your soil is very soft, you can push the light aluminum directly into the ground.

A metal edging may also be made of other materials, such as short lengths of downspout. These can be used to build a very small retaining wall if there is a slope of a few inches between a garden area and a walk. Dig a small trench—and insert the sections. They should touch. Fill with 2 inches of gravel inside and around the outside of the sections. If you wish, plant a decorative ground cover in the sections.

Modular wooden walkways, fast to install, lend themselves to do-it-yourself work.

Raised metal edgings can be made from galvanized downspouts cut down and set in trenches.

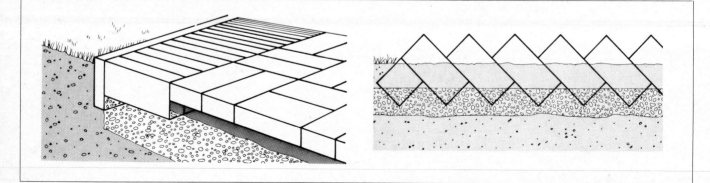

Brick can sit on edge on a gravel-plus-sand sub base to make an attractive edging. Set pretreated lumber or railroad ties in a trench if used as edgings—either flush to patio surface or to a minimum depth of 3 inches. Brick can be angled in trench with 2 inches of mortar or concrete. Use a half brick to end the edging. Extend concrete or mortar a few inches beyond the last brick.

5 HARD WALKS

This chapter will concentrate on the hard materials available for walks, and show you how to build walks using them.

CHOOSING THE MATERIAL

You can choose among a range of hard surfaces, which are usually needed for main entry walks, driveways, and equipment areas (like concrete slabs near the garage for lawn mowers and garden equipment). Sometimes you have a choice between either a hard surface or a "soft" one. For instance, you could use concrete pavers or gravel walks equally well for some garden, informal, or less frequently trafficked routes. The type of material you need will become clear if you think about the function of the walk before you select a material. An entry walk in cobblestone may look good, but heels will get caught in the joints and it will become slippery in the rain. Broom-finished concrete, or an exposed-aggregate concrete surface, would be a safer choice.

Maintenance

Maintenance is also a consideration for walks and other surfaces. A gravel walk where young children play or where there is active traffic—as for sports—will require continual maintenance. You often can improve maintenance and function by adding a border for gravel walks or patios, using cross ties or concrete curbs set several inches above the surface of the gravel. This cuts down on the spread of gravel, although it does not entirely solve the problem.

Temporary Walks

When budget enters into the selection of a walk, as it does in most building projects, you may find that gravel and pavers of any material are easier and cheaper to install than concrete or asphalt. If you need a temporary walk of a durable surface, as well as a material that is cheap initially and easy to remove when you are ready

for the permanent surface, cold asphalt might be a good choice. Or you might use wood—a "soft" walk—which could be saved for another use when you replace it with a permanent walk or surface.

EXCAVATION BASICS

Virtually every construction project involves preparation and most outdoor projects require some excavation. Digging is hard work and it is tempting to rent equipment to make the job easier. However, a small mistake made with excavating equipment can negate the time you hoped to save by using the machinery. You may be better off to do the project with hand tools or to hire an

excavation subcontractor to do it for you. If you gouge out areas due to poor use of a machine, you must fill them again. Shallow depressions and gouges can be leveled with gravel, or you can just let the concrete fill the areas—this is for gouges and depressions of only several inches. Deeper mistakes must be filled with an appropriate soil and compacted. However, building on fill soil is always questionable and may lead to problems.

Avoid building on fill whenever possible. If it is necessary to bring in foreign soil to replace unsuitable soil, check with your local building department and/or HUD. HUD has very specific requirements for building on compacted fill, and

Walks in heavily trafficked areas, such as walks to front doors, should usually be in hard surfaced materials. There are many combinations of materials to choose from.

Exposed aggregate is set in a grid of railroad ties to fit with the landscape.

A poured concrete walk requires a form nailed to stakes and aligned with level string.

Forms and stakes are nailed to withstand the pressure of the concrete. Forms are built with double-headed nails for easy removal.

your building official will know the compaction procedures for your specific project. To simplify drainage problems, you may have to replace heavy, clay soil if you live in an area subject to freezing and frost heave.

CONCRETE WALKS

Concrete is one of the most important building materials of the 20th century. Combined with reinforcing steel, it can be shaped in almost any form imaginable—and it has been. Concrete is very durable and, properly used, will last generations. The ingredients of concrete are available everywhere, making concrete a sensible choice for any project from a garden walk to a skyscraper.

Cost

The cost of concrete, as with any building project—large or small—must be evaluated for the specific project you have in mind. As a walk, for example, if concrete is an appropriate material (a consideration that must be made for all materials), it is cheaper than a pressure-treated wooden walk. Little form work is required for a walk. In a project requiring more form work, such as a long run of concrete steps, the cost of concrete is likely to be high—because you have to use so much wood for the forms. It would be more economical of time and money to build the steps in wood if you cannot rent forms for your steps. In determining the cost of concrete (or any other materials) for a given project, you must also consider all

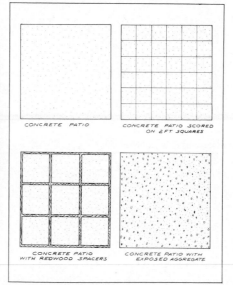

```
CONCRETE  PATIO          CONCRETE  PATIO  SCORED
                         ON  2 FT  SQUARES

CONCRETE  PATIO          CONCRETE  PATIO  WITH
WITH  REDWOOD  SPACERS   EXPOSED  AGGREGATE
```

Redwood (or pressure-treated wood) can be set in forms as a grid to visually break up the expanse of concrete.

the costs associated with building the project.

Advantages and Disadvantages

Concrete is fairly simple to work with, if you understand and follow the requirements of laying good concrete. The ingredients must be selected, mixed, and laid properly, at the right temperature, and with the proper reinforcement—you cannot take short cuts or eliminate steps if concrete is to perform for you.

Concrete lends itself readily to squared-off shapes. Some simple curves and freeform shapes can be made in drives and walks. However, the more complex curved above-ground structures, such as garden walls, may be too much of a challenge for the beginner because of the extensive form work involved. For walks, drives and slabs of any shape, however, concrete is a predictable, relatively inexpensive, and durable material with which to work.

Forms

Forms are a must for containing and leveling the concrete. Form work can simplify your work if you have a fragmented schedule. You can break the work into smaller, more manageable work segments, laying portions of your project separately. The grid is an example of this technique. A drive or walk, laid within a wooden grid of approximately 4-foot squares, can be laid all at once or one grid at a time using construction joints in the grids. You may prefer to leave the grid in place, making it part of your concrete design or pattern. For straight edges, 2x4 or 2x6 form members with 2x4 stakes at 4 foot on center will work well.

Building grids. Most forms are laid out and built almost identically, whether for walks, patios, or drives. The interior form or grid are typically 1-inch members the same height at the edges as the form material. The grid is formed by cutting the wood to the width it must span, then installing it at the desired spacing; for discussion here, we will use 4 feet. Nail these boards flush with the tops of the outside forms; now you can install four-foot boards between the boards just installed, at four feet on center. This gives you a 4x4 foot grid. Check the top frequently with a spirit level. The grid stays in place after the concrete is poured and becomes a permanent part of the surface. It is advisable to cover the tops with masking tape to keep them clean of any concrete.

The wood used for the grid should be durable. Pressure-treated wood is probably the longest lasting choice. Redwood is a close second for durability and you may like its aesthetic appearance over the pressure-treated wood, which is most often pine.

Creating curves. Curved boundaries can be laid out visually with a garden hose, or you can draw them in a rectilinear shape and set them out precisely.

Building the forms. Lay out a freeform shape with the garden hose or rope; the "correct" dimensions will be those that function and look visually correct to you. Set out 2x4 stakes at approximately 1 foot on center along the garden hose or rope. Nail thin ¼ inch plywood to the stakes. Shallow grooves may be cut into the outside face of the plywood so that it will curve easily; ⅛-inch cuts spaced every inch will make the plywood very flexible. The stakes bolster the wood and keep it from bulging once the concrete is poured. Remember that designers find the aesthetic design of freeform shapes more difficult than rectilinear shapes.

Adding Control and Isolation Joints

Control (contraction) joints and isolation (expansion) joints are essential to proper concrete work. All concrete expands and contracts as the outside temperature changes—and concrete always cracks when this happens. Control joints are relatively shallow cuts (less than an inch deep) made in concrete with a special tool called a "groover". These control joints become weak points at strategically located points along the walk or drive, to direct the natural cracking that develops in concrete. The cracks will occur at the control joints if they are properly placed. If you use a permanent wood grid approximately 4-feet square, you may omit the control joints.

Unfortunately, the successful placement of these joints is largely a matter of experience. You should not have any trouble if you place them 4 feet on center for 4-foot walks. For larger expanses, a 4-foot square grid should handle the cracking effectively. If you start looking around at concrete work, you may note that control joints are not generously used

by some contractors—and you may also find a number of unsightly cracks.

If you have a large expanse of concrete, it may be wise to take your drawing to the building department and to let them advise you about control joints. Or consult an architect—it will only take a few

minutes to locate the joints and ensure a better job.

Isolation joints (also called "expansion" joints) differ from control joints in design and purpose. They go all the way through the concrete to the earth. Their purpose is to absorb expansion of lengths

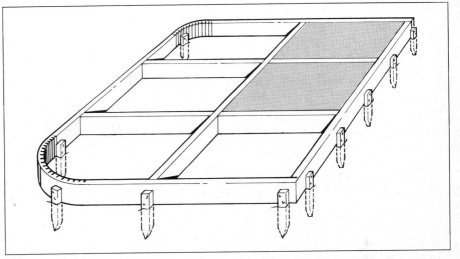

Grids fit into forms after the forms are staked; concrete can be laid in small sections. Curved edges on forms are created by making small cuts in the form board and bending it.

Short, curved forms may be made from ¼ inch plywood staked every 6 inches.

Control joints are cut with a groover tool. Board acts as guide.

Flexible expansion joint material may be bought prefabricated. It is installed between abutting concrete areas to absorb pressure created when concrete expands in the heat.

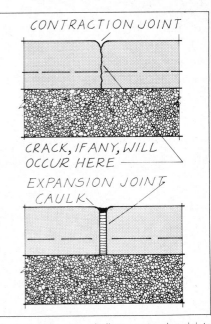

Control joints are shallow; expansion joints reach through the concrete, to the base.

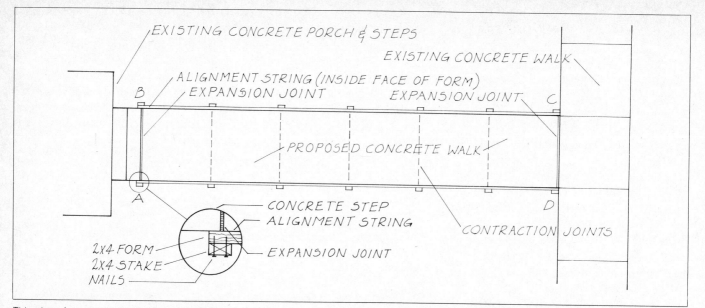

EXISTING CONCRETE PORCH & STEPS

EXISTING CONCRETE WALK

ALIGNMENT STRING (INSIDE FACE OF FORM)

B   EXPANSION JOINT   EXPANSION JOINT   C

PROPOSED CONCRETE WALK

A

CONCRETE STEP
ALIGNMENT STRING

2X4 FORM
2X4 STAKE
NAILS

EXPANSION JOINT

D

CONTRACTION JOINTS

This plan of a proposed walk shows all details needed for a good installation. Expansion joints are placed between new walk and existing steps and sidewalk. Control joints are marked and forms securely staked and nailed along alignment strings.

Set alignment strings carefully so walk will be straight. The final placement and setting of the form boards will be along the line of the string. Check it carefully.

Form boards are installed along the string line and nailed to the stakes.

of concrete that meet existing steps, other objects, perhaps the house foundation wall or some other structure. Isolation joint materials are available at all building supply houses.

Setting Up the Walk Forms

In home projects new work almost always is referenced from some existing point. For the following steps, assume you are laying a simple concrete walk from a porch to a sidewalk at the street. The sidewalk runs perpendicular to the walk, so that the walk intersects at a 90° angle.

Step one: staking. Set stakes at corners A,B,C, and D. The walk butts at the bottom step and runs straight out to the existing sidewalk. The inside edges of the stakes are set for the width of the walk plus the thickness of the wood in forms.

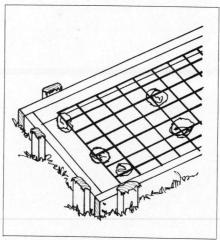

Place small rocks inside the form to raise the reinforcing mesh above the ground when pouring concrete.

Step two: stringing the stakes. Connect the stakes with string. Check the corners, assuring that they are 90 degrees. Nail the string to the centers of the stakes.

Step three: excavating. Excavate as required for the desired finish grade. Plan for 4 inches of gravel and a thickness of 4 inches for the concrete walk. This will vary according to frost depth requirements; check local codes. Cut the soil down 8 inches (in this case) from the top of where the new walk will be. Start at the base of the existing steps. There is little need to reinforce a 4-inch walk unless you know that an automobile or other heavy object will be moved across it. However, once again, check local codes for reinforcing requirements. A typical reinforcement for drives and walks is 6x6 #10 wire mesh reinforcement, set on stones to hold up the mesh.

Step four: checking the slope. Typical walk slopes are 1/8 inch to 1/4 inch per foot, sloping away from the house, garage, or other buildings to some planned drainage disposal point—most commonly the street, but often a swale or ditch and sometimes a catch basin or dry well. Grade and create the pitch before setting up the forms.

Step five: installing side forms. Install the side forms. The top of the forms will be just above the desired finished grade of the concrete. (The concrete will settle.) Set 2x4s on their narrow edge for walk forms. Nail the 2x4s to stakes. Oil the forms for easy removal.

Step six: adding control joints. Mark the location of the control joints on the forms. Control joints are cut into the concrete before it sets. Use a groover to slice thin, shallow cuts that are one-fourth the depth of the concrete. These joints are very thin and require no fillers. Place the joints every 4 to 6 feet. You may use more control joints, letting the lines serve as design patterns.

Step seven: installing isolation (expansion) joints. Because concrete expands when the temperature goes up, you need isolation joints to protect the concrete walk or drive from buckling and to protect the foundation wall (or other object) from damage when the walk or drive pushes against it. Hold the joint strip in place with stakes. Lay it between the edge of the concrete and the house (or other structure). Tap it in place.

Placing Concrete

Step one: remove all organic matter within the formwork. Tamp the soil down; you can buy hand tampers from a building supply house or you can make your own. Use any sturdy handle similar to a long shovel handle and add a wooden weight (about 8x8x12 inches) to the end of the shovel.

Step two: place the base. Lay and tamp the gravel. The thickness of the layer will vary according to local codes. Check before you begin to excavate the walk to the required depth.

Step three: reinforcing. Set the reinforcement, if any, using stones to hold the wire mesh off the ground. Keep the mesh a little closer to the bottom of the slab than to the top, but do not let it touch the ground.

Step four: moistening the form area. Moisten the ground to keep it from absorbing the moisture from the concrete.

Step five: placing and compacting the concrete. Pour the concrete, tamping it for compaction and working it with a shovel. Push the shovel up and down in the concrete in a cutting or slicing—not shoveling—motion. This breaks up the air pockets that form in the concrete when it is first poured. You can further aid compaction by walking around in the concrete in rubber boots. Pay particular attention to compaction at the edge of the forms. Where the drive or walk will be subject to heavy loads, rent a roller tamper to further compress the concrete.

Step six: finishing the surface. Use a length of 2x6 to screed off the excess concrete so it is level with the form tops. Do this with a partner, working the screed across the top of the forms in a sawing motion. Then use a wood float for the first finish of the surface. You can buy or rent a wood float, which is simply a flat wooden surface used to smooth out any raised spots and fill any depressions. A wooden float with a long handle will help save your back. If a rough surface is required, the surface you now have may be satisfactory to you. You also can use a broom to further roughen the texture and to give a rough stucco finish to the concrete. For a smooth finish, work the surface with a steel trowel.

Step seven: freeing the edges. When the concrete begins to set—sometimes within an hour in hot areas—free the outside edges from the form with a steel trowel. This helps compact the edge and prevents chipping. Finish off the edges with an edger to round the edges that guard against chipping.

Step eight: jointing. Form the control joints with a groover. The joints should not be deep. The Portland Cement Association guideline is ⅕th to ¼th of the thickness of the slab or walk. The width of the joints should be ¼ inch, although the jointing tool may result in a ½-inch slot at the top.

Step nine: final floating. Use a hand float, a broom, or trowel (depending on the desired final finish) around the control joints and at the edges.

Step ten: curing. Moisture is essential to the curing process. Curing compounds, sprayed over the concrete after finishing, hold moisture in during the curing period. You can also spray the concrete every day to ensure adequate moisture. Whichever method you use, leave the forms on for at least a week, or longer if possible—they aid in keeping moisture in.

Creating Various Concrete Finishes

All finish work begins after the concrete has been "struck off" (screeded) as described above. There are many finishes besides the basic ones described; others are described in Chapter 4. Instructions for the most popular finishes are provided here.

Using rock salt for a pitted surface. Where new concrete conflicts with the appearance of the existing surrounding materials, or you desire a rustic effect, you can achieve the appearance of an older, weathered and pitted texture by sprinkling common rock salt on the surface of the concrete before it sets. Put the rock salt on once the surface is otherwise finished as you want it (troweled smooth, floated, or broom finished). Press the rock salt into the concrete to about half the depth of each piece of rock salt. You need not do this individually by hand; embed the pieces of rock salt with a hand float and carefully press as many of the salt pieces down at a time as you can. The typical application calls for about 5 to 10 pounds or rock salt per 100 square feet. Tamp the salt in place and leave it in. The nuggets will wear away soon, leaving pits in the surface.

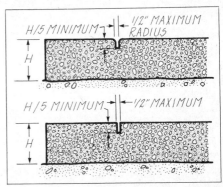

Control joints may have curved or straight finishes and ½ inch widths. Depth varies but a guide is 1/5th the thickness of slab.

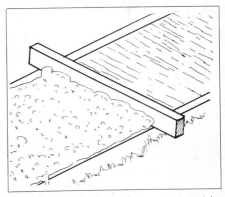

After it is poured (placed), concrete must be leveled by screeding with a 2x4 board.

Rock salt pits fresh concrete. Use this in mild climates only or surface will crack.

Exposed aggregate. Exposed aggregate is a well-known finish; you see it most often with a brown or gray aggregate. Aggregate commonly ranges in size from pea-size to about thumb size, distributed uniformly over the surface. But you may use any color or combination of colors you choose, or vary the size of the aggregate and group it any way you like. You can make mosaic patterns with it. It is probably better to use round or pear-shaped aggregate because the edges of the crushed type are sharp when exposed.

Creating an exposed aggregate surface is a three-step process. First the concrete must be placed and finished to a rough finish before placing the aggregate for the top.

Aggregate is placed on the surface, either scattered or hand set into a pattern, and then pushed gently into the surface of the concrete. Float smoothes the concrete over the aggregate.

Test concrete to see if it is set enough to hold the aggregate firmly, use broom and water pressure to wash the thin concrete surface away. Rent a combination broom and hose, to save yourself time and effort.

In aggregate finishes, it is important to apply the aggregate at the proper time. That time is after you have floated the concrete, while it is soft enough to press the aggregate in with a hand float—but not so soft that the aggregate sinks by its own weight.

Tools. In addition to the basic concrete tools—in this case, a short 2x4 or wood handfloat and a darby or long-handled float—you will need a hand brush and a stiff-bristled push broom with a hose attachment.

Distributing the aggregate. Sprinkle the aggregate over the concrete, in the pattern you want. For an even appearance, sprinkle the whole surface with aggregate before you press it in.

Setting the aggregate. Now press the aggregate in flush with the surface with a short length of 2x4 or a wooden hand float. Float the surface again with a wood float until the aggregate is covered with the concrete mix.

Let the concrete harden a little, testing it now and then with a hand brush. If the brush gouges out cement and moves the aggregate, let it set a while longer. The concrete should be hard enough to hold the aggregate in place while you brush the concrete from the top of the aggregate.

Brushing the aggregate. You can rent stiff-bristled push brooms with hose attachments to provide water near the concrete (where you need it). This is easier than brushing with one hand and holding the garden hose with the other.

Using the hose/broom, brush the surface, gradually exposing the aggregate. Remember, if the aggregate comes out as you brush, the concrete has not hardened sufficiently. Gradually remove the concrete from the surface and expose just the full top portion of the aggregate. Do not expose too much of the aggregate, or it will work loose later when it is walked upon.

Finishing touches. With the aggregate exposed, edge the concrete at the forms and cut any contraction joints. Then use a hand brush to touch up around the joints, if needed.

Timing. The above is not a difficult process, but it requires careful timing. Pour the concrete early in the morning to allow for mistakes. Lay out a test section somewhere (4 feet x 4 feet) and practice before you call out a ready mix truck and have to learn under pressure.

BRICK WALKS
Brick Patterns, Sizes, Joints

Most of the patterns used in brick walls may also be used in paving, as discussed in Chapter 4. There are many standard patterns, or you can design your own.

Closed vs. open joints. Brick sizes vary enough so that patterns with closed joints, where the brick butt against each other without mortar, may not remain square. Size variations in the brick cause the joint lines to waver. You could correct this condition with an occasional open joint, but this solution might be as visually disconcerting as the wavering joint line. In general, the larger the area to be paved, the more difficult closed joint patterns become. In narrow walkways it is less of a problem. If you use open joints, you can make the joints a little larger or smaller, as required for an even look. For patterns like running bond, in which the joint lines are not as obvious, closed joints serve well.

Forms for Brick Walks

Any brick pattern you choose will be better realized if you consider the formwork as part of your pattern. All paving needs some manner of formwork to look best. The form may be just a boundary, or it may be part of the paving design. For example, joints in brick patterns define the pattern; formwork can be used in the same way, as in a tight grid on wide walkways or terraces. Forms may be made of wood, brick, concrete, cross ties, stone, or other substantial form material. Forms define paved areas, serve as reference levels for excavation and base materials, and help keep the paved units at a uniform height. They also aid in laying the pattern.

Step one: staking the boundaries. In building forms for brick, or any material, first decide on a reference point from which to work. For example, if you are planning a walk from steps at the back of the house to a patio some distance away, a good reference point would be where the finished surface of the new brick walk touches the existing back steps at the ground.

Stake the outline of the walk on the ground and mark the boundary with string. Then determine the depth of your excavation.

Step two: excavating. If the walk is brick on sand, then you need to dig for the thickness of the brick, plus 2 inches for the sand, plus gravel—if you need gravel. A standard brick is about 2⅔ inches high. Gravel bases are typically 4 inches deep. So the excavation for the above example with brick on sand and with a gravel base would be 8⅔ inches beneath the point where the riser of the lowest back step touches the ground.

The best way to keep this depth even is to mark it on a stake which you can use as a ''ruler'', checking the depth as you excavate. All of the above assumes that your walk will follow the contour of the ground as it exists. If the ground is too steep, you will have to dig out (cut) some earth to get the walking surface as you want it. If the ground is too low, you will have to add earth (fill) before you lay your walk. Our example is based on a 4-foot-wide walk that follows the contour of the lawn as it exists. Excavate the area just a little wider than the walk materials. Backfill later as needed.

Step three: excavating the staked section. Excavate the walk from the back steps to its end, using the dimensioned stake and a spirit level to keep the bottom of the excavation level and at the right depth. A long-handled, pointed shovel will get most of the earth out; use a long-handled, square shovel to do the finish leveling.

Step four: planning the forms. For brick, you may use a cross tie outer form with 1x6 redwood cross pieces every 4 feet or so. You could instead use 2x6 redwood, or pressure-treated pine for the side and forms and 1x6s for the cross pieces. These are just two examples; there are other alternatives. For the purposes of demonstration, we will deal with 2x6 side forms with 1x6 cross pieces 4 feet on center.

The planning involves locating where the cross ties go, and the number needed. One typical way to handle the forms is to use 2x6 side forms that are 12 feet long. For the first 12-foot length of walk, you will need two 12-foot 2x6s and four 4-foot lengths of 1x6s for the cross pieces. Sketch your walk on paper, to scale, and figure out how much lumber you need.

Step five: setting the forms. The stakes should be 2x4s of redwood or pressure-treated lumber. Cut the ground ends of the stakes to a point and drive them two feet deep with a sledge hammer

(they should stick up enough so they can be sawed flush with the top of the forms). For a brick walk 4 feet wide, measure the exact widths of the nominal size 2x6 side forms and add this to the 4 feet. This gives the distance between the inside faces of the 2x4 stakes. Drive the stakes in place at 4 feet on center on both sides of the walk excavation—do not stake out more than 12 feet at a time. As you move along with your 12-foot lengths, frequently compare heights of the stakes to strings stretched along the forms on both sides—reaching from the step where you began to the destination points of the walk—to be sure the side forms line up.

Step six: laying the base. When the forms are in place, shovel gravel in, enough to do one 4-foot section at a time. Screed the gravel level, 4 inches deep. A screed can be made with a 2x6 or 2x8 by notching each end so that the underside reaches to where you want the level of gravel. Work the screed along the forms, leveling the gravel. Now you are ready to add a sand base and to lay the bricks. The following section is a summary of the above, with instructions for laying brick on sand over gravel.

Brick on Sand

Step one: staking the walk. Stake out the area to be paved.

Step two: preparation of the surface. Prepare the surface by cutting or filling as required and compact the soil, using a hand tamper. The surface should be smooth and level. Add the gravel base, as described above.

Step three: building the formwork. Construct the forms using some reference point from the house; a door, stoop, another walk, etc. Set the forms so the finished pavement will drain where you want it to.

Step four: laying the base. Shovel sand in the formwork as evenly as you can, then screed it level, to about 2 inches deep. A screed can be made from a 2x4 or 2x6 by notching each end so that the underside extends the desired sand level. Work the screed along the forms, leveling the sand.

Step five: moistening the surface. Spray a fine mist over the sand with the garden hose to settle it. Then add more sand if necessary and screed level again. It looks easy to lay bricks in sand and it is, but if the base of sand is not settled and level, the bricks will soon pitch a dozen different directions.

Brick (pavers shown here) may be installed over a smooth sand base for an attractive and durable walk.

Check bricks frequently with a level to ensure that you are maintaining the even surface you need for your walk. If brick does not maintain level, remove and reset the sand base.

Step six: laying the brick. Lay the bricks gently on the sand, being careful not to let the brick dig into the sand. Work a row at a time of whatever pattern you have chosen, using the screed to help you keep the pattern consistent within the forms. Lay the screed across the top of the bricks and tap with a hammer to level the bricks with the top of the forms. Use a spirit level as a frequent check. Continue in this manner until the paving is complete.

An individual brick may be leveled by tapping it gently with a padded object.

Step seven: filling the joints. Sprinkle a light topping of dry sand over the bricks. If the sand is not dry, let it stand on the bricks an hour or so before you try to sweep it in the joints—it will be easier to sweep and it will fill the joints more evenly if it is dry. Sweep the sand into the cracks. Avoid standing on the bricks while you do this. Wet the bricks with a gentle spray to settle the sand in the joints. Repeat the process if it appears the joints will hold more sand. When the sand drys, sweep the surface free of excess sand.

Brick on sand requires a permanent border. Otherwise, sand will escape at the edges and the bricks will begin to droop. Any forms suitable for asphalt (discussed in Chapter 4) also can be utilized for brick walks, terraces, steps, and ramps.

Brick on Concrete

Where it is desirable to have a smooth brick surface, first lay a concrete base and then place the brick on the concrete. The underlayment concrete does not have to be the typical 4 inches thick, as it does for concrete drives and walks. However, it should not be less than 3 inches thick and it is easier to work with at 4 inches, if you do not mind spending the extra money.

Another reason for using brick over concrete, and perhaps a more typical one, is to give a facelift to old concrete surfaces.

Step one: building forms. Build a form border at the edge of the concrete walk for terrace.

Step two: preparing the surface. If the concrete surface is smooth, rough it with a dilute muriatic acid wash. Clean and rinse it and brush on a light cement paste. On rough finished concrete, simply clean and dampen the surface.

Step three: laying a mortar bed. Cover the concrete with ½ inch of mortar, using the screed action as in leveling sand. Do not lay down so much mortar that it begins to dry before you get the bricks on it. The bricks and the concrete should be moistened with a fine spray before laying the mortar.

Step four: placing the brick. Set the bricks on the mortar, following the desired pattern. Start in one corner and work across. Butt bricks together if you want closed joints, or space them appropriately if the joints are to be mortared later. Press the screed across the bricks to level them. Check with spirit level.

Closed or sand joints. Let the mortar set for a minimum of 24 hours. If adding sand, sweep it into the joints. It is best to stay off the pavement for several days to let the mortar cure.

Mortar joints. Let the mortar base set for about 4 hours. Trowel mortar into the joints. When the joints are thumbprint hard, finish them out with a joint tool. Do not remove too much of the mortar. Fully mortared joints are suggested for regions with severe winters.

Brick with Dry Mortar Joints

Step one: laying the bricks on sand. Lay the bricks on a level bed of sand 2 inches deep (the sand may be on top of 4 inches of gravel, if required). Leave a minimum of ¼ inch of space for the joints and not more than ½ inch.

Step two: spreading mortar. Be sure the bricks are dry—the mortar will stick to the surface if the brick is damp. Spread the dry mortar mix over the bricks. Sweep it into the joints. Use a hand brush to work the dry mortar fully into the cracks. Then sweep off the excess with a broom.

Step three: finishing the mortar. Sprinkle the surface with a light spray

Sweep sand into the closed joints to finish your walk. Sprinkle sand lightly over the surface and sweep into joints. Keep adding more sand and sweeping until joints are tightly filled.

from the garden hose; let the mortar set about 2 hours. Clean the mortar from the brick surface with a wet, heavy cloth. Work as neatly as you can when using dry mortar; it is difficult to clean off once it is on the brick. When you have wiped away all the mortar that you can with the cloth, use a mortar cleaner, following the manufacturer's instructions.

Cutting Masonry

It is best to save all the masonry cutting until last. The cutting is a skill. It is easier to get the rhythm and technique down all at once, rather than trying to get the feel for it as you go along. Masons are able to cut brick with a trowel, but less skill is required for the following:

(1) measure the length and shape unit required;
(2) cut a groove with a scribing tool along the line to be cut;
(3) lay the unit on a level wood scrap—a 2x6 is ideal;
(4) place a mason's chisel along the line to be cut, holding the chisel so the cut bevels slightly away from the end to be used;
(5) strike the chisel firmly—the brick should split;
(6) have extra brick on hand, because brick sometimes breaks unevenly.

ASPHALT PAVING

Everyone is accustomed to asphalt streets and driveways. They are a utilitarian necessity. But asphalt as a low-cost design material for gardens and lawns has not realized its full potential. In many instances asphalt can do the same job that concrete does, at less cost. In fact, asphalt is cheaper than almost any other material of similar durability. It also is one of the easiest to install. Whether you do it yourself or hire a contractor to do part or all of the work, asphalt is a bargain.

Asphalt is ideal for paths and walkways. Just lay it and let it weather. If you do not like the black color, you can offset it by rolling on colored toppings such as gravel or crushed brick. You can cover whole areas with it, or you can combine it with walks of other materials like concrete and brick. Use the concrete and brick for the high-use areas—for sitting and cooking, and around entries to the house—and the asphalt for the surrounding areas and walks to more secluded, less-visible areas. Specially manufactured asphalt paints are available in a range of colors to contrast or blend the asphalt with the surroundings.

Types of Asphalt

Hot asphalt. Also called asphalt concrete, it is made by coating crushed rock with hot asphalt cement. It bonds much as concrete does. This is the kind of asphalt you see when the city repaves a street. Paving contractors use special equipment to compact the rock and spray the hot asphalt. It is difficult work, and is not for the amateur. Unless you have some special condition that requires hot asphalt, you probably could not justify the extra cost of using it. If you do choose it, find a contractor.

Cold asphalt. This version can be bought in premix form. It is spread out and then tamped or rolled in place. It can easily be worked by a homeowner.

Laying Cold Asphalt

Step one: building forms. Prepare the surface to be paved with asphalt, just as you would for concrete. Pay special attention to the form work; it will be permanent because the edges of asphalt crumble unless they have an edging. For the permanent frame, use cross ties, brick on concrete, plain concrete, stone, or nearly any other material, as long as it is substantial enough to hold asphalt in place. It is not recommended that you use members less than 2 inches thick. All wood should be preservative-treated. For thicker edges, which are recommended, use higher forms and excavate an extra six inches at the outside edge to permit a one-foot-wide thickening.

To cut brick, begin by measuring the size needed and scribing a line on the surface of the brick at the point you want to cut.

Set the edge of a mason on the scribed line. Hold the chisel firmly and tap the handle with a firm stroke.

The brick should break cleanly. However, brick will sometimes shatter; have extra bricks. Experience will improve your skill.

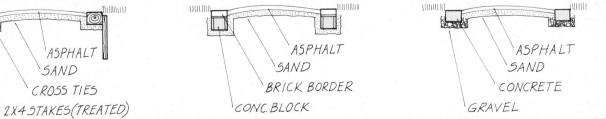

ASPHALT
SAND
CROSS TIES
2X4 STAKES (TREATED)

ASPHALT
SAND
BRICK BORDER
CONC. BLOCK

ASPHALT
SAND
CONCRETE
GRAVEL

Asphalt is an excellent material for walks and drives; however, the edges must be reinforced or they will break down quickly.

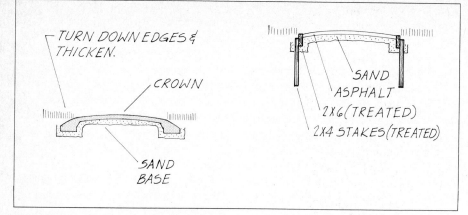

Asphalt edges may be thickened asphalt, concrete curbing, brick, timbers or railroad ties. The choice will depend upon your needs—for economy, pattern and appearance desired.

Step two: laying a base. Spread 2 inches of sand uniformly over the area to be paved.

Step three: spreading the asphalt. Spill the mix out in small mounds on the area to be paved. Rake a few mounds level with a garden rake to get used to handling the asphalt. Then dump out some more, but not more than enough to do a few feet of walk at a time. Rake the asphalt to about 2 inches thick. Build the depth up at the center or slope it to the side toward which you want to direct the runoff. Do not let any area become less than 2 inches thick. Thicken the edges to about eight inches, so that there is a one-foot-wide, 8-inch-thick rim around the perimeter.

Step four: leveling the asphalt. You can rent power and manual rollers and tampers to tamp or roll the asphalt. Rolling probably assures a smoother surface, but it still may be necessary to tamp some areas.

Before you begin rolling, brush the roller with water so the asphalt will not stick to it. You can use an old broom with burlap tied over it if you do not want to rent or buy a roller. Roll the surface until it is smooth and compacted, tamping any high areas. Use an asphalt tamper or make a tamper with a foot-square piece of ¾ inch plywood nailed to the end of a 1x3.

Step five: finishing or adding to the surface. It will take several rollings to reach the tight compaction needed for asphalt walks. Before the final rolling, you may wish to top the asphalt with sand, gravel, crushed brick or a similar finish. Sprinkle the surfacing material over the rolled asphalt evenly or in a pattern you like, and roll the material flush with the asphalt. This can be very

effective because the dark asphalt serves as a backdrop that emphasizes whatever topping you use on it.

Surface characteristics. One major difference between asphalt and concrete is asphalt's flexibility. Asphalt is a very malleable material. This makes the material easy to work with. If the grade changes are not too steep, the asphalt takes on the contour of the lawn. Any hollows that occur in the laying can easily be leveled later. Also, due to this flexibility, asphalt can be laid thinner than the minimum thicknesses required for concrete. Nevertheless, asphalt will accept the normal weights of garden use.

This thinness and flexibility may sometimes work against you, unless you are very careful about the base preparation. Asphalt will eventually reflect every ripple on ground you fail to smooth. Therefore, you must be especially careful with the base. If the soil shifts or sags for any reason, the asphalt will follow suit. Mud and moisture will work through the asphalt without a sand base of about 2 inches. In particularly wet areas, it may be necessary to use a deeper sand or tamped gravel base.

Maintenance and protection. Asphalt requires more maintenance than concrete, but the repairs are easier to make. The edges, unless a sturdy retainer is used, are particularly subject to crumbling because asphalt has no structural strength. If a wood edging is used, it should be pressure-treated for below-ground use. (Refer to the section on wood paving for information on pressure-treated wood.)

If not well compacted, asphalt will soften enough in hot weather to become dented by sharp objects such as iron chairs, tables, wheelbarrows, and skates.

Oil and gasoline dissolve asphalt. If you are planning a driveway or a parking space, you should leave an open space as groundcover where the oil will drip. You could instead pave that area with brick or concrete or gravel. Or you could paint the area where the car will be with one of the specially manufactured paints for asphalt.

Curing. Asphalt mix contains an agent that must evaporate for the asphalt to cure. This curing will take place within a week or so for walking purposes, but it may take as much as six months for it to cure enough for furniture placement and complete usage. Therefore, the best time to lay asphalt is just after it gets too cool to sit outside comfortably. By the next spring, it will be almost as hard as concrete.

PAVING WITH SOIL CEMENT

Soil cement paving uses the existing soil as one of the ingredients. The soil *must* be sandy or granular; clay does not combine well with the cement mixture. Soil cement gives the appearance of hard-packed soil and the surface remains rather gritty. It is best for informal areas, garden walks, stepping stones. It can be used as a drainage aid such as rounded curbs, shallow depressions for drainage of surface water, and areas where you do not want the less-natural look of concrete. It is even hard enough to be used for driveways, and it is very inexpensive. You can easily test whether you like the results and whether this type of surface will work. If you are pleased by the effect, but your soil is not sandy enough, you can remove about 4 inches of soil and replace it with sandy soil.

Installing Soil Cement

Step one: preparation. Rototill or dig up 4 inches of soil, removing rocks and organic matter. Install forms and/or borders for neat, long-lasting edges. Whether or not you use borders, thicken the slab edges to 8 inches and make the 8 inch edges about a foot wide all around (as recommended for asphalt also). The forms and/or borders can be like one of those described for concrete, brick, and asphalt surfaces.

Step two: installing cement. Spread the dry cement evenly, per the manufacturer's instructions. Work it into the soil with the tiller or with garden tools. Drag off the loose surface by pulling a heavy wood member across the surface, such as a 4x4 or a 4x6. Compact the soil smoothly; then replace the loose soil. Continue this process of dragging and compacting until the soil is at the level you want it with proper drainage. When the surface is the way you want it, wet it down with a fine spray. Let it soak in and repeat until the soil is thoroughly wet, but not runny.

Step three: finishing the walk. Roll the soil when it has dried enough so that you can work it without its sticking to the roller. At this stage, you should be able to press on it without leaving marks. Keep it lightly watered for several days and do not walk on it until it hardens—a week or so.

USING FLAGSTONE

Flagstone is expensive, but it is a classic paving material that offers a beauty many people are willing to pay for. The stone colors are pleasant—mild earth colors: yellow, brownish yellow, orange, red, gray. However, designing in color is always more difficult than in monotones; therefore, cast concrete flagstone is often used instead of the real thing. The imitation stone enables greater control of color, surface texture, and shape. For some, however, only the genuine stone will do.

Laying Flagstone

On sand. The thickness of individual stones varies, but when laying flagstone on sand, the stone must be at least two inches thick. Flagstone has uneven edges that create larger joints, which may make flagstone on a sand bed a nuisance unless the joints are filled with mortar (you cannot keep sand in wide joints). Mortared joints for flagstone are handled the same as brick in the ''Brick on Concrete'' section. The stones are cut the same as for other masonry.

On the ground or over sand-and-gravel base. Flagstone can be laid directly on the ground and this is often done for walks where a highly uniform surface is not required. For larger areas, more formal areas, areas subject to frost heave, and areas where people will congregate, you will need to prepare a better base.

Excavate enough soil to permit you to install 4 inches of gravel, and 2 inches of sand underneath the stone. Plan carefully so that the finished stone surface will reach to the elevation you desire. Before

you lay the gravel, level the soil well and tamp it with a hand tamper. Level and tamp the gravel.

On concrete or other surfaces. You can lay flagstone on any surface you can lay brick or other pavers. Stones thinner than 2 inches can be used on concrete. For an additional discussion of stone size and selection, refer to Chapter 4. Check that you have the flagstone correctly laid out before you fill the joints with mortar.

Using ground cover. As an alternative to mortar, you can use wider joints plus extra soil. Plant a hardy ground cover between the stones. Most ground covers would not grow in the joints if the stones were laid over concrete, however; the ground cover solution would work for flagstone laid over earth or for a 2-inch bed of sand with an earth base and sandy-earth joints.

QUARRY OR CERAMIC TILE

Outdoor tile is available in a number of sizes and finishes. Typical sizes are from 4x4 inches to 12x12 inches. They also come in octagonal and other geometric shapes. Those with glazed finishes give a highly formal appearance and, generally, should be used sparingly unless they fit with the character of the surrounding materials and design. Not all glazed surfaces are suitable for a walking surface. Check with the supplier about usage. Glazed surfaces are good for vertical surfaces that might otherwise become stained—such as vertical surfaces around outdoor cooking pits. Quarry tile is the color of the natural clay from which it is made. Ceramic tile includes many types and sizes of tile, both glazed and unglazed.

Thin tiles are more difficult to work

Ceramic quarry tile is a very attractive material for exterior walking surface. Care must be taken in choosing tile that will look appropriate and will not be slippery when wet.

with than the thicker ones. Tiles can be as much as 2 inches thick, and it is preferable to use these, if possible.

Laying Ceramic or Quarry Tile

Planning the design. Although tile dimensions need not define your design, you can cut down on unnecessary tile cutting—assuming an inch or two does not affect your project—by planning the walk and design as multiples of the tile size. Allow about ¾ inch (maximum) for the larger tile joints and ½ inch for the smaller ones. If you were planning a four-foot walkway in 12x12 tiles, the walk would be 4 feet plus three ¾-inch joints or 4 feet and 2¼ inches, plus whatever border you have chosen.

Cutting the tile. Tile is hard-fired, brittle, and difficult to cut smoothly by hand. If you have curved areas where considerable tile must be cut, you should leave those areas for last, if possible. When you are ready, mark the tiles with a pencil and take them to a stoneyard where they can be cut smoothly with a diamond saw. Saw cuts give crisp, accurate edges. For small cuts, you may use a tile nipper and cut away ⅛ inch at a time. Ceramic tile outlets often will lend a ceramic tile cutter, asking for only a refundable deposit.

For smaller areas and areas where the line value is not important to your design, cut the tile yourself, by hand. Draw the line to be cut with a pencil. Lay the tile on a wood scrap as you would to cut brick.

With a small chisel and a hammer, start well back from the line and chip away the tile, a little bit at a time, until you approximate the desired shape. Scratching the line of the cut as deeply as you can will offer some insurance of a better edge when you chip the excess tile away.

If the tiled area is to have a raised border, you can avoid cutting entirely by lapping the border material over the surface of the tile, using the border to define the edge, rather than the tile.

Tile on sand. Only thick tiles should be laid on sand. Tiles 2 inches thick can be laid on a 2-inch bed of sand. Thinner tiles become less and less stable in the sand. The sand itself should be on well-compacted soil (tamped), a gravel base, or a concrete base. To set the tile:

(1) stake out and prepare the area to be paved, as for brick on sand;

(2) level a ½ inch bed of sand with a screed, as for brick on sand;

(3) set the tiles in place, leaving the form in place to help contain the sand and tiles.

Tile on mortar. In areas of the country where the weather is very mild and where the soil is stable, you can lay a bed of mortar 1 inch deep right over the soil. The tile is carefully worked into the mortar; the joints are filled with mortar and tooled as desired. However, mortar on earth is not suitable for areas of extreme cold. Here is a step-by-step breakdown.

1. Stake and prepare the area to be paved as for brick on sand. Since the mortar right on the earth, assure that the earth is smooth, level, and very well compacted; tamp as needed. Otherwise, the tiles will move underfoot, causing the mortar joints to crack.

2. Lay a 1-inch mortar bed, using a screed. Do not put down more mortar than you can cover in about an hour, or it will harden before you get to it.

3. Sprinkle cement lightly over the mortar bed.

4. Soak the tiles in clean water for at least 15 minutes before laying them. Stand them on edge to drain off excess water before placing them.

5. Place the tiles, using a screed to level them. Lay the screed across the top of the tiles and the top of the form edges and press down to help level the tiles.

6. Use a hammer handle to gently tap down individual tiles that still are not level.

7. Do not stand on or apply any pressure to the tiles at this point.

8. Mix a joint mortar thin enough to be poured into the joints. Pour the mortar into the joints.

9. When the joint mortar is the proper consistency, tool the joints with the appropriate jointing tool.

10. Clean up mortar splatters immediately with a damp cloth.

11. Do not walk on the tile for about a week.

Tile on concrete. For outdoor use, concrete provides the best subsurface for tile. To lay tile over concrete:

(1) prepare the surface as for brick on concrete, including a border form;

(2) set the tile in a ¾ inch bed of mortar;

(3) fill the joints with mortar, as above;

(4) tool the joints and let the surface set before walking on it.

This walk is of quarry tile rubble. The pattern created looks like small flagstones. Combined with the cross tie divider strips, the material fits suits the garden space.

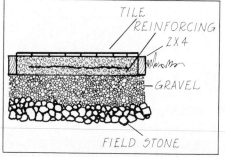

To prevent tile cracking from frost heave, provide a well drained, reinforced base.

Tile on wooden surfaces. Tile may be used on wooden walkways, steps, and ramps. Existing wooden areas to be paved must never sag. Any sag will cause the tile joints to crack and sometimes will cause the tile itself to crack. You could use professional consultation to advantage here; otherwise, you might easily waste more money on a tile project than the professional service would cost you.

To tile on wood:

(1) make sure the surface is level;

(2) place a layer of waterproof building paper over the wood;

(3) attach stucco mesh;

(4) apply a 1-inch mortar bed;

(5) dust the surface with cement;

(6) set the tiles, using a screed or length of board to help keep tiles level;

(7) check frequently for level with a spirit level.

INTERLOCKING PAVERS

Concrete pavers offer as much versatility (or more) as conventional poured concrete. Where the soil and climate permit, pavers may be laid right on the ground. As with most concrete blocks, they are relatively inexpensive.

Choosing a Subsurface

Over concrete. Pavers may be laid over a concrete slab. When this method is used and the joints are mortared and finished with a joint tool, the surface has a smooth, highly finished appearance with a line value similar to that of a brick surface.

Over sand. Pavers on a bed of sand can have either sand or mortar joints. If sand joints are chosen, note that concrete pavers are good in areas where there are trees. The pavers lift up when the tree roots grow, rather than break and crack as would a concrete slab. Concrete pavers with sand joints also allow drainage down to the roots of the trees and shrubs.

Design and Strength

Patterns and joints. Concrete pavers can be laid with closed joints (each paver butted against the other with no joints). Pavers may be grouped within wooden grids in the same manner as poured concrete. They may be laid in basketweave, ashlar, grid, running bond, or nearly any pattern you need. Usage, climate, and soil conditions will deter-mine the best type of joint and the preferred method of installation, as these conditions do for any lawn surface.

Installing Pavers

Pavers used for patios and walkways are split in the same manner as common brick. However, their installation is a little different than that of other materials, in that the grade is first set in coarse sand and the bricks laid on top of it. The workman always adds the next rows by working on top of the brick he has laid.

Excavating and grading. For those interested in the process, excavate 4 inches for the gravel and sand, plus the depth of the paver plus 2 inches, all the way across to allow for grade. Add the gravel layer. Then spread a base of torpedo sand at least 2 inches thick across the entire patio area. Check the grade in the sand using a level and a long, straight 2x4. If you need to adjust the grade, add more sand. Once the grade is set, do not step back onto the sand. If you must step on the sand again, regrade it. Tamp the sand thoroughly.

Laying the pavers. Starting from a corner, lay four or five pavers in line and work straight to the next corner, standing only on the blocks you have laid and not on the sand.

Adding the sand. When complete, sweep fine mason's sand onto the paving stones and wet the sand. The pavers will now interlock to form a continuous, firm surface. Repeat this process. Do not use portland cement mix on the pavers. When the patio is done, finish the edges with railroad ties or end blocks. Some paver manufacturers make special end stones for the purpose.

Finishing the surface. Finally, sweep the patio well, wash it down with the garden hose, and apply a good coat of cement sealer to extend the patio's life.

Quantities needed. Pavers, depending on their shape, are usually needed at a rate of 2½ per square foot.

MATERIALS LIST FOR SEVERAL TYPES OF 4 FT.X25 FT. WALKS

Material	Number Needed*	Gravel	Coarse Sand	Fine Sand
Brick	470	1 yard	1 yard	3-4 bushels
Patio Block	110	1 yard	1 yard	3-4 bushels
Paving Stones	270	1 yard	1 yard	3-4 bushels

(No figure is given for flagstone because its size varies from quarry to quarry)

*Extra blocks should always be purchased at the time of installation to ensure later color and texture match of repairs.

Concrete pavers, sometimes called patio block, come in various colors and surface textures. The blocks can be scribed and cut like bricks and used in walks or as edgings.

6 SOFT WALKS

Soft walks include loose paving and wooden pavings. They serve better than hard surfaces in some lawn and garden situations. For example, around children's play areas—where there may be swings and other play equipment—a hard surface would be dangerous and inappropriate, and a live groundcover could not survive. However, a bark mulch in such an area of high activity gives a relatively soft surface to protect children if they fall.

Modular sections of pressure-treated wood may be laid as a walk or grouped in a patio area. Slight spacing between boards provides good drainage.

A bark and wood chip walk runs parallel to a heavy railroad tie fence. The soft material is held in place by an edge of 2x4s set into the ground.

In gardens and areas where you want to preserve a natural appearance, bark or wood chips look more appropriate than concrete or other hard-surface walk materials. These natural materials also benefit the soil as they decompose.

Another important advantage to these materials is their relatively low cost. Economy can be a factor in selecting a soft walk, since the materials are cheaper to buy and easier to install than hard surfaces.

HOW TO USE LOOSE MATERIALS

Loose aggregate paving is best for informal areas, where the traffic is not great and where the soil readily absorbs rainfall. It is not appropriate for tennis, volleyball, badminton courts or other backyard athletic areas because the surfaces slip under pressure. The pieces will scatter. In regions with good drainage conditions, loose aggregates may be laid directly on the earth. The existing drainage patterns will be maintained because the rainfall will filter through the aggregate and run off as before, assuming that adequate weep holes have been installed at the grade level of any border or edging material. You can lay loose aggregate on a shallow bed of gravel, slightly above grade. All loose aggregates require permanent borders to keep them in place (see "Edgings", Chapter 4).

TYPES OF LOOSE AGGREGATE
Gravel

Gravel does not absorb water as do organic materials and thus is a good drainage material. Where you wish to use organic materials (bark or wood chips, for example) and the soil drains poorly, a base of gravel under the organic material will improve drainage.

Size and shape. Gravel is available crushed or whole in various sizes. The crushed gravel is typically ¼ inch to ¾ inch—although it can be found in much larger pieces or stones. Crushed aggregate is usually not a good walking surface because the edges of the crushed material are sharp on bare feet. However, it acts as a good drainage base. Whole gravel is available in nearly round form and in smooth, irregular forms, ranging from ¼ inch to 2 inches and larger to stone sizes. The larger pieces are not comfortable to walk on but are good for decorative purposes such as a cobble-like edging. Crushed or whole, gravel packs best when there is a mix of sizes from about ¼ inch to an inch—and this mix will compact into comfortable surface for walking. Uniform sizes do not pack well, and will move around when walked on.

Other Crushed Stone and Brick

Crushed granite comes in a variety of sizes and thus packs well—but again, crushed aggregates are not the best walking surfaces.

Crushed brick may be used as a loose aggregate. However, it is relatively expensive, has sharp edges, and the color is sometimes more showy than desirable for the normal low-key and service uses of loose walks and pavements.

Bark and Wood Chips

Bark blends in well with natural surroundings. In kitchen gardens, the bark becomes a useful mulch as it decomposes. The old bark, when decayed, can be transferred to the compost pile and replaced with new bark. It is a good way to obtain paths and mulch at the same time.

Fir bark is a warm, dark bark that does not splinter readily. Therefore, it is an excellent material to use in children's play areas—around swings, slides, etc. It will last as long as three years with a little maintenance. The soil beneath may be sterilized if you wish, in order to cut down on weeding. When using loose materials, however, it is probably best to avoid soil sterilizers and to just pluck the weeds that come through.

Other soft aggregates include wood chips and shavings, sawdust, even pecan and walnut shells. These materials are relatively cheap, but they do not function as well as bark for paving.

All organic paving is susceptible to bacteria and insect infestation and thus decomposes and "wears out". If you do not have a use or disposal area, organic paving may not be for you.

WOOD PAVING

Pressure-treating techniques have made wood a durable, versatile, relatively cheap, and easy-to-install pavement. Pressured-treated wood may be installed below ground, on grade, or raised to allow the existing drainage to remain essentially unaltered. Wood is an especially pleasing material for home use. The scale, color, texture, feel—and even the sound it makes when you walk over it—are pleasing and comfortable. Projects done in wood are easier to design around than those done in any other material. However, for the most economical and durable projects, choose wood given the best preservative treatment for each usage.

Treated Wood

Specification markings. Pressure-treated wood is available in all sizes, enabling a wide range of paving designs. There are established standards for wood treatment quality. Treated wood should be stamped with proper usage information. Pieces marked LP-22 ABOVE GROUND USE ONLY .25 should be used only where the wood will not be in direct contact with the earth, as for walks on stringers above ground. Pieces marked LP-22 GROUND CONTACT .40 may be used for on-ground projects and some in-ground projects, such as fence posts. FDN FOUNDATION .60 means the wood is suitable for use completely un-

Two feet square modular sections are set to create a standard four foot width walk.

Pressure-treated lumber is marked to indicate proper usage for your convenience.

Wood walks of almost any design may be created by setting boards on stringers.

A bed of coarse crushed stone is laid near this fence. It provides a good drainage bed and a relatively firm surface for stacking firewood or other material.

derground—in some cases, even in building foundation work. The decimal figure indicates the amount of treatment per unit area of wood.

Using treated wood. The timbers can be laid on gravel or sand and staked at the outside timber. Installing a 1x3 spacer at regular intervals—about four feet on center—helps keep the timber exactly parallel as you install it.

Laying 4x6 timbers on the 6 inch side, parallel to the direction of the walk, draws the eye along the lines of the grooves. Such a walk would be good for an entry. There is a degree of visual direction in such a walk. For a more static appearance, the same timbers may be cut into 4 inch sections and laid in a bed of sand. The procedure for construction is much the same as for brick on sand. As for all pavements laid in sand, add a permanent border, as discussed in Chapter 4.

For another variation using the same timber size, lay stringers on a gravel bed and nail 4x6 timbers across them. In this case, stringers are sections of 4x6 running the length of the walk. They should be set into the gravel about 2 inches to secure the walk in position while supporting the cross members. This is a slightly raised walk.

Building Modular Wood Paving
One of the simplest and most versatile paving units is a 2x2 foot wood module that can be assembled as a walk, or just about any outdoor area. The wood should be pressure-treated. The following describes the building procedure and gives material requirements for a 4-foot walk that is 36 feet long.

Tools and materials. You need a pencil and a carpenter's ruler, a hand or power saw, and a hammer. Each block is made from two 8-foot lengths of 2x4 lumber and twenty-four 8d galvanized nails; the galvanizing resists rust. For this walk size you need thirty-six 2x2 foot modules.

Assembling the modules. From each piece of 2x4 cut three pieces one foot 11½ inches long for top boards, and one piece 2 feet long for a stringer. You will have a total of 6 top boards and 2 stringers from both 2x4s. Lay the top pieces on the two stringers; space them evenly, allowing ¼ inch on the sides and ends of the runners.

Use four 8d nails, two on each end, to attach each top board to the bottom stringer. You may nail from the top or bottom depending on whether you want the nails to show. Install the nails at least one inch in from the ends and sides of the lumber to avoid splitting the timber. For easier nailing, holes may be predrilled using a ³/₃₂-inch drill bit. The modules can be built inside the house, or outdoors, and stored in the garage or basement until it is convenient to lay the walk. With blocks this size, almost any job goes quickly.

Installing Modular Wood Units
Tools and materials. To prepare the ground for the 36 feet of walk, you will need a ruler, shovel, garden rake, six 80 lb. bags of sand, 144 square feet of 6 mil black polyethylene, four 2-foot stakes, some string, and four 12-foot 2x6s.

Preparing the base. Prepare the walk area by pounding 2-foot stakes into the ground to mark each corner and by running string between stakes to outline the walk. Remove the topsoil to a minimum depth of four inches and smooth the surface with the rake. Lay a two-inch base of compacted sand in the excavated area. Install the perimeter 2x6s set on edge, butted together at the corners and nailed at each end with two 8d nails.

Cover the sand or gravel with 6 mil polyethylene film to eliminate weed growth and then cover the film with a 2-inch base of sand. The black polyethylene will not be noticeable. Use a heavy nail or rod ¼ inch in diameter to punch drainage holes about 12 inches on center across the surface.

Setting the modules. Level the sand with a rake. Start placing the modules, working from a corner. Butt each one snugly to the next. After the modules are in position with the walk perimeter, backfill around the edges of the walk to create a smooth transition from the lawn to the walk.

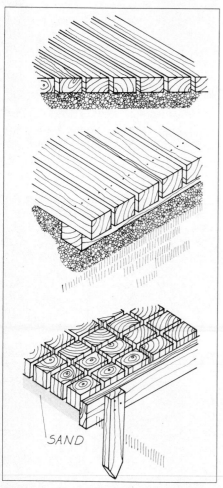

SAND

In some areas wood walks may be laid directly on gravel; sturdier walks are nailed to stringers—parallel cr perpendicular to the walk; timber sections may be set in sand.

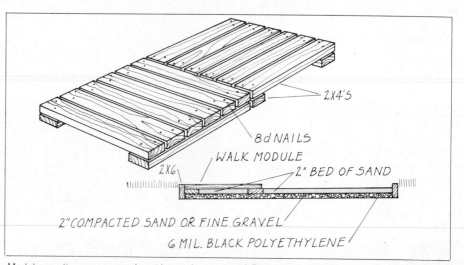

2X4'S

8d NAILS

WALK MODULE

2X6

2" BED OF SAND

2" COMPACTED SAND OR FINE GRAVEL

6 MIL. BLACK POLYETHYLENE

Modular sections are properly set in sand over gravel. Plastic sheet is laid over the gravel and sand is placed on sheet. Puncture the sheet for drainage.

7 STEPS, RAMPS & BRIDGES

Grade changes in a yard may make the area more interesting, but may make whole areas of your yard unusable. Here, wood steps and a large landing cover a grade change.

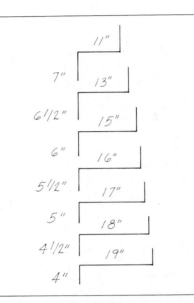

The relationship between treads and risers may be different from what might be logically expected; the higher the riser, the shallower the tread. Low risers combine with deep treads.

There are some very specific, technical requirements for design and construction of steps and ramps. You must understand these details before attempting to build. However, steps and ramps can, in addition to being very functional elements, be visual assets to your total design. The purpose of all steps and ramps is to allow the movement of people and equipment from one grade to another in safety and comfort. Before you begin determining riser heights or ramp slopes, consider the following:

(1) What do I want these steps or ramps to do?
(2) Who will use them?
(3) How can I make the steps and/or ramps contribute to the total design?

DEALING WITH SLOPE CHANGES
Evaluating Your Options

If you keep the major questions in mind, the technical solutions will fall in place. For example, there is no set width for steps, and no "best" material. The primary requirement is that the steps work for you and look right for your project. If you have a big house and plan extensive outdoor entertaining on a large, multi-level patio or in the yard, a single, 4-foot-wide flight of steps between levels will not do the job—functionally or aesthetically. In this case, steps that extend the entire length of the patio (or several separate steps) would work and look better. Depending on circumstances and the grading, however, you may actually need a ramp rather than steps. A gentle slope would not require steps.

Ramps. Ramps perform the same function as steps, but if you or a guest happens to be in a wheelchair, any flight of steps is not a comforting sight. If your slope must be climbed by people in wheelchairs or with canes, children on bicycles and tricycles, or anyone using wheeled lawn equipment, you may find that a ramp is a more feasible option. Some circumstances may require a combination of ramps and steps.

Proportions and size. A large house with a wide patio calls for steps and/or ramps on a similar scale. However, if you have a small, intimate patio right outside a bedroom, wide steps would look ridiculous. Study your needs and the scale of the surroundings carefully before you begin designing steps and ramps.

Design Guidelines

People designing for typical urban and suburban environments have found that certain guidelines on tread/riser relationships and ramp slope relationships can be very helpful. Here are some notes on tread/riser relationships.

1. Many experts believe that the best tread/riser proportion for the garden is a 15-inch tread with a 6-inch riser. This ratio is probably the most popular, but it cannot always be achieved, nor is it always appropriate for your needs.

2. If steps join a walk or are part of a walk, the steps should be the same width as the walk.

3. If possible, where a flight of steps abuts a walk or drive at right angle, the steps should be set back at least 2 feet from the walk.

4. The tread/riser relationship should be consistent throughout the flight.

5. The treads should be pitched forward approximately ⅛ inch per foot to assure adequate drainage.

6. Landings should be the same width as the treads, and not less than 3 feet long.

7. Stair railings are recommended for flights in which the rise is greater than 30 inches.

8. Avoid risers that are less than 4 inches and more than 7 inches—for stepped ramps as well as flights of steps.

9. Avoid treads that are less than 11 inches deep.

10. Treads and risers should not be tapered. For example, if you have a 6-inch riser, it should be 6 inches along the entire width of the steps; the same is true for treads.

11. All sections of ramps falling between risers (treads) should be the same length.

Gentle changes of grade may be handled with sloping walks (ramps) or combinations of steps and ramps (stepped ramps). The length of ramp sections should be consistent.

Steep slopes will require the construction of steps. This slope is climbed on steps that cover the slope on an angle. There are landings wherever the steps change direction.

Sizes mentioned in Notes 8 through 11 are commonly used relationships, even if not acknowledged standards. Variations from these relationships are uncommon and, therefore, unexpected. Changes from standard proportions could cause an accident. You should design on a larger scale for outdoor steps and walks and ramps than you would for inside steps. Space indoors is usually at a great premium. Small steps tend to look small and out of scale on generous suburban landscapes; but if you are designing for a small, intimate, urban lot, your step space may be at as much a premium as indoors. The basic requirement always remains the same: steps and ramps and walks must be wide enough to accommodate the traffic they will have. A 4-foot garden walk usually is adequate for one person to stroll comfortably, but a five-foot or greater walk is needed for two people. If at all possible, never reduce the width to less than 1½ to 2 feet and then do so only for short lengths of passageways or steps.

Figuring Step Requirements

First, find the slope of the intended ramp or flight of steps. As shown in Chapter 3, the slope is found by dividing the height of the rise by the length of the run. To determine these dimensions, stake a line to the top of the slope and stretch it tightly across to a tall stake on level ground at the bottom of the slope. Use a line level to check for level. For example, if the distance along the line from the top of the slope to the proposed edge of the last tread is 7 feet 6 inches, you would install six 15-inch treads along the horizontal distance (or run) of the slope (90 inches divided by 6 treads=15 inches). If the distance down from the level line to the ground is 3 feet, you will need six 6-inch risers.

The following plan is for a simple flight of steps that can be built straight down any convenient point on a slope. It may be part of a walk or merely provide access between any changing lawn levels. There are many cases where the step solution will be this simple, so that you will be able to use the ideal tread/riser relationship shown. However, there are times when you may have to deal with a more difficult slope than the one described above. To create steps that will be comfortable and convenient even though the slopes are steeper and longer than the ideal, you will have to manipulate the route of your steps as it works its way down the slope.

Handling steeper slopes. When the slope or grade is steep, you have to change the layout of the steps or ramps to increase the amount of run relative to the rise of the slope. This means your route down the slope will not be a straight one. For example, you may be able to solve the problem of getting an acceptable tread/riser relationship by simply running the steps diagonally across the slope. As an alternative, you may use a series of slights and landings.

There are other ways to deal with steep slopes or extreme changes in grade due to retaining walls or other grade controls. A flight of steps can be raised on stilts. More complex versions of this solution might incorporate a series of landings to

jog down the slope. This same idea also can be employed in designing any run of ramps. If necessary, the slope itself may be modified by cutting from the top and filling at the bottom.

DESIGNING AND BUILDING RAMPS

Ramps are used where a grade transition is too gentle for comfortable steps or too sloped for the run to be called a "walk". A surface with a pitch of more than 5 percent is considered a ramp. Of course, ramps are indispensable for the handicapped and the elderly, and they are convenient for any wheeled equipment that must be moved from level to level in the lawn. Ramps rarely replace stairs

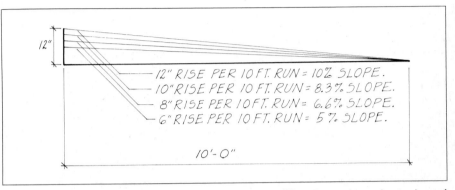

Any walk with a slope of 5% or more is considered a ramp. When the grade reaches a slope of more than 8.3%, a ramp must be combined with steps for comfortable walking.

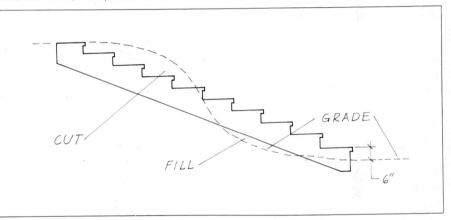

If a grade is very steep and short, you may have to cut away the upper section of the slope and move soil, as fill, to the lower level of the slope. Do this carefully and compact the fill. Anchor steps into firm subsoil with a foundation at the top and bottom steps.

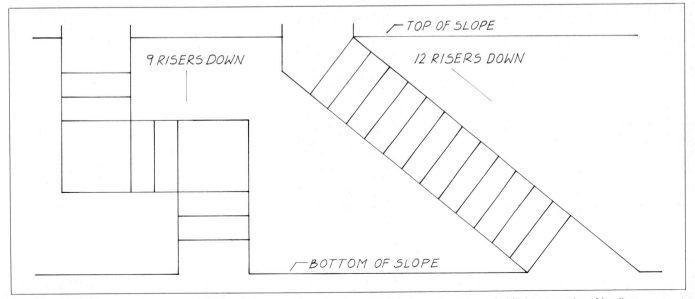

A steep slope may be handled in more than one way. Here the same slope is traversed in either an angled flight or a series of landings.

unless absolutely necessary, since some people find them hard to use.

Designing Stepped Ramps

Some grades will require a combination of a ramp and steps, called stepped ramps. The ramps may utilize single risers, pairs of risers, or longer flights.

The selection of steps and/or ramps is a compromise between your terrain as it exists and the slope you have to give it to obtain good tread/riser relationships. For fairly gentle slopes, use stepped ramps with single risers; when you use stepped ramps with single risers, the grade should be no more than would lie on an imaginary line connecting the bottom of the upper riser of each pair of risers.

(1) Ramps and stepped ramps should be the same width as the walks they meet when they reach ground level.

(2) Risers should not be higher than 6 inches.

(3) Treads (similar to landings) are most comfortable to walk on if they provide space for one or three comfortable paces—approximately three or nine feet.

(4) The maximum gradient for a ramp of any extended length should not exceed 1:12 (8.33%), not including curb ramps.

(5) Handrails should extend a minimum 18 inches beyond top and bottom of ramp.

(6) The minimum clear width of any ramp is 3 feet. Where ramps are heavily used by pedestrians and service deliveries, there should be sufficient width to accomodate both, or provisions made for alternate routes.

(7) The bottom and top approach to a ramp should be clear and level for a distance of at least 5 feet, allowing for turning maneuvers by strollers, dollies, or wheelchairs.

(8) Plant materials should be located so that shadows do not prevent sun from melting snow and ice on ramp surfaces.

(9) Ramps should be designed to carry a minimum live load of 100 lbs. per sq. ft.

(10) Low curbs along the sides of ramps and landings (2 inches) should be provided as surfaces against which wheeled vehicles can turn their wheels in order to stop.

(11) Ramps should be illuminated to an average maintained light level which ensures their safe use in darkness. It is important that the heel and toe of the ramp be particularly well illuminated.

(12) Ramps should be maintained properly to keep them from being hazardous. Debris, snow, and ice should be kept off the surface. Handrails should always be securely fastened.

BUILDING WOODEN STEPS

Most home projects are easy to lay out because there are so many reference points from which to start. Stepped ramps and walks, for example, often lead from front sidewalks to some entry at the house. The final grade of the new project can always be related to a prominent existing point. Use the techniques discussed in this section and in the wall and walk sections, to locate and lay out your projects. Do rough "thumbnail" sketches to help you work your way through the functional requirements and problems you will encounter and to help you see the possibilities in design and material. Then move on to more accurate, dimensioned drawings or sketches to scale. One step-building technique calls for a 2x12 stringer notched to accomodate the treads and risers.

Sizes and Dimensions

Finding the stringer length required. Measure the slope along the ground to determine the length of the stringer material. If you were building steps down from a retaining wall, you could find the stringer length arithmetically: slope squared=run squared+rise squared (see accompanying chart). The slope in this example is just over 8 feet. Therefore, you must use the next standard board length, 10 feet, for your stringer. Cut the board to the length desired.

Another way to find the stringer lengths is to do a scale drawing on paper of the slope. Since it is recommended that you

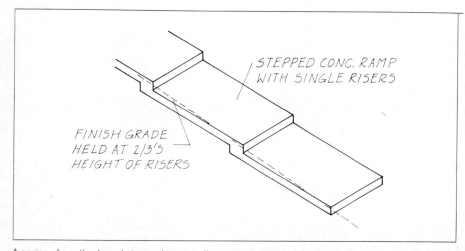

A series of gently sloped stepped ramps allows good control of the grade. The longer ramp treads allow for several steps to be taken on each for a more comfortable walk. For maintenance of a natural pace, the tread should allow for an uneven number of strides.

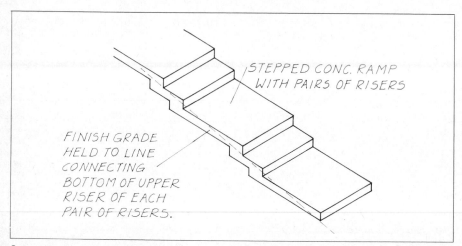

Some slopes may require combinations of steps and landings. The landings should allow the user to take at least three walking steps to maintain the most natural stride.

always work out an accurate drawing before starting any construction, this is a good way to begin.

Building Wooden Steps with Notched Stringers

If you work out a good drawing, you can prefabricate the steps and then set them in place. You also can build them on location and draw in the tread and riser notches on the stringers.

Step one: figuring riser heights. Measure the vertical difference in elevation that the steps must span and divide by 6 inches. For example, if the difference in elevation is 5 feet 1¼ inches, divide by 6 inches, to find you need ten 6⅛ inch risers. All risers should fall between 6 and 7 inches.

Step two: figuring tread depths. Assume the run (horizontal length) of your slope is 11 feet 5¼ inches. Dividing by 15 inches, each tread turns out to be 15¼ inches. The risers of 6⅛ inches and the treads of 15¼ inches are close to the ideal outdoor relationship of tread to riser, which is 6 inches for the riser and 15 inches for the tread.

Step three: planning stringer notches and the foundation support. Lay out your stringers to measure the treads and risers. Remove enough slope (or fill) so that the stringer will span the slope after a base of 4 inches of gravel has been laid. Stringers may be notched to fit over a concrete foundation at the top and rest on a concrete foundation at the bottom. This is the preferred system. The foundation at the top can be a patio, house foundation or retaining wall—whatever conveniently located feature exists—and the foundation at the bottom may be a walk, or another patio or wall. Cross ties (railroad ties) may be substituted for the lower foundation by recessing them in the ground on a bed of gravel. For the top foundation, the ties can be bolted to an existing structural member, and the stringers notched to fit as for concrete. In temperate climates (with no frost heave) you can use a concrete block foundation. Check local codes. (Do not yet secure the stringers to the foundations.)

The type of foundation and the way the stringers meet and are secured to the foundation will vary from project to project. Always try to have as much bearing surface between the stringer and the foundation as possible. The bearing

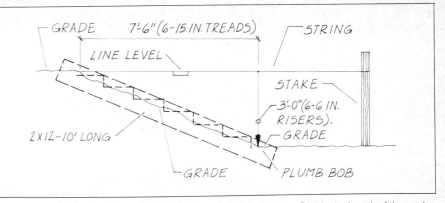

Divide the height of the slope by 6 to determine the number of risers. Divide the length of the run by the number of risers to determine the depth of the treads.

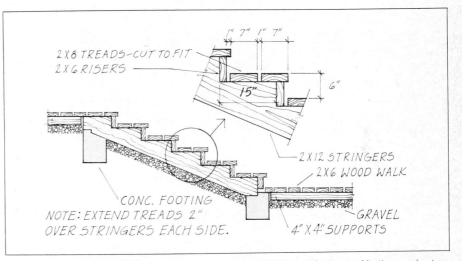

Grade level wood steps should be anchored to concrete footings at the top and bottom and set on a bed of gravel. Use pressure treated wood for maximum durability.

surface is simply that portion of the stringer that touches the foundation and supports the steps. Determine these bearing surfaces before you mark the tread and riser cuts.

Step three variation: building a concrete block foundation. Lay a row of 8x8x16 inch concrete blocks equal to the width of the steps and fill them with concrete. When the concrete is stiff, but not hard, insert a 9 inch long, ½ inch diameter anchor bolt as close as possible to each of the outside edges and another bolt in the middle; the bolt should go about 6 inches into the blocks and protrude about 3 inches above the top of the block. The bolts in each row will be anchored to a 2x6 plank laid across the top of the blocks. The planks will provide a base for notched stringers to fit over and be nailed to. If your steps are wider than four feet, install anchor bolts no more than 2 feet on center, with an anchor at the outside edges of each step.

Step four: marking the notches. Brace one stringer temporarily in place

with stakes or concrete blocks. Measure, locate and draw the tread and riser cuts. To draw the cuts, use a spirit level, a carpenter's square, and a pencil. Mark the cuts, measuring off the tread depths with the carpenter's square. Use the level to be sure the carpenter's square is even. When you hold it along the tread line, you can mark both the tread and riser positions.

Step five: cutting the notches. Use a handsaw or rotary saw to saw out the notches on the 2x12 to form the tread and risers. Use the notched stringer as a pattern to cut the other stringers. Lay the notched stringer on the others and draw along the tread and riser notches.

Step six: securing the stringers. Reposition the stringer on the slope to be sure it can be secured to the foundation as you want. Metal anchor clips, available at any building materials house, can be used to secure the stringers in position. Fasten the stringers to your foundation.

Step seven: attaching the steps. Nail the tread and riser members to stringers.

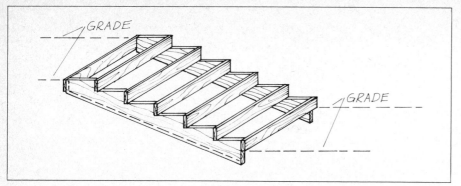

Concrete steps are durable and can be built to almost any size. However, they require the construction of forms nearly as complete as a full set of wood steps.

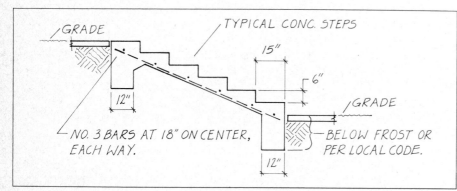

Footings are thickened sections of concrete at the top and bottom of the run and should extend below the frost line. Unit is reinforced horizontally and vertically as shown.

Concrete steps are finished with a float as soon as the concrete has set enough to hold without the face form board.

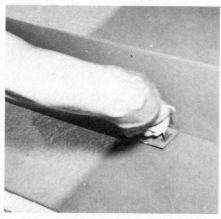

A special tool creates a clean edge between the back of the tread and the bottom of the riser. Riser should angle forward slightly.

An edger shapes the concrete and frees it from the form board at the same time. This prepares the concrete for final finishing.

Form boards are released so that the riser face can be finished. The steps must cure for at least one week before they can be used.

Building Wooden Steps with Support Cleats

You may also build steps in which the treads mount between the stringers on 2x4 cleats, eliminating the 2x6 risers. This will give a more open, airy appearance to the steps. This method does not have as much strength in the steps as in notched stringers. The cleat blocks support the treads; they are nailed to the stringers under the ends of each tread. Otherwise, the building procedures are the same as for the notched-stringer steps.

CREATING CONCRETE STEPS

To build the steps of concrete, follow the same design and layout procedures as for wooden steps. The framework of the wooden stringer steps can be used as the form for the concrete steps. All that is needed is side braces to support the form against the weight of the concrete.

This illustrates a basic problem of poured concrete construction. Concrete seems to be the most plastic of all building materials. When this appearance and durability are important, nothing else will work as well. However, the process of building concrete structures often requires that nearly the entire structure be constructed first in wood forms to create the desired shape in concrete. In large projects this form work entails considerable expense. It may cost less to just build wooden steps instead.

If the soil base is firm, the reinforcement shown may be eliminated, or wire mesh substituted for the rods. Check with your building department concerning reinforcement and safety requirements. The codes are designed for your safety and health; do not arbitrarily decide to reduce reinforcing without consulting the codes.

BUILDING STEPS WITH BRICK

Brick, when used for steps, is probably best used as a veneer. Brick has no more strengths as a foundation material than cheaper materials. You can use brick with a wood framework as described above, or over concrete steps, or in some combination of the above. The main appeal of brick as a step veneer is its warm appearance, variety of patterns and durability.

Using Brick on Wood Steps

Combined brick and wood steps can be built with only little more effort than is required for plain wooden steps.

Laying brick and wood steps.

(1) Compute the heights of the treads and risers. Remember to include the brick thickness in your riser computation.

(2) Saw the notches on the 2x12 stringers, as discussed previously.

(3) As an alternative to a concrete foundation, you can use 4x4 posts to secure the stringers. If you use posts, set a minimum of 18 inches deep in a bed of gravel; then fill the hole to slightly above grade with concrete (a full discussion of post anchoring is included in the fence section).

(4) Lay the stringers on a 4-inch bed of gravel.

(5) Nail the stringers to the foundation posts.

(6) Nail 2x12 sidewalls to the string-ers so that the bottom of the sidewall is flush with the bottom of the stringer.

(7) Nail the risers to the 2x12 stringers.

(8) Fill the area within the stringers and sidewalls with gravel—the gravel will give you a base on which to lay the brick.

(9) Unless you plan the treads so that the space from front to back will be filled by two bricks, plus whatever joint you use, you will have to cut bricks.

(10) Cut them by scoring each with a nail and striking the scored mark with a brick set (chisel) with a hammer.

(11) Lay the brick treads even with the stringer notches on the gravel base and check regularly with a spirit level.

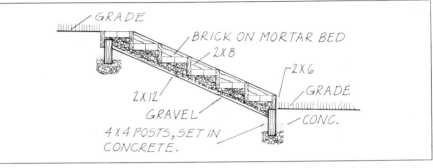

Brick steps may be laid with wood risers and be secured to stringers to maintain level.

These steps combine railroad ties and brick for an attractive pattern and a durable flight of stairs. The ties are nailed together and set into the ground.

RAILROAD TIE (CROSS TIE) STEPS

Cross ties (also called railroad ties) may be laid directly on the ground, but it is difficult to keep them neat and level without a base. If a more informal, less hard-edged design is appropriate, lay the cross ties directly on the ground and stake them from the sides at the ends or on the front (riser side). A gravel base is suggested for good drainage and longevity. The installation techniques are:

(1) build the foundation as above;
(2) saw the notches in the stringers;
(3) lay the stringers on a bed of gravel;
(4) nail the stringers to the 2x6 plank over the foundation blocks;
(5) Nail 2x6 risers to the stringers; then toenail the cross tie treads to the 2x6s (see illustration).

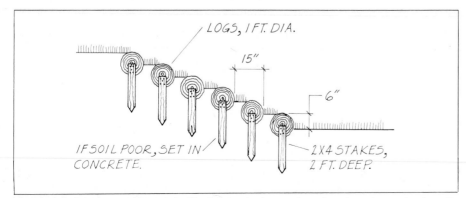

Cross tie steps can be built with notched stringers. The ties provide a durable tread surface. The stringers must be secured firmly to concrete block or poured concrete footings.

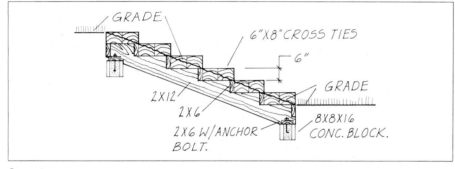

Because they are heavy and stable, cross ties may be set into firm soil as step risers, and the top as part of the tread. Grass, gravel, or other fill may complete the tread.

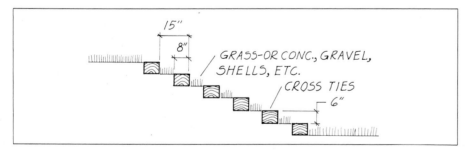

Logs, set in trenches and secured with stakes, can be used as step risers in a natural, rustic landscaping plan. Place the logs so they will provide firm footing for users.

CONSTRUCTING LOG STEPS

Logs make long-lasting steps and provide an attractive, informal appearance and walking surface. To create a flight of log steps, first compute your slope rise. Figure the tread/riser relationship, as discussed previously. Then begin work on the excavation.

1. Use a pointed shovel to dig out rough treads and risers directly in the earth. Your logs, which should be pressure-treated, probably will vary somewhat in diameter. Excavate to size.

2. After you have the earth roughly shaped like steps, dig out the necessary depth so the tread surface of the logs will be at the level you want. If there is one side of a log that is more nearly flat than another, you will put that side up. Remember that your base must allow for the shape of the logs. Dig your trench large enough for the greatest circumferance.

3. It is always wise to put 4 inches of gravel under any wood installed below grade; to add 4 inches of gravel under the steps you must first add 4 inches to your excavation. The log treads, from riser face to riser face, should be about 15 inches.

4. At the ends of the logs drive stakes 2 feet into the ground. The stakes must be long enough so that, after being driven into the ground, the tops of the stakes are even with the center of the logs. Nail the stakes securely to the logs. Use 16d or 20d (3½ or 4 inch) nails.

Part of the tread will be the surface of the log. However, since the logs curve, you will need to add some kind of filler. In areas informal enough for log steps, the best (most appropriate) filler is earth planted with a hardy groundcover. Other fillers—gravel, bark, wood chips—may be used. You might, of course, use cut brick or poured concrete. If you use brick, concrete, or any hard surfacing material between the logs, you should cut and square off the logs where the hard surfaces will meet the logs. This will avoid a feather edge that would chip or break away in time.

Railroad tie variation. It is possible to create steps with railroad ties using the same methods. Because the ties are squared, they will provide a surface for the tread as well as the riser. See illustration.

FREE-STANDING STEPS

Sometimes you must deal with a severe grade change that you cannot or do not want to alter, so that you must build steps to bridge the grade change comfortably. For instance, you may need steps to lead from a retaining wall to another grade, or a layer of rock may form a grade change and you may not want to remove the rock. In cases like this, you can build free-standing steps between the different grades.

Construction and Installation

Building free-standing steps. First, measure your grade change and slope distance; compute tread/riser relationship. The foundation, in this example, is a concrete base at the foot of the slope and 4x4 pressure-treated posts at the top.

(1) Set the 4x4 posts a minimum of 2 feet deep on a bed of gravel—this assumes a three foot vertical grade change. The posts should extend above the upper grade; cut them later to fit the stringer.

(2) Pour concrete to an inch above grade at the posts and slope it away from the posts for proper drainage.

(3) Pour the concrete base footing, using an oiled wood member form that has a notch for your stringer. After the concrete sets, remove the oiled member.

(4) Secure the stringers to the top posts with four ³⁄₈ inch diameter bolts at each post. Secure the stringers at the concrete base with metal anchor clips. You should have three stringers for 4-foot-wide steps.

(5) Trim the posts to the appropriate height. Notch the stringers and nail on the treads and risers.

ADDING A FOOT BRIDGE

A foot bridge is sometimes necessary in order to cross narrow depressions, creeks, or other grade irregularities that you cannot, or do not wish, to level or fill. If you have help, a footbridge is a heavy, but possible, construction job.

Building a Small Bridge

A simple foot bridge can be built with railroad ties for supports, 2x4s for decking and handrails, 4x4s for the posts, and ¹⁄₂ inch diameter anchor bolts to hold the structure in place. The following describes a 4-foot-wide bridge to span a 4-foot creek or depression.

Step one: positioning the posts. Pairs of 4x4 posts on 4-foot centers are 7 feet on center on opposite sides of the depression. To be sure the post hole locations are square, lay the railroad ties across the depression as visually parallel and square as possible, as close as possible to their final position. On one side of the depression lay a 4-foot-long 2x4 across the ends of the ties so that the 2x4 overhangs by 4 inches on each side. Using the ties' outside edges as guides, stake the locations of the posts; repeat on the other side. Remove ties; dig post holes to at least 18 inches deep.

Step two: installing the posts. Set the 4x4 posts in a bed of gravel (see the fence section for detailed post installation). Pour concrete an inch or so above grade at the support post. Slope the concrete away from the post for good drainage. The posts should reach above the planned top level of the railroad ties.

You can trim the posts a ... ties are in place. When t... you are ready to lay the r...

Step three: installing railroad ties against the ... with the posts outside the ties; the ties will extend beyond the posts by 4 inches. Check the ties for level with a spirit level. Make minor adjustments by placing stones under the ties to level them. When the ties are level in the position relative to the posts, toenail them to the posts with 60d nails. Trim the posts off flush with the top of the ties.

Step four: securing ties and decking. With the ties secured to the posts, drill two ⁵⁄₈-inch holes through the posts and the ties where the posts meet the ties—then secure the ties to the posts with ¹⁄₂-inch diameter bolts. Nail the 2x4 decking across the top of the ties, 2-inch side up. The 2x4s should overlap the ties 8 inches on each side. Keep the decking square by starting at either end of the ties with the first 2x4 flush with the end edges of the ties. Space the 2x4s 1 inch apart;

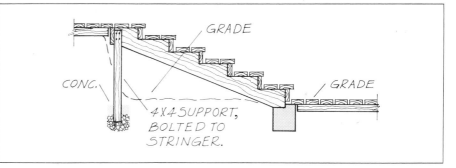

Free-standing steps only touch grade at the top and bottom anchors of a steep slope.

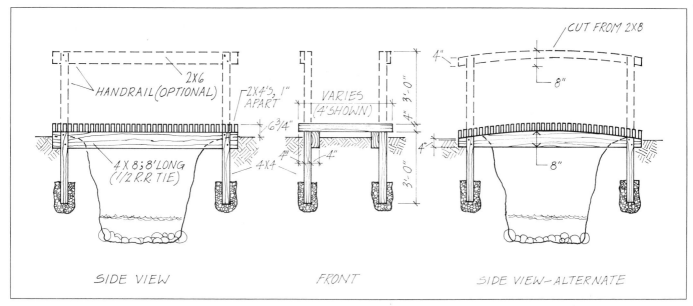

A footbridge with a short span can be built by the home do-it-yourselfer. The support for the surface is provided by an 8x8 cross tie split lengthwise or two 4x8 landscaping timbers. The span members are bolted to 4x4 posts embedded in concrete. Walking surface is of 2x4s.

A small footbridge spans a narrow section of a pond. Such a bridge may add visual variety to a yard, provide alternate access to certain areas, and complete a landscaping theme.

These cross tie steps give direct access to the water. Although the chain handrails are essentially decorative, they demonstrate one of the alternatives to common wood handrails.

keep them equally spaced with a spacer scrap. Toenail 2x4s to ties with 20d nails.

The decking will be even more secure if you tie it all together by nailing 1x4 spacers between each 2x4 as you lay the 2x4 deck members. The 1x4s should be as long as the 2x4s.

Design Variations

Handrails. If the codes permit, you may wish to omit the handrail. For a handrail, extend the 4x4 supports above the top of the ties by 3 feet or to height specified by the local code. Attach a 2x4 or 2x6 handrail, 2-inch side up. Handrails should be bolted with a minimum of two $^3/_8$-inch diameter bolts at each post.

Lumber alternatives. Railroad ties are 8x8, or larger. It is assumed in the example that it is cheaper in your area to cut a railroad tie in half than to buy landscaping timber. If not, or if you prefer to use landscaping timber rather than the creosoted ties, it is suggested you use pressure-treated landscaping members. You may also substitute two 2x8s for each of the ties or landscaping members.

Arched bridge. If you wish a foot bridge with a slight arch, use two 2x8s in place of each tie or landscaping member.

Cut the tops of the 2x8s in an arc (curve) that drops from the full width at the center down to 4 inches at the ends. Handrails can be arched in the same manner. Unless you have a good workshop, you would be better off to have the curved sawed at the lumber company.

Materials List: Foot Bridge 8 feet long

1–8 foot railroad tie split in half
  lengthwise
    or
2–4x8 landscaping timbers, cut 8 feet long
4–4x4 posts cut 4 feet long
38–2x4s cut 4 feet long for decking
8–½ inch diameter anchor bolts
60d nails
20d nails
  gravel and concrete for post support

8 WALL FOOTINGS AND FOUNDATIONS

BUILDING CONCRETE FOUNDATIONS

A good foundation, properly laid and protected against the weather, is critical to the longevity and strength of all walls. Before you can create a concrete foundation, however, you must learn how to:

(1) mix the right type of concrete mix (or order it) for your regional and structural needs;
(2) prepare the earth so that you can lay concrete on it;
(3) build forms to shape, hold, and support the concrete until it sets;
(4) place the concrete so that it will attain the strongest structural properties;
(5) guard against frost action and prevent crumbling or other damage;
(6) cure the concrete so that it attains its full strength.

Concrete is created by a chemical reaction between the cement, the aggregate, and the clean water. You will see later why clean water is called for. You must aid this chemical process by mixing and pouring the concrete properly during acceptable weather conditions. To help you do good concrete work, we will examine each of the ingredients briefly, starting with cement.

Cement

The cement most used today is portland cement, a powdered mixture of limestone, shale, clay, or marl (a natural mixture of limestone and calcium). The most common types of portland cement in use are Types I through III and air-entrained.

Type I cement. This mixture is used for general construction: pavement, sidewalks, pipes, concrete building blocks and bricks, soil-cement mixes, and many other residential, commercial, and industrial uses. Type I cement generates con-siderable heat during the curing process and is therefore good in cold weather, where the heat generated helps prevent freezing. Obviously, this heating characteristic works against you in hot weather. Type I cement should not be subjected to sulfate hazards. Sulphates of calcium, sodium, or magnesium in the soil—or water—react chemically with concrete, causing it to corrode and disintegrate. Determining if the ground in your yard has sulphates is a good reason to do a soil test before progressing too far in planning. You can buy a soil test kit from your garden center. Do the test even if you do not need to determine suitability for plantings. If you discover sulphate concentrations in your soil (.10 parts per million or more), ask your architect or building inspector to recommend a sul-phate-resistant cement. If the soil contains alkali salts, you will need advice about alkali-resistant cement.

Type II cement. This cement generates less heat in curing than Type I. It is often used when pouring in high temperatures. Type II resists sulphate concentrations, such as those found in drainage culverts and pipes. It is also used in large structures to cut down the amount of heat generated in the curing process.

Type III cement. The advantage of Type III cement is that it develops strength early. Using it in cold areas cuts down on the cost and bother of keeping the concrete protected against cold during the curing process.

Air-entrained portland cement. In air-entrained cement, an agent has been added that causes the finished concrete to

The foundation for a wall, whether of masonry or of concrete as shown, must always extend beyond the wall on each side. Check local code for the minimum extension requirements.

be filled with untold numbers of tiny air bubbles. These air bubbles allow water to freeze and expand without damaging the concrete. This can be crucial in very cold regions, and is very useful in areas where severe frost is a problem. The "bubble agent" can be added to Types I, II, and III portland cement. Check with a concrete supplier for help in choosing the proper cement for your concrete project. Successful mixing of air-entrained concrete requires a power mixer. Do not hand mix.

Aggregate

Aggregate is mixed with cement and water to form concrete. Some common aggregates are sand, pebbles, gravel, and crushed or broken stones.

Sizes. Aggregates are roughly divided into two sizes: fine and coarse. Fine aggregates are those that will fall through a ¼ inch screen opening (and, under some definitions, a ⅛-inch opening). The ideal aggregate mix includes a variety of sizes ranging from fragments of sand up to pebbles or stones over 3 inches. The coarsest aggregate in most concrete for residential purposes is about 1½ inches in size. The size of the ideal aggregate mix varies with the job—a retaining wall 2 feet thick can accommodate larger aggregate than a 3-inch garden walk. There is not a single "best" aggregate; there is one that will be best for your job. Fortunately, you do not have to know everything about aggregates to do good concrete work—most concrete contractors do not know all the answers, either. What you need to understand is that aggregate mix is important and that one mix will not do for all jobs. Describe your project to your concrete supplier so he will know what you want the aggregate mix for.

The purpose of the aggregate. The strength of concrete comes from the structural makeup of the aggregate, bonded together by the cement paste. The voids between the aggregate, in a good mix, are completely filled with cement paste. The water is an important factor: too much water will make the cement paste too thin to hold the aggregate together; not enough water will leave tiny pockets of dry aggregate and will weaken the concrete. Cement paste is just that—a kind of high-strength paste or glue that holds the crushed stone, gravel, and sand together in the tightest possible manner. Dirty water, water with organic particles

The slump cone is 12 inches high, with a base diameter of 8 inches and a top diameter of 4 inches. Set the cone on a firm surface and hold down by placing feet onto the projections. Fill the cone with 3 layers of concrete. Tamp each layer 25 times before adding the next layer.

of oil, or other materials, interferes with the bonding of the aggregate.

Pouring concrete from too great a height or excessive use of vibrators can disrupt the balance between the graded aggregate sizes. If clusters of aggregate that are the same size become grouped together, the cement paste will be distributed too heavily in some areas and too thinly in others—weakening the concrete.

Water

The proper amount of water results in a cement paste that coats every particle of aggregate, cementing each to the other. Both water and aggregate must be thoroughly clean, and drinkable water is often specified for mixing concrete.

MIXING CONCRETE
Tools Needed to Mix by Hand

To mix concrete by hand, you need a helper, two shovels, a watertight platform about 10x12 feet, a measuring box, and a measuring bucket.

Estimating Material Quantities

First, you must find how much cement, sand, and aggregate you need. You can easily compute the number of cubic yards of concrete you need for your job. For example, if you are laying a 4-foot-wide concrete walk that is 4 inches thick and 36 feet long: 36 feet x 4 feet x ⅓ foot = 48 cubic feet (4 inches = ⅓ foot). Dividing by 27 (for a cubic *yard*), you get 1.8 cubic yards. For practical purposes, you need 2 yards of concrete. If, for example, your job calls for 1:3:5 concrete (1 part

Level off the concrete when the cone is filled. Lift the cone and allow the concrete to settle. Stand the cone next to the concrete in order to measure. A large slump indicates a wet consistency; a slight slump is due to a stiff consistency. A good slump is 2 to 4 inches.

cement to 3 parts sand to 5 parts aggregate), you can figure the exact quantity of each concrete ingredient you need.

However, the easiest, fastest, and surest way to determine quantities is to call a concrete supplier and give him the dimensions of your wall so he can compute your concrete ingredients instantly and tell you the costs. Have him price it out both for delivered and "will call". Some concrete suppliers figure concrete by volume and some by weight, but *all* the suppliers have computation tables that enable them to save you time, effort and mistakes you might make because of unfamiliarity with the arithmetic.

Mixing by Hand

Mix the sand and cement together by first spreading the sand over the platform. Spread the cement over the sand, then place another layer of sand over the cement. Arrange the remaining cement over the sand. Layering the materials like this cuts down on the shoveling. Usually, you and one helper should not mix more than about one cubic yard at a time.

Face your helper across the materials and, working from the edges to the center, gently and evenly turn the materials with a shovel. Add the aggregate as you turn the sand and cement. Work the aggregate in as evenly as possible. A uniform color means you are ready to add water.

Adding the water. Form a "bowl" in the center of the mixture and add the correctly measured amount of water—drinkable water. Turn the dry materials, folding them into the water. Repeat the process, adding measured amounts of water until the water has been used and the mix is appropriate for the job. The platform must be watertight and no water must be allowed to run off its edges. Build a lip around the platform with 2x4s to prevent spills. Obviously, mixing your own concrete is appropriate and cost-cutting for small jobs. Mixing your own becomes more difficult and questionable as the size of the job increases.

Determining the amount of water needed for the mix. There is a general proportionate rule for cement. You can expect to use 6 gallons of water for each bag of cement. However, this is not precise for each job. In order to determine the amount of water needed, you should perform a slump test.

Performing a slump test. Obtain a slump cone, a metal cone open at both ends that is 12 inches high and has an 8 inch diameter at the bottom and a 4 inch diameter at the top. Make a careful note of the proportions used in the mix. Set the cone on a firm, flat surface and fill it with your concrete mixture. You should add the concrete a shovelful at a time and tamp the concrete 25 times between every two or three shovelfuls. When the cone is filled, level off the top and remove the cone by lifting straight up.

The concrete will settle. After a few minutes the concrete will have settled as far as it is going to. Place the slump cone next to the concrete and lay a flat board or straight dowel across the top of the cone. Place a ruler vertically on the concrete to measure the distance from the top of the concrete to the top of the slump cone. A good mix will produce a slump of between 2 and 4 inches. If your concrete slump is more than this, reduce the amount of water in your mix. If the slump is less than this, increase the amount of water until you achieve a good slump to your concrete.

Using a Portable Concrete Mixer
A portable concrete mixer is often a good solution for home projects. Renting a portable mixer is cheaper than ordering a ready-mix truck. Portable mixers are widely available, and fairly inexpensive to rent. With a mixer you can make larger batches than with handmixing, mix them better and faster, and save your strength. Portable mixers looks like miniature mix

If you don't have a cone for a slump test, measure the concrete consistency by making ridges. If too stiff, ridges will not form easily; if too wet, ridges will slide away.

trucks without the cab. They operate in the same way. They can be towed with an automobile. The machines and their operation vary somewhat, but they are quite simple; check the machine for operation instructions—if they are not printed on the machine, ask the rental company for a copy of the instructions.

LOCATING THE FOOTING/FOUNDATION
Before you lay concrete, you must prepare the earth to receive it. This involves cutting the earth in a shape that closely resembles the finished shape of the concrete. Then forms of the exact, final shape are placed within the earth. To make the earth cuts and to accurately build the forms within, a system of reference points must be used. The preferred system is to use batter boards to guide you in excavating and in setting up forms.

Setting up Batter Boards
If you were to mark the points needed to build your masonry walls or walks exactly where the work was to be done, the marks would soon be covered with earth or damaged or lost. Batter boards are like an extension of the drawing board—they can be considered T-squares for the field. Batter boards are located several feet back from the actual work, and they offer a means of locating and recording the needed reference points so they can be checked when needed. The batter boards

Use of a power mixer enables the homeowner to mix larger batches faster, and with less strain. It is a cost-effective alternative to ready-mix truck delivery.

may be single or combined. Generally, batter boards are made up of two stakes, driven in the ground and preferably braced with additional stakes. A horizontal member (a leveled 1x4 or 1x6) is nailed across the stakes.

To understand how batter boards are set up and used, consider a simple example of building a masonry wall in your back yard. You want the wall to be the same width as the rear portion of the house. First locate, either from your survey or with the services of a surveyor, the four corners of the lot and stake them—A,B,C, and D. Stretch lines between the stakes at the sides of your house and across the back. Measuring as accurately as you can from the lot line strings, drive stakes at the approximate positions of the proposed wall corners—Points 1,2,3, and 4.

Erecting corner batter boards. Now erect a corner batter board four feet out from Corner Number 1. To do this, Line 1-2 must be extended 4 feet beyond Stake 1. Do the same with Line 1-4. The extensions create two sides of a square. Complete the square—use a carpenter's square to insure right angle corners. Then, in the corner that is diagonally opposite Stake 1, pound in another stake. This is the basis for the batter board construction. Drive another stake eight feet along Line 1-2, and four feet away from Line 1-2. Drive a third stake in the

same relative position along Line 1-4.

Attach a horizontal member between the corner batter board stake and the stake outside Line 1-2. Nail it at a convenient height, a foot or so off the ground. Level it with a spirit level. Run a string between the two outside stakes. The string should be level with the top of the horizontal

member. Attach a second horizontal member between the corner stake and the stake outside Line 1-4. Its top should be level with the string.

You should now have created a level, right angle guide. Now add support stakes and boards to the second and third stakes as shown.

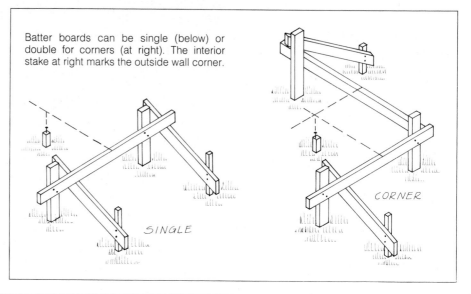

Batter boards can be single (below) or double for corners (at right). The interior stake at right marks the outside wall corner.

SINGLE

CORNER

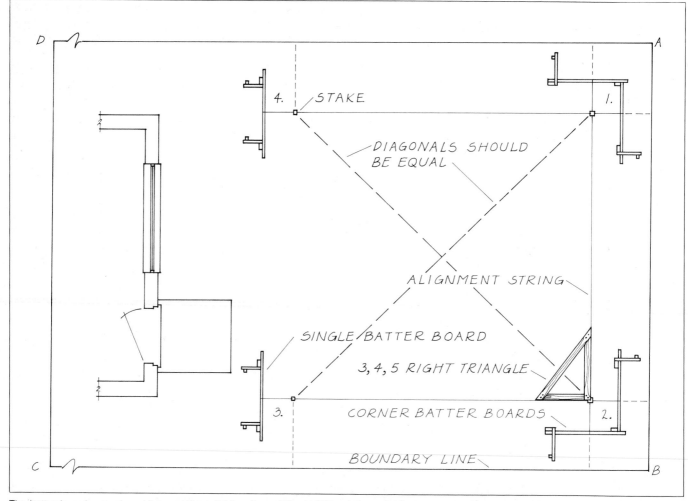

The batter boards are placed beyond the outside edges of the wall foundation as reference points and markings.

Erect another corner batter board at Corner Number 2. Erect single batter boards (as opposed to double) at Points 3 and 4, keeping them level with batter board Number 1.

Marking the boards. Find someone to help you hold a line and ask a third person to mark the batter boards. Stand on line AD and have your helper on line BC (refer to the illustration). Stretch the line over the batter boards and through Points 1 and 2, and measure the distance between line AB and the intended foundation face of the proposed wall. Do this by measuring as accurately as you can along line AD from line AB. Have your helper do the same along line BC from line AB. It sounds complicated but it is not. This distance to the foundation wall may be the setback distance you desire, or that the code requires. Hold the line so it stretches tightly over (just touches) the top of the batter boards at Points 1 and 2. The third person should now mark the position of the line onto the batter boards. This mark registers the foundation wall face—at the rear of the wall—on the batter boards.

It is good practice to notch these marks on the batter boards with a saw and to identify them on the boards using pencil marks, but do not notch them yet. Tie the lines in place across the batter boards at the foundation wall face registration marks.

Follow the same procedure for the side foundation wall setbacks from lines AD and BC. With these marks, you can find any other vertical surface on the wall without having to go through the same location procedure.

Stretching the lines. Stretch lines between Points 1,2,3, and 4. Check the lines with a line level; make any adjustments needed. Check the corners to be sure they are square. Do this by measuring the diagonals across the wall stakes. If the diagonals are perfectly equal, the corners are square. You may check individual corners by measuring 6 feet along the line from a corner stake, then 8 feet along the opposite line. The distance, measured from outside corner to outside corner (hypotenuse), should be 10 feet if the corner is square. This is the 3, 4, 5 right triangle method. You may also make up a 3, 4, 5 triangle with wood members to quickly check each corner.

Notching the stakes. When you are sure the lines are level and the corners

square, use a saw to notch the position of the lines across the batter boards. These notches represent the outside edge of the foundation wall (not the footing). These points are now permanently registered on the batter boards. In this example, the outside edge of the foundation wall of the new garden wall is in line with the face of the house foundation wall. You are now ready for excavation.

EXCAVATION PROCEDURES

Excavation can be done manually or with machinery. The "best way" to do an excavation depends on your physical ability to do manual work, your ability to handle machinery effectively, your budget, and the value of your time.

Using Excavation Machinery

Small back hoes and trenching machines can be rented for footing excavation. Small dozers or graders will serve for shallow excavation. Excavating machinery can save considerable time and labor, if you are good with machines and can learn to operate them quickly, without making costly and time-consuming mistakes. A small mistake—gouging a footing trench too deep, or grading a walk bed unevenly—can quickly take away the time and labor savings.

Excavating by Hand

If you pace yourself according to your physical condition, the cheapest way to

get small excavating jobs done is to do them yourself with hand tools. If you are not in good condition and you push yourself too hard, you can easily hurt your back or strain yourself and spend the saved money on medical expenses.

Hiring an Excavator

An alternative to manual excavation or operating the machinery yourself is to contract the excavation on an hourly basis. Small excavating companies sometimes advertise in the newspaper, or a contractor equipment supplier or building materials supplier may be able to find an excavator for you.

Digging the Footing Trench

When digging footing trenches, be sure to keep the bottom level at the right depth. If the trench is too deep, it will have to be filled with concrete, not earth. The footing depth required is the depth of your frost line plus the depth of the footing. The top of the footing should be beneath the frost line, where possible. In cold areas, where the frost line is too deep to dig below economically, you must set the footing on a bed of gravel. Contact your building department for frost line depths and methods of stopping or minimizing frost heave action. It should be noted that concrete block is not an acceptable material for foundation walls in regions where frost heave occurs. The width of the footing depends upon what you are build-

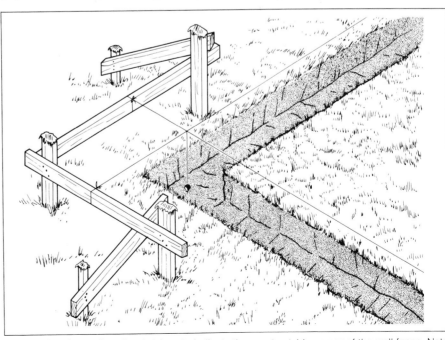

A plumb bob hangs from level strings to indicate the exact outside corner of the wall faces. Note that this is inside the excavation; the foundation extends beyond the wall.

ing and how large the construction will be. Get advice from your building department.

While working, keep the bottom of the trench at a constant depth by frequently checking it with a plumb bob hung from the alignment string. Make the excavation wide enough so that you can accommodate the footing, foundation and forms. You will also have to provide enough space for working room between the forms and the side of the excavation. You will need enough room to to drive nails into the forms and support stakes. An area three times the total width of the footing should be sufficient for most excavations. You will be able to tell by studying the proposed width of the footing and the depth of the footing and foundation. The size of the foundation—like the footing—is an engineering problem. Check codes.

Preparing the Soil

If the soil is firm enough, and not too rocky, you can use the earth itself as a "form". Concrete requires moist conditions for good curing. Shallow excavations often require that the ground be dampened with a garden hose so that dry soil does not draw the moisture from the concrete and weaken it. For footings and foundation walls, lack of moisture is usually less a problem because the below-surface earth is damper than that near the surface. If for some reason this is not the case, and the earth is dry, dampen it with a fine spray from the garden hose. Another way to help the concrete maintain moisture while it cures is to leave the forms on as long as possible. This holds moisture in and keeps the earth from drawing it away.

Coping with Frost Heave

In very cold climates, frost action, also called frost heave, is a problem that cannot be ignored. When you excavate for concrete work, it may be necessary to remove soil particularly subject to frost heave and replace it with soil less likely to be affected.

What does "frost heave" do? Frost action or "frost heave" is not fully understood. When water freezes, its volume increases; when moisture in soil freezes, its volume increases. The soil swells up and it returns to its original volume upon thawing. However, the expansion of soil due to frost heave is greater than the mere expansion of frozen water would indicate. This movement is very powerful, enough so in some areas of extreme cold that it can endanger buildings. One of the functions of foundations, beyond providing a firm base for walls or other structures, is to negate frost action. Wherever economically practical, therefore, footings are laid below the frost line. The frost line is the depth to which the soil freezes. When the foundation rests on a footing that is below the frost line, the structure is held in place while the soil moves up and down.

Placing footings above the frost line. In some areas of very deep frost penetration it is impractical to carry foundations below the frost line, as this could result in more wall beneath the surface than above it. For these conditions, it is recommended that the wall foundation be laid on a well-drained gravel pad. The pad prevents the collection of significant moisture, which in turn keeps frost action to a minimum.

You do not need to use footings under walks or drives to hold them in place against frost action. Paving may be laid on a bed of gravel or coarse sand, whichever is the appropriate base for the

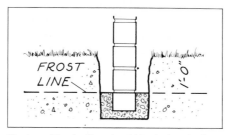
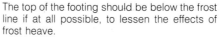

The top of the footing should be below the frost line if at all possible, to lessen the effects of frost heave.

walk material itself—poured concrete, concrete pavers, brick, wood, or other surface. As you can see, the control of frost action is largely a matter of controlling soil moisture through good drainage.

Since soil conditions and temperatures vary so greatly across the country, there is no single best way of dealing with frost action. The basics discussed here will alleviate most problems. Just keep wall and other foundations below the frost line where economically possible, provide subsurface materials that drain well, and provide good surface drainage. Builders everywhere have had to learn the cheapest and easiest methods for dealing with frost action in order to survive in business. You may be able to get advice from a builder. However, always check with your building department for area codes.

CONSTRUCTING FORMS

As stated earlier, excavation involves cutting the earth so it resembles the finished shape of the concrete as closely as possible. However, more accurate forming is needed within the excavation for structural stability and an aesthetically pleasing job.

If forms are used, and they are suggested, first restring the alignment strings on the batter boards. Remember, the strings represent the outside face of the foundation wall. From the intersection of the lines, hang a plumb bob to the excavation floor. Drive a stake there. Raise the plumb bob so it just touches the top of the stake. Center a 4d or 6d (1½ or 2 inch) nail in the stake, letting the nail project just enough to hold the string. This point represents the exact outside corner of the foundation wall.

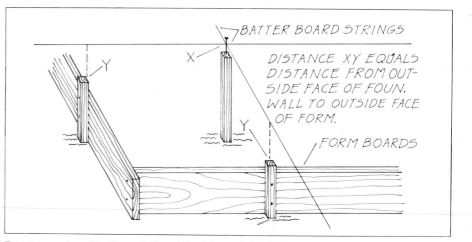

The distance from X to Y equals the width of the wall plus thicknesses of the form boards. String is attached to the ends of the batter boards indicate placement of the stakes.

Setting Up Outside Form Boards

Working toward the outside walls of the excavation, measure from the nail in two directions, marking off the distance to the edge of the footing plus the thickness of the form material. Drive 2-inch-thick stakes into the ground. On one stake, mark where the top of the footing form will be, working from the registration marks on the batter boards. From that point, stretch a line to the other stake and level the line with a line level. Mark the level point on the stake. At intervals that suit your form material length, drive stakes around the footing area, checking often for level. Mark on each stake where the top of the footing form will be. Brace all the stakes with diagonal 2x4s or 1x4s, and check for level and square corners. Adjust as necessary.

Install the form boards, nailing from the inside of the form boards to attach to the stakes. Check the form boards frequently with a spirit level to be sure they are plumb. When the form boards are installed, cut the stakes off flush with the top of the form boards. Now you are ready for the inside forms.

Inside Form Boards

At one corner, measure from one inside face of the outside form by the width of the footing plus the thickness of the form material. Now do the same from the other face at the corner, establishing the position of the inside corner stake. Do the same at the other corner. Set the stakes for the inside forms using the same method as the outside forms. Attach the inside forms, leveling them with the outside forms with a spirit level. Oil the forms for easy removal.

Reinforcement. Your masonry wall probably will need reinforcement. If your wall is fairly low, the building department may be able to give you enough information. But taller walls need the attention of an architect or engineer to design your reinforcement and to show you how to place it. (See illustrations for sample reinforcement.)

The reinforcement is secured before you pour the footings. Steel reinforcement bars come in lengths approximately 20 feet long. Take one of the lengths at a time and hacksaw it into 1 foot sections. Drive these short sections into the bottom of the footing trench to support the reinforcement. For example, if the rein-forcement is to be 3 inches off the ground, 1 inch from each edge the footing, and 14 inches apart (your architect or engineer should supply the specific dimensions for your job), then you would drive the 1-foot support sections in pairs, placed so you can wire horizontal continuous reinforcement bars to them. They should reach just high enough above ground so the continuous reinforcement bars can be wired to them. Support bars spaced approximately 3 feet on center should be sufficient. After you secure the reinforcement, check the inside of the forms for nails, heavy splinters or anything that would embed in the concrete and make the forms difficult to remove.

CONCRETE BASICS
Placing the Concrete

Big jobs, calling for ready-mix concrete, require preparation for the truck (it is big and it is very heavy) and adequate labor when it arrives. The driver delivers concrete—he does not help lay it. Your site must be accessible and you must have enough help to handle a large amount of concrete. Be certain that the route to the excavation does not pass over a septic tank—the truck can crash through.

Before placing the concrete, sprinkle the excavation with water. If the height from the chute to the edge of the excavation is more than four feet, some additional chute or tube must be arranged to shorten the distance of fall.

Do not allow the concrete to mound up in one area and then flow along the form. You can avoid this condition by moving the ready mix chute along as it pours, or by distributing the concrete along the length of the area to be poured in layers of 6 inches or so. To further prevent mounding, pour from the corners, working toward the center of the form. These precautions help keep the gravel uniform within the cement paste.

Settling the concrete. For deep foundation walls, it may be necessary to use a vibrator to get the concrete settled in the forms. Vibrators can be rented from contractor equipment supply houses. There are external vibrators that operate on the form itself and internal vibrators that can be immersed in the concrete. Choose the one most convenient to your operation. But do not over-vibrate. Over-vibrating brings the cement paste to the top, leaving the gravel in the bottom.

Notching the footing. Concrete foundation walls in areas of frost action should have a notched or keyed footing. The key form is removed from the footing when the concrete hardens. When the foundation wall is poured over the footing, it runs into the key, which increases the stability of the foundation wall.

Finishing the Concrete Surface

The footing top should be floated flat —this leaves a rather "gritty" surface, which is a good surface on which to build

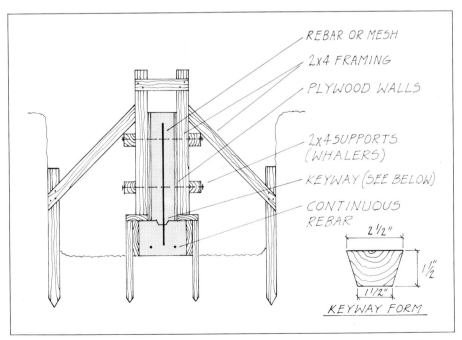

REBAR OR MESH

2x4 FRAMING

PLYWOOD WALLS

2x4 SUPPORTS (WHALERS)

KEYWAY (SEE BELOW)

CONTINUOUS REBAR

2½"

1½"

1½"

KEYWAY FORM

Insert the keyway form on the footing right after pouring, but after drilling a hole through which you can insert the vertical reinforcing that will extend up through the foundation.

the foundation wall, because it gives the masonry a good bonding surface.

Curing Concrete

Concrete requires time to cure after it has set. Do not think that because it is hard, the concrete has cured. Curing temperatures range from 40 degrees F. to 70 degrees F. Concrete should not be poured if temperatures are out of this range or may be out of it during the week or so it takes the concrete to cure. Moisture is important also. Keep the concrete moist during the curing period. Leave the forms on for a week or so if you can—this helps retain moisture. You may also wish to use a curing compound.

Using Masonry Materials

Concrete block should be dry when it is laid because it tends to crack upon drying if it is laid wet. Brick, on the other hand, needs to be dampened before use because dry brick draws the moisture from mortar, weakening the structure. To control the amount of water in the brick, spray it uniformly with a fine mist; do not let rain drench it. With the above in mind, it is best to store all masonry materials—concrete block, concrete brick, and clay

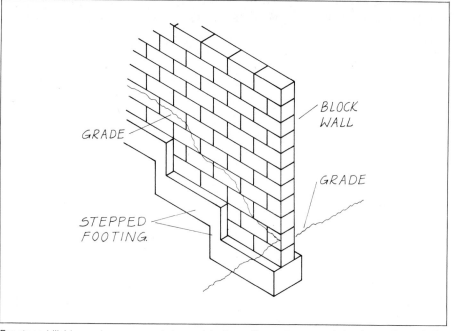

For steep hillside grades, you need stepped footings. Excavate stepped depths, and match the forms to them. The final, finished top of the wall remains level.

brick—in a dry place.

Masonry foundation walls depend on mortar to bond them together. Mortar is a mixture of cement, hydrated lime, sand, and water. It may be hand or machine mixed. As with concrete, unless the job is a very small one a power mixer is preferable. The mix used depends on the area of the country and the design of the wall.

For construction of the foundation with masonry units, follow the same procedures as for laying a masonry wall (see Chapter 9).

9 MASONRY WALLS

Fences and walls enclose outdoor space and offer security and privacy. Perhaps the most important difference between walls and fences and screens is the increased sense of stability and permanence offered by the wall. Study your objectives for enclosing a space before deciding between a wall, a masonry fence or screen, or a wood fence or screen.

BUILDING SOLID CONCRETE-BLOCK WALLS

Concrete masonry walls are built of units composed of portland cement, graded aggregates, and water. The standard units are concrete-colored, but they may be bought in a variety of colors, weights, shapes, sizes, and configurations. Regional availability will vary considerably. A trip to the local supplier is necessary before you design the wall. However, if you have a block shape in mind that is not available locally, the supplier may be able to order it for you—at extra cost.

Concrete blocks with 25% or more of their cross-sectional area open are called "hollow". This includes the typical hollow concrete block seen in residential, commercial, and institutional work. The hole sizes vary according to usage. Although you can buy concrete blocks that are completely solid, they need not be completely solid to be called "solid".

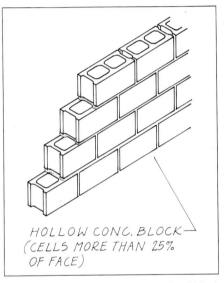

Commonly used in construction, "hollow" block has open areas (cells) of more than 25% to help reduce the weight and cost of the wall.

The openings in a brick screen wall permit passage of light and air while providing visual privacy. The perforations can be arranged to complement plantings and design schemes.

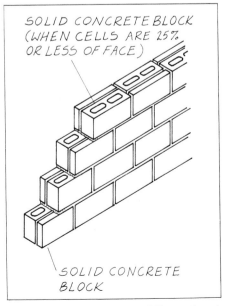

Concrete blocks are called "solid" even though they may have openings, if those openings are 25% (or less) than the face dimensions.

A parge coat of plaster can be troweled to a smooth or textured stucco finish. Joint patterns may be added to emphasize, or to provide, design impact.

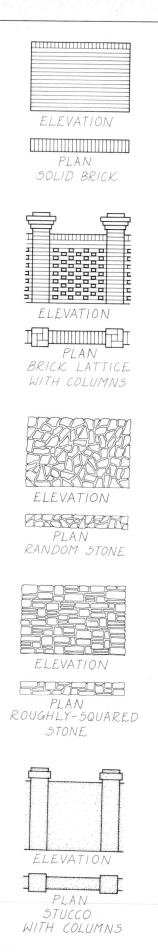

ELEVATION

PLAN
SOLID BRICK

ELEVATION

PLAN
BRICK LATTICE
WITH COLUMNS

ELEVATION

PLAN
RANDOM STONE

ELEVATION

PLAN
ROUGHLY-SQUARED
STONE

ELEVATION

PLAN
STUCCO
WITH COLUMNS

Drawings and Plans

Concrete masonry units are usually based on 4- or 8-inch modules. A ³⁄₈ inch or ½ inch mortar joint has become standard in practice. This is the nominal size. The actual size is 7⅝ x 7⅝ x 15⅝ inches. The exterior dimensions of masonry units are actually reduced by ³⁄₈ inch to allow for the joints. This allows you to plan the size of your wall dimensions in 4 or 8 inch modules. However, the larger, nominal sizes (such as 8 x 8 x 16 inches) also are available. Whether nominal or modular, there are slight inconsistencies in block size, usually no more than $\frac{1}{16}$ inch. These inconsistencies are evened out by the joint lines when you arrange the base before mortaring.

Drawing a plan. First, work out a scale drawing of the wall in plan (overhead or birds-eye view), accurately locating the wall on your lot. When you see a neat set of working drawings for a house, you are looking at the *result* of many sketches and calculations. So do not expect, or try, to turn out a finished working drawing of your wall without some trial-and-error work. Working drawings, incidentally, are just that: fully detailed and dimensioned drawings used to guide you through the actual work.

Drawing an elevation. Draw the entire length of the wall. The elevations should show where the grade meets the wall all around the perimeter. Any doors or other openings should be noted on the elevations. Also indicate on the elevations the brick or block patterns or other design features. Draw in all pilasters, control joints, and reinforcement.

Drawing a foundation plan. A foundation is designed to support what you want to put on top of it. You cannot plan the foundation until your plan drawings and elevation drawings are complete so you can see what the foundation must support. When you are satisfied with the plan and elevations of your wall, draw a foundation plan that will accommodate the wall. Sharp grade changes may require a stepped footing, because the footing itself must be kept level. Pilasters may require that the footing be expanded for them, or you may have to build piers, (sturdier integral support columns). The foundation plan should also show any reinforcement.

Planning the masonry pattern. These elevation drawings will serve you better if you draw in the masonry pattern in detail. You will learn how many masonry units and what type of unit you need. For example, there are special blocks available for corners, pilasters, and the top (head) of the wall. The corner blocks have a flush end for a finished appearance. Pilaster blocks are designed to fit smoothly with other blocks in the wall; they are hollow so that you may add reinforcing steel and concrete, if needed. Blocks specially designed for the top (head) course, have a flush, finished top.

Horizontal dimensions are given in multiples of full nominal height of the block. In your drawing, work out the corners first, and proceed toward the center of the wall. Odd sizes are taken care of by "closure blocks" located near the center of the wall. Closure blocks are discussed more fully in the discussion of how to lay masonry for a wall. Working from the corners allows you to preserve a 4- or 8-inch module that prevents ragged corner conditions.

The accompanying drawings show some typical uses of concrete block in

Longer, thinner units of concrete block work well on lower planters and borders.

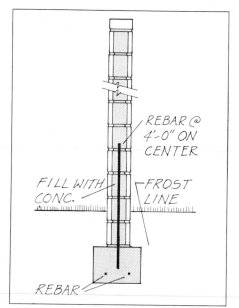

REBAR @ 4'-0" ON CENTER

FILL WITH CONC.

FROST LINE

REBAR

Vertical reinforcing bars are inserted into the hollow cells and then mortar is placed around them to tie the courses together.

masonry walls, including some typical corner conditions and other block patterns, a few of which are also typical for brick walls.

Using Pilasters

When the word column is mentioned, most people will think of the columns in front of churches, banks, colonial homes, and similar buildings. These are free-standing columns. Pilasters are less visible but perform a function similar to these columns. Pilasters can be built into garden walls to provide lateral strength. They also permit the construction of higher and thinner walls and cut down on the amount of steel reinforcement needed in the wall.

There are many pilaster shapes, sizes, and configurations (such as corner pilaster blocks) available in concrete masonry. A pilaster unit will blend in with the surrounding wall masonry.

Hollow pilaster units can be grouted full and may contain steel reinforcement. Grouted pilasters should have all vertical

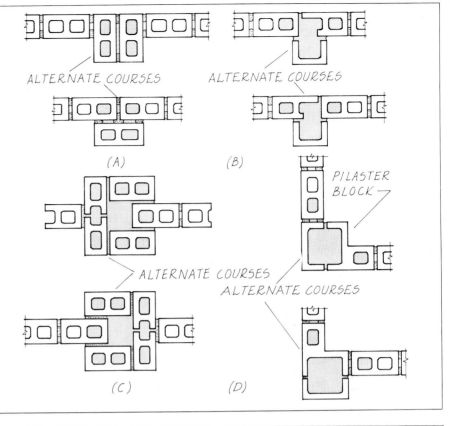

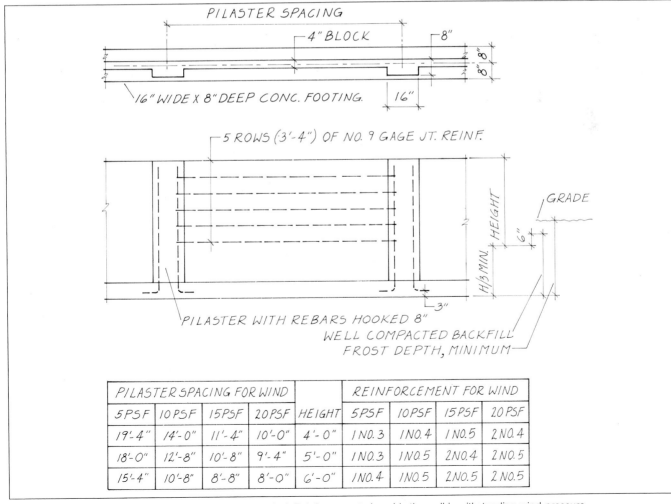

Pilaster spacings depend upon the wind-resistance needed. Reinforcement also aids the wall in withstanding wind pressure.

PILASTER SPACING FOR WIND				HEIGHT	REINFORCEMENT FOR WIND			
5 PSF	10 PSF	15 PSF	20 PSF		5 PSF	10 PSF	15 PSF	20 PSF
19'-4"	14'-0"	11'-4"	10'-0"	4'-0"	1 NO.3	1 NO.4	1 NO.5	2 NO.4
18'-0"	12'-8"	10'-8"	9'-4"	5'-0"	1 NO.3	1 NO.5	2 NO.4	2 NO.5
15'-4"	10'-8"	8'-8"	8'-0"	6'-0"	1 NO.4	1 NO.5	2 NO.5	2 NO.5

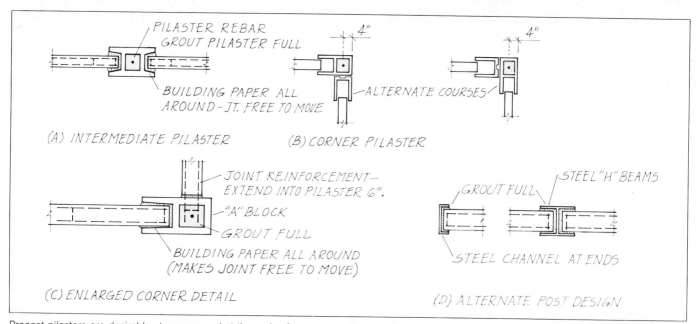

(A) INTERMEDIATE PILASTER

PILASTER REBAR
GROUT PILASTER FULL
BUILDING PAPER ALL
AROUND—JT. FREE TO MOVE

(B) CORNER PILASTER

4"
ALTERNATE COURSES

(C) ENLARGED CORNER DETAIL

JOINT REINFORCEMENT—
EXTEND INTO PILASTER 6".
"A" BLOCK
GROUT FULL
BUILDING PAPER ALL AROUND
(MAKES JOINT FREE TO MOVE)

(D) ALTERNATE POST DESIGN

STEEL "H" BEAMS
GROUT FULL
STEEL CHANNEL AT ENDS

Precast pilasters are desirable at corners and at the ends of masonry walls, as well as on both sides of any openings in the wall.

joints fully mortared and the horizontal joints should be reinforced with steel ties.

Long, fairly high walls need pilasters along the length of the wall. The number of pilasters will depend on the height and thickness of the wall, the amount of reinforcement, and the wind. In short, low walls, you may be able to construct the wall without pilasters. It is often desirable, both from structural and aesthetic standpoints, to end the walls with pilasters.

Other conditions where pilasters are needed. The free ends of serpentine walls may be closed off with a pilaster or by turning the wall in a sharper radius than the radii along the wall. This gives extra lateral strength at the ends. The pilasters should be in scale with the wall and be visually pleasing. Pilasters may be needed at openings in masonry walls. They may also support gates.

Leaving Wall Openings

Where there is masonry above an opening in a masonry wall, you will need a lintel of some kind. Concrete blocks come in special shapes that can be filled with concrete and reinforced with steel to accept the load. Brick and block are often supported with a steel angle over openings. Also, control joints may be needed above the openings. You need professional consultation to design for these situations.

Adding Control Joints

On a small project, like a short, low

For control joints, building paper or roofing felt is inserted in continuous joints that are created with a combination of full and half-length blocks.

garden wall, you may be able to avoid using control joints—or even pilasters—if the wall is thick enough or is reinforced. But on long stretches of wall, control joints will be needed.

All masonry walls develop stresses that may result in cracks in the wall. Control joints are intentionally weakened vertical sections in masonry walls located where these cracks are likely to occur. Control joints transfer cracks to areas where they are not visually conspicuous. The exact places where cracks will occur cannot be pinpointed, and there are no meaningful rules that will apply to every wall; there are too many variables. Experience shows, however, that cracks are likely to occur at changes in wall height (where the wall steps up or down a grade, for example), and at points where the founda-

tion steps up or down, and at changes in wall thickness—such as at a pilaster. Long lengths of wall may crack because the wall contracts more than the foundation it sits on, among other reasons. Therefore, it is common to see control joints at all these points, and periodically in long lengths of wall.

If the block (or brick) is covered with stucco or bonded with a veneer of brick, the control joint should be extended through these materials.

Types of control joints. There are several ways to add control joints, but in concrete masonry the Michigan type, the tongue and groove, and the premolded rubber insert are the types most widely used.

The Michigan joint. The Michigan control joint is built using a flanged concrete block. You fold a strip of building paper on one side of the joint position. The core between the two blocks that make up the joint is then filled with mortar. The building paper allows the mortar to bond only to the units that are touched by the mortar. The mortar plug in the core prevents wall movement from side to side, but it allows up and down movement. Regular block coursing is used in this method. Where the joint occurs, the block is cut to fit.

Tongue and groove joint. The tongue and groove control joint is made with special block units shaped as the name implies—that is, one block is channeled and the other block has a tongue that fits into the channel. This coupling keeps the wall together but allows some movement at the joint.

Premolded joints. Premolded control joints use rubber inserts shaped like a plus sign (+) that fit in grooves formed in the specially made concrete blocks.

Caulking the control joints. All control joints should be caulked. When the mortar in the joint becomes stiff, rake it out about ¾ inch. Building supply stores offer concrete block sealers and bond breakers. Use a sealer to coat the sides of the joints; grease the back of the joint with a bond breaker. Caulk will now adhere to the sides of the joint without drying out but will still slide up and down against the back of the joint.

Inserting Reinforcement

Plain masonry walls are those without reinforcement. The term a "reinforced wall" refers to one in which the reinforcement is an indispensable part of the wall structure.

The paper or felt must be cut wide enough to extend across the joint. This keeps mortar from bonding on one side to create the joint.

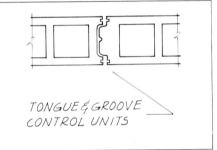

Tongue-and-groove control joints do not require insertion of any kind of paper or felt because the joint is molded into the block.

Continuous horizontal metal ties in masonry joints prevent obvious cracks due to shrinkage and temperature movement. There will still be cracks, but they will be too small to be easily noticed. Joint reinforcement is placed on the bare

Blocks with control joints cast into them are available. The tongue-and-groove ends shown give lateral support.

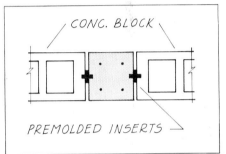

Rubber inserts, shaped like plus signs, fit between the blocks to prevent bonding and to enable movement without structural damage.

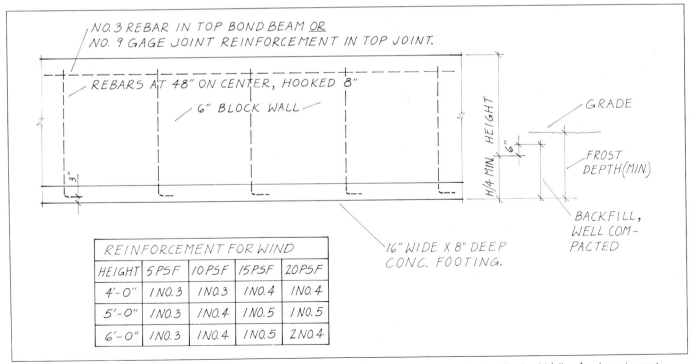

Although general guidelines and preferences are given here, bars inserted to reinforce concrete block walls should follow local requirements.

REINFORCEMENT FOR WIND				
HEIGHT	5 PSF	10 PSF	15 PSF	20 PSF
4'-0"	1 NO. 3	1 NO. 3	1 NO. 4	1 NO. 4
5'-0"	1 NO. 3	1 NO. 4	1 NO. 5	1 NO. 5
6'-0"	1 NO. 3	1 NO. 4	1 NO. 5	2 NO. 4

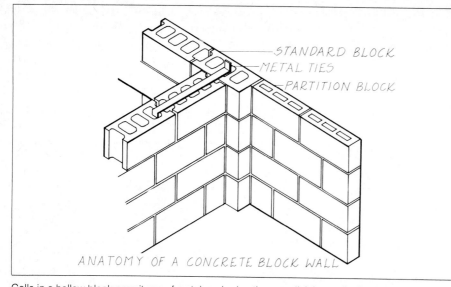

ANATOMY OF A CONCRETE BLOCK WALL

STANDARD BLOCK
METAL TIES
PARTITION BLOCK

Cells in a hollow block permit use of metal anchoring ties on adjoining walls. Partition walls are not subject to stress and need not be as thick or have as much reinforcing.

block, then covered with mortar. At the corners, prefabricated corner and T-type reinforcement is preferred although it can be job-fabricated. Joint reinforcement is especially important at wall openings (such as vents) or above doors and gates.

Footing needs. Concrete wall footings often need continuous steel bars or wire mesh reinforcement. Where a poured concrete or reinforced block foundation wall is required, or in the case of a concrete retaining wall, it is often necessary to use steel dowels turned up from the footing; the foundation wall is poured over the dowels.

Requirements for hurricane and earthquake areas. There are special reinforcement requirements for hurricane and earthquake areas. If you live in an area subject to either of these severe conditions, discuss these requirements with your building inspector and/or your architectural consultant. When you complete your design, the local code requirements must be included in your plan.

Other special requirements. The variety of designs and individual usage requirements make it impossible to present other than a few typical examples of steel reinforcement. However, most projects are subject to the provisions of local building codes. Local HUD offices also provide guidelines. If you are unable to get the information you need from the city building official or HUD, seek professional design consultation.

Coloring Concrete Blocks
The type of aggregate, cement, and mix

ingredients determine the natural color of concrete block. You do not have to use only gray blocks. In considering color, bear in mind that most block becomes darker with age. Since block color varies from batch to batch, try to buy all you need at one time.

Painting is still the typical way to add color. This avoids the concern about color uniformity. However, it is possible to buy units with integral color, or which expose the natural colors of the aggregate. The manufacturers have special machinery that grinds the surface of the block, giving the block surface a finish similar to terrazzo floors. Some standard colors of integral-colored concrete block are tan, buff, red, brown, pink, and yellow. Green, blue, black and gray may also be available. Mortar colors are available to match the colors you choose for the block.

Textures Available
Surface texture of concrete block can be varied by aggregate, mix, wetness of the mix, and compaction. Textures are generally classified as open, tight, fine, medium, and coarse. Usage determines which classification is best; stucco, for example, clings best to a coarse-textured block. A fine texture is more easily painted than a coarse texture.

There are also "prefaced" units available in many colors, patterns, and textures. They may be scored, patterned, or dappled. Ceramic and mineralized glazes, which may be combined for desired design effects, also can be found.

Mortar Mixtures
Masonry foundation walls depend on mortar to bond them together. Mortar is a mixture of cement, hydrated lime, sand, and water. It may be hand or machine mixed and, as in concrete, unless the job is a very small one it is preferable to use a power mixer. The mix used depends on the area of the country and the design of the wall. The types most frequently used are Type M and Type S. These are for exterior application only, and come pre-mixed. Building supply houses are usually knowledgeable about the mix used for building projects in their localities; ask them to recommend a mix for your project. You might want to ask the building department for confirmation.

Storage of Materials
Store all masonry materials, whether block or brick, in a dry area. Concrete block should be laid dry. Use protective coverings if necessary.

Preparing Foundations for Masonry
A good masonry wall will be plumb, all the units will be in the same plane, and the wall will rest on a straight, level foundation. Such a wall requires precise, but not difficult, design. If it is designed and executed carefully, it will not sink, lean, or crack noticeably.

If the foundation wall is of masonry, such as concrete block, the top of the footing should be flat, presenting a good surface on which to lay the wall masonry. Smooth the top of concrete footings with a wood float. This finish is just rough enough to provide a good bonding surface for masonry. If you live in an area of extreme cold, masonry is not a good choice for foundation walls, because it does not hold up against frost action as well as will concrete foundation walls. Footings should be notched, or "keyed" to receive concrete foundation walls. Let the footings cure before starting the foundation wall. Concrete block, concrete brick, or clay brick may be used for foundation walls in areas not subject to frost heave.

Snapping chalked guidelines. To begin the first course, locate the foundation wall corners. Snap a chalkline at the corner points on top of the footing. Chalklines, sold at most building supply houses, are coated with a colored chalk.

Secure the line between two points, in this case the corner points on top of the footing. Nails can be used to attach the line. Pull the line taut and then lift it up in the center; let it snap against the top of the footing. The chalk mark remains on the footing. Lift the chalked string and repeat the process, so you have an outline of the foundation wall on the footing. Check the lines on the footing to be sure they are square. The foundation wall blocks should be centered on the footing. Before laying any block, clean the surface of the footing. Then lay out the first course of block without mortar to establish spacing; joints may have to be increased or decreased due to slight inaccuracies in block lengths.

Laying Concrete Block

Placing the first block course. Trowel on a full bed of mortar. Lay the first block at a corner, in the mortar bed. However, if the wall is to be grouted—the hollow cores filled—keep the mortar out of the cores so the grout can adhere to the footing. Keep the block plumb, level, and flush with the chalkline on the footing.

Butter the end of the second block and set it in line with the first one. Level the block and check that the joint is full. Butter several more blocks—about three—or approximately the length of your level. Place them in line and level them together. Lay the rest of the first course.

Creating corner leads. As you lay the block, apply mortar only to the horizontal and vertical face shells of the block, leaving the cores open. Lay the mortar on the horizontal surface of the blocks of the first course that will support the lead.

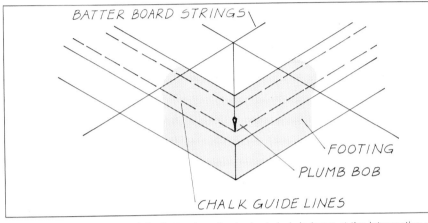

Strings attach to the ends of the batter boards. A plumb bob is hung at the intersection of the strings to show exact outside corners of the foundation's position on the footing.

Furrow full mortar bed with trowel for lots of mortar at bottom edges of first course.

Carefully position a block at the corner. Lay the thicker end of the shell face up.

For vertical joints, butter ends only. Lay blocks on end for fast mortar application.

Lay 3 blocks; check with a level. Adjust as necessary for correct alignment.

With a full mortar bed, keep the mortar from falling into the hollow centers.

This will be only four blocks: two around each side of the corner to form a right angle. Do not try to lay mortar all along the first course at this time—it would only get in the way. As you build up the lead, butter the vertical faces of the blocks just laid and butter the vertical faces of the next blocks before you lay them in line—this gives the best mortar contact for the best joints.

Be very careful in your work as you build up these leads because these blocks help you line up the future courses. If you have poorly laid leads, the whole wall will be off later. Carefully check each block as you lay it with a level, keeping all blocks plumb and aligned in a flat plane at the outside surface.

Horizontal joint consistency is maintained with a story pole. A simple story pole can be made with a 1x3 wood member, marked at 8 inch intervals. The story pole may be secured against the corner block or used as a frequent check, like the level. Even more accurate story poles can be obtained at contractor supply houses. If your project is small and you do not anticipate building more walls, a wooden story pole should suffice. But check the story poles available at the building supply houses—a ready-made story pole may be worth the cost to you for the convenience you gain. You also may be able to rent one.

When the first corner is built up, move to the next corner and, using strings from the first corner to keep the courses level, build up the second corner.

If you do not use L-shaped corner blocks, place an 8x8x16-inch block on the outside corner and a concrete brick inside to fill.

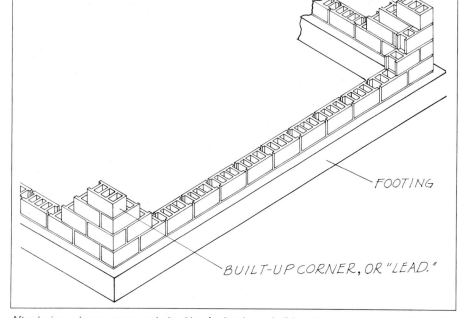

Step each course by half a block. Use a story pole diagonally across the corners of the block to verify alignment and spacing.

After laying a base course and checking for level, you build up three course corner "leads" to provide a convenient check of both level and plumb as you fill in the walls.

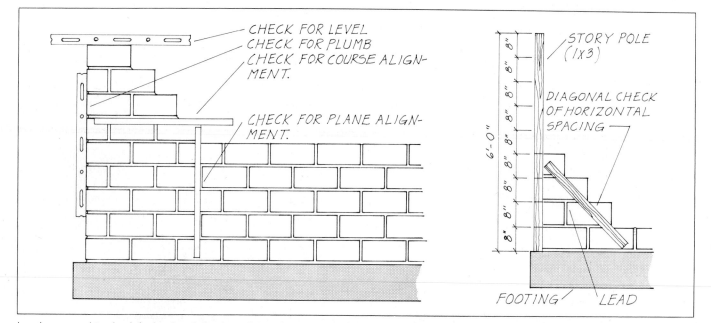

Levels are used to check for level and plumb, and to make sure that the faces of the blocks are all in the same plane.

Filling between the corners. Stretch a line between the top corner blocks of your leads. The line should be stretched so that it is an extension of the top, outside edges of the top lead blocks. The line will be used to align the blocks you lay between the leads. The line can be secured with a small nail driven into the corner blocks, or with a mason's line. One alternative calls for nailing wooden story poles at several points along the lead (one story pole at each lead). The line can then be raised on the story pole to align with each course. Still another way to align the courses is to drive stakes (2x4s) a foot or so away from the leads and to attach the line between the stakes so that it can be moved up as you lay the courses.

The blocks are leveled and aligned with the string; tap them with the trowel handle if you need to align the outside face.

Keep the work clean, but do not try to wipe mortar drippings off the wall while they are wet. Let them stay until they are almost dry, then flick them off with a trowel. Bits of mortar will still remain—let them dry, then rub them off with a piece of concrete block. Remove any remainder with a stiff-bristled, but not a wire, brush.

Reinforcement. Most of the steel reinforcement for block walls functions in similar ways. Ladder reinforcement, the most common horizontal reinforcement, is made of steel in small diameters, shaped like a ladder. It is about as wide as the block. The steel ladders are laid continuously along each course in the mortar. Another steel reinforcement shape typical for block walls is the truss design. As the name implies, the steel is formed like a truss; it is placed every other course or so in the block wall. Vertical reinforcement bars, placed in the cells of a concrete block, are usually "deformed billet" bars. Grout or mortar is placed around the bars. Whatever the shape of the reinforcement, its purpose is to tie the wall together firmly. Call the building department or an architect and describe your project to find out whether or not reinforcement is needed. If the project calls for some reinforcement, but not for professional design help, go to a concrete block supplier and take a look at the reinforcements available.

Setting the closure block. The last block laid in a course, called the closure block, will have to be cut or sawed unless the overall dimension of your wall is a multiple of the block size you are using. For example, the 16-foot base course in the illustration is made with twelve 16-inch blocks. The second course is eleven 16-inch blocks along the course, with two blocks turned on end at the corners. The next course would be another twelve 16-inch blocks laid end to end, and so forth, up the wall.

Suppose, however, that the wall were some length greater than 16 feet—such as 16 feet 8 inches. Then you would have an

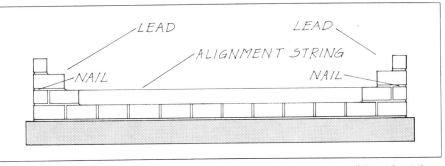

Rather than laying each full course, build first up the corners (called "leads") by at least three courses and then attach guide strings at each course level.

Once corner leads are built up, attach nails and alignment strings to serve as guides for level as you fill in the rest of the course.

An offset jamb block sometimes can be used at control joints, with a noncorroding metal tie bent in an open "Z" across the joint.

Lower closure block (last block in course) carefully. If mortar falls out, remove closure block. Re-apply mortar; reposition block.

odd block size—8 inches—somewhere. That "somewhere" is easier to deal with along the interior of the course than at the corners. The best way to locate closures is to do a scaled elevation drawing, or schematic sketch.

In the drawing, first lay out the overall dimension of the wall in question, such as the 16⅔ foot wall. Then draw in the blocks to scale, starting at the corners. Locate the closure for the base course in the center. Draw the next course, again starting from the corners and working toward the closure block in the base course. You will notice that unless you use two 12-inch blocks on the second course you will be forced to lay one vertical joint on top of another. This is not a good practice because vertical joints weaken the wall. Put the joint of the two 12-inch blocks over the center of the 8-inch closure block on the base course.

You will follow this closure pattern all the way up the wall: base course with an 8-inch closure block, then two 12-inch closure blocks over it, then an 8-inch closure block on the next course, then two 12-inch closure blocks, and so forth up the wall. Headers are commonly used for the top course of garden walls—this topping may be referred to as a coping. You also can buy precast concrete copings at most concrete block supply houses. A variety should be displayed.

Doing a good job. To build a good wall, the frequent checks with level,

strings, and plumb bob should become work habits. This is essential. Short-cuts and haste in checking will show up negatively in the appearance of the wall. There is considerable planning in even a small, simple wall. The skills needed to construct a wall are habit to a professional mason, but they are not habit to the rest of us. Patience and careful planning must substitute for experience for the amateur mason.

Finishing the Joints

Mortar joints are important to the appearance of your wall. You can "tool" mortar joints to a variety of finished appearances. Tooling refers to the final finish you put on mortar joints with some kind of joint tool. The tooling is important where watertight joints are needed. When the blocks are laid, mortar oozes slightly from the joint. This is due to the weight of the block, adjustments of the block, and because you always put a little more mortar on the block surfaces than you need. Tooling compresses this excess, bringing it into tighter contact with the block and making the mortar surface denser to resist the weather.

After you have laid a wall section, test the mortar by pressing it with your thumb. If your thumbprint remains but the mortar does not stick to your thumb, the joints are probably ready for tooling.

Tools for and styles in jointing. There are various joints to select from,

First tool the horizontal joints and then use a small S-shaped jointer to strike the vertical joints.

When finishing and compacting a V-shaped mortar joint, you can produce your own tool from a ½-inch-square bar.

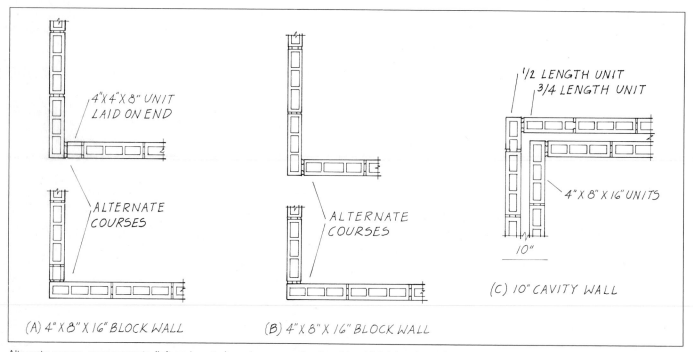

(A) 4" X 8" X 16" BLOCK WALL

4" X 4" X 8" UNIT LAID ON END

ALTERNATE COURSES

(B) 4" X 8" X 16" BLOCK WALL

ALTERNATE COURSES

½ LENGTH UNIT
3/4 LENGTH UNIT

4" X 8" X 16" UNITS

10"

(C) 10" CAVITY WALL

Alternate course arrangements (left and center) produce a running bond in which joints in each course center on blocks above and below.

each of them having a function and an aesthetic effect of its own. Concave, vee, raked, and beaded joints are typical. Metal jointers are used to finish most joints. Flush, struck, and weathered joints may be done with a trowel. Plexiglass jointers should be used for white or light-colored mortar to avoid stains.

Concave joints contribute to a flat wall appearance, where this is desired. Vee joints emphasize shadows. Flush joints are desirable where stucco will be used to finish the surface. Raked joints leave the mortar perpendicular and recessed almost a half inch (but not more); these joints create dark shadows. Beaded joints are like extruded joints but with a more formal appearance, achieved with a special tool. The extrusions create strong shadow lines. Struck joints and weathered joints, like the raked joint, create dark lines on the wall.

Joint types can be mixed for a desired aesthetic effect. For example, you may combine flush vertical joints and extruded horizontal joints to produce long lines of horizontal shadow. However, mixing joint types is difficult, even for a professional.

Mortar color and mix. Mortar color also affects the appearance of walls. All batches of mortar mix must be kept uniform in color and the hardness of the mortar consistent. Mortar mix is affected by moisture; if you are interrupted by rain, wait for the block to dry before starting up again, or the mortar color will not be consistent.

Regardless of how careful you are, some joint patching will probably be necessary due to human error. It is best to work while the mortar is still plastic. But if you must after the mortar hardens, gouge out the joint about a half inch, wet it, and patch with fresh mortar.

Functions of joints. In addition to their visual effects, masonry joints have different functions. Concave and vee joints drain well. Flush joints lack the compressed quality of other joints; they are good for stucco—when they are not covered with stucco, they soak up water.

There are negative aspects to some of the joints. Raked joints collect water, snow and ice. Beaded, struck and extruded joints are not good water joints. These negative qualities are perhaps not as important in garden walls as they are to walls you count on to keep out the

weather. In areas of extreme weather, however, they can result in the early deterioration of your work.

Dry block is a must—a word of warning. Please note a final caution about concrete block. Store block where it will stay dry and *always* lay it dry. Walls that are laid when the block has excess moisture tend to crack as they dry out.

Adobe Walls and Slump Concrete Block Walls

Adobe brick. Laying up a wall of adobe brick involves the same steps as for a wall of concrete block. Adobe bricks are a mixture of sand and clay and straw. Emulsified asphalt is added to waterproof the bricks. Clay is the binder in adobe bricks; sand is the aggregate. The straw is not for strength, but to help prevent cracking. It is best to avoid hay; it is usually too porous and too large in diameter to do the job as well as straw. The straw is cut to 4-inch lengths before mixing with the adobe.

Slump block. Adobe is, of course, common in the Southwest. In other areas of the country, you may have to make your own. Another option is use of slump block. Slump concrete blocks are specially shaped concrete blocks that look much like adobe bricks. The slump blocks are widely available and are laid using the construction techniques for regular concrete blocks. However, if your project requires creation of authentic adobe, first research the material carefully.

CREATING A STUCCO SURFACE

Stucco is a beautiful material that can be applied over many different surfaces. It

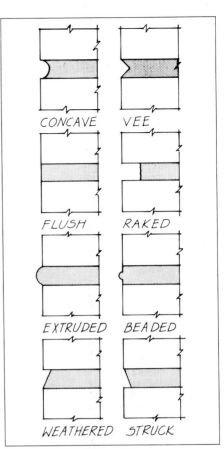

Each mortar joint type requires a different tool or depth to achieve a desired effect.

Concrete block with a three-dimensional relief pattern offers both dynamic design and traditional solidity and strength.

Plain concrete walls of block can be disguised with unusual textures and designs using application of several layers of stucco plaster.

works well on any kind of masonry wall. It may be used as a surface for a new masonry wall or as a face-lift for an old one.

Stucco is a mixture of sand, portland cement, lime, and water. Color may be mixed into stucco, or you can apply it in its natural gray and paint it later. A wide variety of textures is possible; these rougher textures tend to hide minor imperfections on wall surfaces. Stucco seems to be especially appealing in warm climates, where the sun lights its surfaces. Stucco is a durable, long-lasting material applicable in many climates, if it is applied properly. The material does, however, require some application skills. Stucco is a material for the advanced handyman.

Mixing the Stucco

The stucco mix you need varies depending on the material you are covering and whether or not you use a wire mesh. Wire meshes especially made for stucco are available at building supply stores.

Mixing stucco is similar to mixing concrete or mortar. And, as with concrete or mortar, a power mixer is best. All ingredients must be thoroughly mixed with water until the stucco is workable. The stucco ingredients arrive at a uniform color after several minutes of mixing. You should not mix more than you can use in about 2½ hours. A little water may

be added occasionally to maintain plasticity. Do not attempt to re-use stucco that has dried on your mixing platform.

Using wire mesh. If the surface is a pitted and scarred old masonry wall, nail the mesh to the surface at about 8 inches on center each way, and spread the stucco thoroughly through the mesh. Then apply a second and a third coat of stucco. New concrete block can be covered with two coats of stucco without using mesh.

Applying the Stucco

New concrete masonry walls provide a good base for stucco. The wall should be free of dirt or any material that might reduce the bonding effect. The wall should be damp, but not wet, before applying stucco. A sprayer offers the best means of dampening the block. If the water is not readily absorbed, or droplets appear even though you are not spraying enough to wet the surface, use a bond agent to prepare the surface (1 part portland cement, 1 to 2 parts sand, plus enough water for a heavy, paintlike mixture).

Stucco may be applied over concrete block by hand in two coats. The first coat is ⅜ inch thick and the second coat is ¼ inch thick. Apply the stucco with trowels and a mortar board. You may instead use a machine sprayer, although its use is probably best left to a contractor. The sprayers require skill to use; when you

make mistakes, they tend to be big ones. If you can handle the sprayer, the work will go more quickly and the rental expense is relatively small.

CONCRETE-BLOCK SCREENS

Concrete masonry walls with over 25% open area may be considered screens or fences. They are visually lighter and more decorative in character than solid masonry walls, and obviously let in more light and air.

Structural Needs

Conventional concrete block may be used for screen walls by leaving voids or by laying the block on the sides—but this method often looks heavy and awkward, defeating the decorative aspect of the screen. Concrete block comes in many sizes, cut-out patterns, shapes, colors, and textures in addition to the conventional block. Before planning a wall in a particular decorative block, you should check availability in your area.

Screen walls are usually less structurally sound than solid masonry walls and, in spite of the open areas, need steel reinforcement both horizontally and vertically to protect them against wind loads. Experts recommend that screen units have a minimum compressive strength of 1,000 psi on the total area when tested with their hollow cells parallel to the direction of the wind load.

The structural design requirements for a concrete masonry screen wall are a combination of features of both masonry walls and fences. Lateral support is usually provided by posts of concrete or steel, or by piers built from some arrangement of concrete block similar to the piers used in solid masonry walls. The screen panels between the posts are reinforced in the horizontal joints at a spacing determined by block thickness, anticipated load, and height. Practical size of screen openings will depend upon the size of your wall. The longer and higher the wall, the smaller the openings must be. The panels may have a reinforced bond beam (see art below) at the top, with fully grouted joints. The panels are anchored to the posts either with steel connections or with grout, depending on the arrangement of the posts.

Mortar. Type M or S mortar is recommended for exterior screen walls. There are five types of mortar: types M,

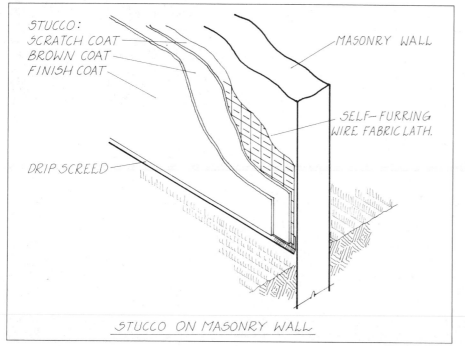

STUCCO:
SCRATCH COAT
BROWN COAT
FINISH COAT

MASONRY WALL

SELF-FURRING
WIRE FABRIC LATH.

DRIP SCREED

STUCCO ON MASONRY WALL

A stucco finish consists of several coats of plaster that are applied over lath that has been attached to a masonry wall.

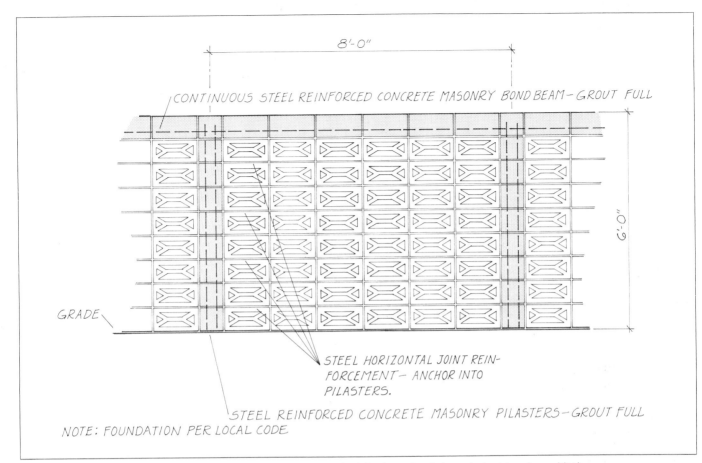

8'-0"

CONTINUOUS STEEL REINFORCED CONCRETE MASONRY BOND BEAM - GROUT FULL

6'-0"

GRADE

STEEL HORIZONTAL JOINT REIN-
FORCEMENT - ANCHOR INTO
PILASTERS.

STEEL REINFORCED CONCRETE MASONRY PILASTERS - GROUT FULL

NOTE: FOUNDATION PER LOCAL CODE

Bond beams are hollow to accept steel reinforcing and grout. Vertical reinforcing extends from plaster into a beam block.

In order to ensure sufficient bonding and structural strength, screen patterns require careful planning before building them.

Some concrete block comes with designs and cutouts already cast into each unit.

Although masonry screen walls offer visual privacy, they do not block sound.

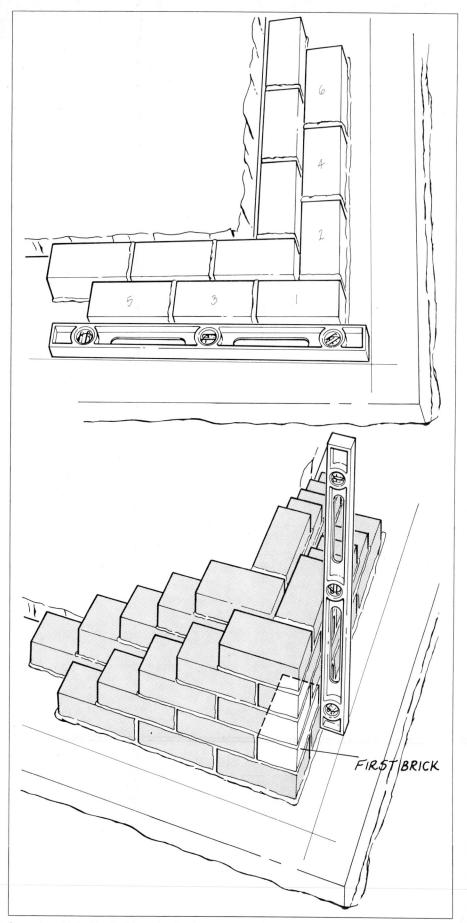

Spread mortar inside chalklines. Lay Brick 1 and work alternately from side to side. Build up corner lead. Lay header to start second course and to create the running bond.

S, N, O, and K. Types M and S are particularly suited for these types of masonry walls. All the types should be available at building supply stores.

Building the Screen Wall

The layout and construction process for a concrete masonry screen wall is the same as for a solid masonry wall, although more reinforcement is generally required in thin screen walls than in thicker, solid masonry walls. The precise selection of reinforcement for high screen walls (over 4 feet) should be done by an architect. An accompanying illustration shows typical placement of steel reinforcement within the wall, plus a bond beam on top. The bond beam is a specially cast, but readily available concrete block that is open at the top. The reinforcement is placed inside and the bond beam filled with grout. The end result is a beam along the top of the wall that ties into the pilasters, which are in turn attached to the steel wall reinforcement.

In this way, the whole structure of the wall is tied together by a network of steel reinforcement. The steel in the wall is placed every other course, tying in at the pilasters. An alternative system uses steel channels.

BUILDING BRICK WALLS

The techniques for laying clay brick and concrete brick walls resemble those for concrete block walls, especially the layout and coursing techniques. Walls covered with another material—such as stucco or plaster—or walls that will be painted would be more easily and economically built using concrete block.

The typical brick garden wall is two parallel walls of brick (called ''wythes'') laid to the same thickness as the length of one brick. This leaves a cavity in the middle for reinforcement and/or for grout. The top is usually capped with a row of bricks laid perpendicular to the wall across its top.

Patterns and Bonds

Brick patterns often have structural purposes, as well as decorative ones. The word ''bond'' is important in understanding the structural function of brick patterns. ''Structural bond'' refers to the way individual bricks are laid to aid a structural need for strength. The plan of decorative layout of brick positions is called pattern bond. Therefore, laying a brick wall using individual bricks in a pattern to help hold the whole structure together, is something like building an interlocking puzzle. Although this sounds complicated, remember that practical masonry is merely a series of practices that, once you know them, are quite simple.

Using reinforcement. When steel reinforcement is used, less attention need be devoted to structural function of the surface patterns. Many building codes allow steel bonding ties in brick walls. Typical steel joint reinforcement for brick

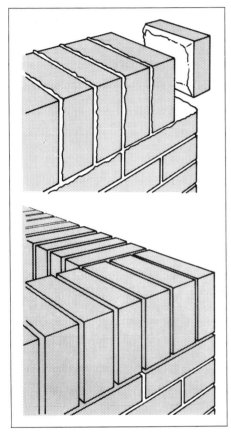

Cap courses with rowlocks in order to seal the flashing and unite the two wythes. Set any partial brick (needed to fill) 4 or 5 units from the end.

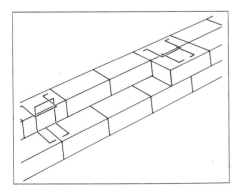

Adjustable mini-trusses handle different heights of brick wythes. Install every 2½ sq. ft. in a thick mortar bed.

walls is ³/₁₆-inch diameter steel ties placed at a maximum separation of 18 inches vertically and a maximum of 36 inches horizontally. The ties come in Z or rectangular shapes and are placed on the mortar. Stagger the ties so that they do not line up vertically—staggering makes the wall stronger. It is suggested you use grout to fill the cavity in the center of the brick wall. If using vertical "deformed billet" bar reinforcing, place the bars in the mortar of the joints, between bricks.

Brick orientation and terminology. Knowing the names of the various parts of a brick wall and of the traditional pattern bonds is necessary before you can plan the work.

Courses and stretchers. A "course" refers to one horizontal layer, or row, of bricks. One brick in this course, laid flat, is called a stretcher. If laid on edge, it is called a "rowlock stretcher."

Headers. A "header" refers to a brick laid perpendicular to the courses of the wall. Headers may be used singly, set in the wall between the stretchers or, more frequently, in a recurring pattern. Sometimes they alternate with stretchers. They may be laid side-by-side the length of a course—in which case, you have laid a header course. Headers strengthen walls by tying the parallel courses together, but they also may be used for purely decorative purposes. In the discussion above, the headers were laid flat, as were the stretchers. A header laid on edge is called a "rowlock header".

Soldiers and sailors. A brick laid on end (with the narrow side as the face of the wall) is called a soldier—courses of bricks laid on this manner are called soldier courses. A brick laid on end with its wide side as the face of the wall is called a sailor.

Running bond. This is the most common pattern. It consists of courses of all stretchers. The vertical joints are staggered for strength.

Common bond. Common bond consists of running bond with headers at some interval. There may be an entire course of headers at vertical intervals (set by local code requirements) or you may have a header alternating with a stretcher for the full length of the course.

Flemish bond. In Flemish bond, each course alternates individual stretchers and headers for the full vertical height of the wall.

English bond. English bond consists of alternating courses of stretchers and headers. The joints in the alternating stretcher courses line up with each other vertically; the headers are centered over the stretchers.

English cross. The vertical joints between the stretchers in alternate courses do not line up vertically in English cross. Instead, the joints are centered on the stretchers in the courses above and below.

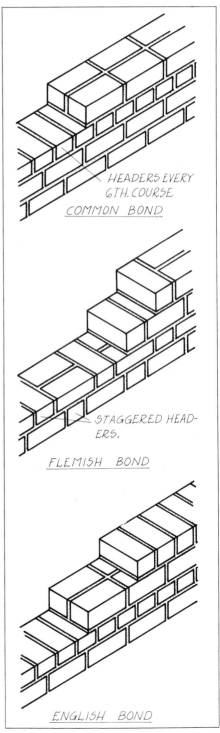

Vary placement of headers to create common bond, Flemish bond, and English bond.

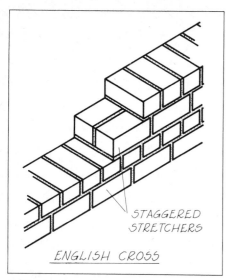

ENGLISH CROSS

English cross calls for alternating courses of stretchers and headers. The stretcher courses are staggered relative to each other.

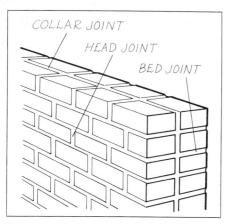

A bed joint is horizontal between courses; A head joint is vertical between bricks; A collar joint is vertical between wythes.

The header joints, however, do align vertically.

Stack bond. Stack bond is an example of a pattern that has almost negligible structural qualities. All the vertical joints line up, the bricks being literally stacked one on the other. A wall built with a stack bond pattern depends almost entirely on metal reinforcement to hold it together. The typical reinforcement used for stack bond is pencil-shaped steel rods placed in the mortar of each horizontal joint. Check with your building department for local practice.

Building a Two-Wythe Garden Wall

A two-wythe-thick cavity wall is built using the same techniques as are used for a block wall. Essentially, you will build two walls next to each other. Construction begins at the corners and leads are built up in the same way as with concrete block.

A two-wythe wall may either be left as a cavity wall or filled. If it is left hollow, you must provide drainage weep holes to prevent moisture accumulation in the cavity. If the wall will be subject to a great deal of wind or other stress, it is advisable to fill the cavity with mortar grout and install vertical reinforcing rods. Horizontal reinforcing wall ties are used whether the cavity is filled or not. These ties are placed every six courses, staggered from course to course, set on 24-inch centers.

The top of the wall is finished with rowlock headers. These headers cover the cavity, complete the top, and help tie the two walls together. If you prefer, you may finish the top with stone or precast concrete copings.

Brick Panel and Pier Wall

One of the simplest, cheapest brick walls is the brick panel and pier wall. A pier is a column built within the wall for support; it often is thicker than the rest of the wall. (Information presented here was prepared from data provided by the Brick Institute of America.) A brick panel and pier wall requires only half the amount of bricks of the double garden wall discussed above.

Designing the wall. Sketch the design, showing a pier at every corner or turn in the wall. Locate intermediate piers so that the panel spaces between the piers will be nearly equal. If the wall is tied to the house, a pier will not be needed at that point unless desired for aesthetic considerations. When you are satisfied your plan meets your needs, dimension the drawing.

Staking the location. Stake out the piers and wall foundations. In temperate areas the bricks are laid directly on the ground. In areas of extreme cold, you will have to check with your building department for local foundation underlayment standards and design the foundation to your required standards. Dig the pier holes; Table 3 shows the depths required.

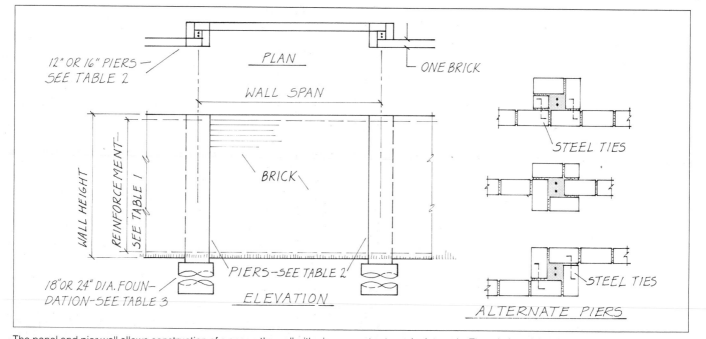

The panel and pier wall allows construction of a one wythe wall with pier supports at regular intervals. The relation of the piers to the wall face may vary to have one side flat, have the piers protrude equally on each side, or have the piers alternate.

TABLE 1 — PANEL WALL REINFORCING STEEL

WALL SPAN, FEET	VERTICAL SPACING, INCH.								
	WIND LOAD, 10 PSF			WIND LOAD, 15 PSF			WIND LOAD, 20 PSF		
	A	B	C	A	B	C	A	B	C
8	45	30	19	30	20	12	23	15	9.5
10	29	19	12	19	13	8.0	14	10	6.0
12	20	13	8.5	13	9.0	5.5	10	7.0	4.0
14	15	10	6.5	10	6.5	4.0	7.5	5.0	3.0
16	11	7.5	5.0	7.5	5.0	3.0	6.0	4.0	2.5

NOTE: A = 2 - NO. 2 BARS; B = 2 - 3/16 IN. DIAMETER WIRES; C = 2 - 9 GAGE WIRES.

TABLE 2 — PIER REINFORCING STEEL

WALL SPAN, FEET	WIND LOAD, 10 PSF			WIND LOAD, 15 PSF			WIND LOAD, 20 PSF		
	WALL HEIGHT, FT.			WALL HEIGHT, FT.			WALL HEIGHT, FT.		
	4	6	8	4	6	8	4	6	8
8	2 NO.3	2 NO.4	2 NO.5	2 NO.3	2 NO.5	2 NO.6	2 NO.4	2 NO.5	2 NO.5
10	2 NO.3	2 NO.4	2 NO.5	2 NO.4	2 NO.5	2 NO.7	2 NO.4	2 NO.6	2 NO.6
12	2 NO.3	2 NO.5	2 NO.6	2 NO.4	2 NO.6	2 NO.6	2 NO.4	2 NO.6	2 NO.7
14	2 NO.3	2 NO.5	2 NO.6	2 NO.4	2 NO.6	2 NO.6	2 NO.5	2 NO.5	2 NO.7
16	2 NO.4	2 NO.5	2 NO.7	2 NO.4	2 NO.6	2 NO.7	2 NO.5	2 NO.6	2 NO.7

NOTE: WITHIN HEAVY LINES 12 BY 16 IN. PIER REQUIRED. ALL OTHER VALUES OBTAINED WITH 12 BY 12 INCH PIER

TABLE 3 — REQUIRED EMBEDMENT FOR PIER FOUNDATION.

WALL SPAN, FEET	WIND LOAD, 10 PSF			WIND LOAD, 15 PSF			WIND LOAD, 20 PSF		
	WALL HEIGHT, FT.			WALL HEIGHT, FT.			WALL HEIGHT, FT.		
	4	6	8	4	6	8	4	6	8
8	2'-0"	2'-3"	2'-9"	2'-3"	2'-6"	3'-0"	2'-3"	2'-9"	3'-0"
10	2'-0"	2'-6"	2'-9"	2'-3"	2'-9"	3'-3"	2'-6"	3'-0"	3'-3"
12	2'-3"	2'-6"	3'-0"	2'-3"	3'-0"	3'-3"	2'-6"	3'-3"	3'-6"
14	2'-3"	2'-9"	3'-0"	2'-6"	3'-0"	3'-3"	2'-9"	3'-3"	3'-9"
16	2'-3"	2'-9"	3'-0"	2'-6"	3'-3"	3'-6"	2'-9"	3'-3"	4'-0"

NOTE: WITHIN HEAVY LINES 24 IN. DIAMETER FOUNDATION REQUIRED. ALL OTHER VALUES OBTAINED WITH 18 IN. DIAMETER FOUNDATION

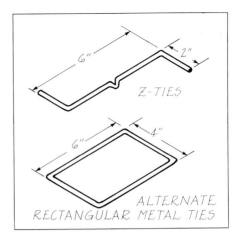

Wall ties vary in type. Check with your building code for type required in your area.

Once the mortar is thumbprint hard, use a jointing tool to smooth the mortar joints.

Preparing the base. Prepare the earth for the base of the panels. Remove earth several inches down and scrape the excavation floor smooth and level. Remove any debris, dirt clods, or protruding stones. Tamp the earth smooth.

Laying the bricks. In temperate areas, lay the first course of bricks on a one-inch bed of mortar placed directly on the smooth earth. This course (and perhaps additional courses) should be below ground level. The more courses below ground, the larger the foundation will be. In areas subject to ground freeze, you must build a foundation. Check with your building department for foundation depth and preparation requirements.

The piers and the brick panels are built up at the same time; the wall courses tie into the piers as you work upward. The piers themselves are hollow-core, square columns that are part of the wall, which may connect with the pier at one side, at the center, or alternately at the front and back faces of the pier. (See the illustration for types of piers and the wall unions.)

After laying mortar for the second course, place the horizontal steel in the mortar before laying the bricks in the second course. Continue laying the brick, installing the reinforcing according to Table 1. As the panel rises, grout the center opening in the pier with mortar, to which sufficient water has been added so that it will flow readily and completely surround the vertical steel. Your local lime and cement dealer will supply grout and can tell you what mix is used in your region.

Table 3 is based on soils with an allowable bearing pressure of 3000 psi or more. For poorer soil, additional engineering analysis of the foundation is necessary. Ask your building department to refer you to a soils engineer.

Materials for your wall. For greatest durability and strength use ASTM C270, type S brick made with 1 part portland cement, ½ part hydrated lime and 4½ parts sand by volume. Use No. 2 and larger bars of reinforcing steel with a minimum yield strength of 40,000 psi. No. 9 gauge wire and 3/16 inch diameter wire must have a minimum yield strength of 60,000 psi.

Workmanship. Vertical (head) and bed joints must be filled solid; pack the joints fully and do not rake them out. The

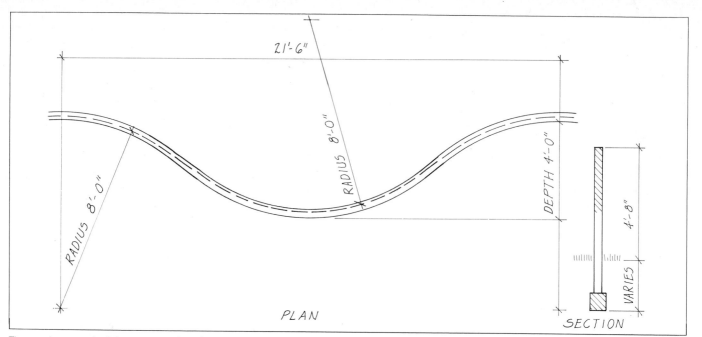

The maximum and minimum proportions for a serpentine wall have been carefully established in order to fulfill structural needs.

grout in the piers must surround the steel and completely fill the pier.

Constructing a Serpentine Wall

The wavering form of the serpentine wall serves a functional as well as decorative purpose: the shape provides lateral strength, allowing the wall to be built only 4 inches thick. Where the depth of the curve does not present a space problem, the serpentine wall is a relatively cheap way to build.

Determining the curve. In general, the radius of curvature of a 4-inch wall should be no more than twice the height of the wall above finished grade. This is a general rule to ensure that the curvature of the wall is not so shallow—and, therefore, weak—that the wall will topple. In other words, if the curve is too shallow it resembles a straight wall. A straight 4-inch wall that would need steel reinforcement to be stable. So, if you needed a wall 4 feet 8 inches high, your radius of curvature should not be more than 9 feet 4 inches. Another guideline is that the curvature radius should not be less than half the height. For a 4-foot 8-inch wall, the radius of curvature should not be less than 2 feet 4 inches. These limitations also seem to produce the most visually pleasing walls.

Laying out the wall. Laying out a serpentine wall calls for precision techniques. The longer the distance of the wall, the more obvious any mistakes will be. These directions are for walls

that—even though they are serpentine—extend in one direction only. If the walls must jog around obstructions, the layout problems are multiplied and you would be wise to call a surveyor and have him stake

out the centerline of the wall for you. (This is a good idea for any wall of this complexity.) Have a sketch to show him so that he will know what kind of wall you have in mind and where you want it

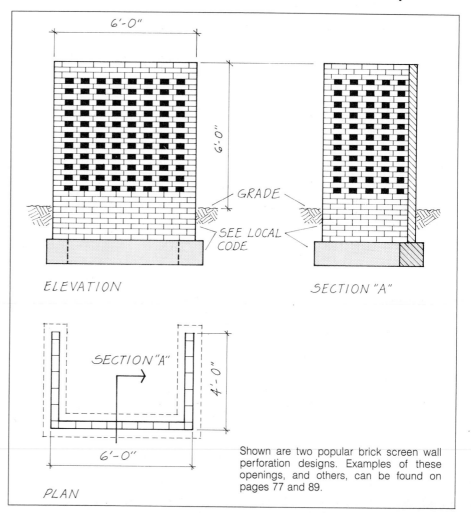

Shown are two popular brick screen wall perforation designs. Examples of these openings, and others, can be found on pages 77 and 89.

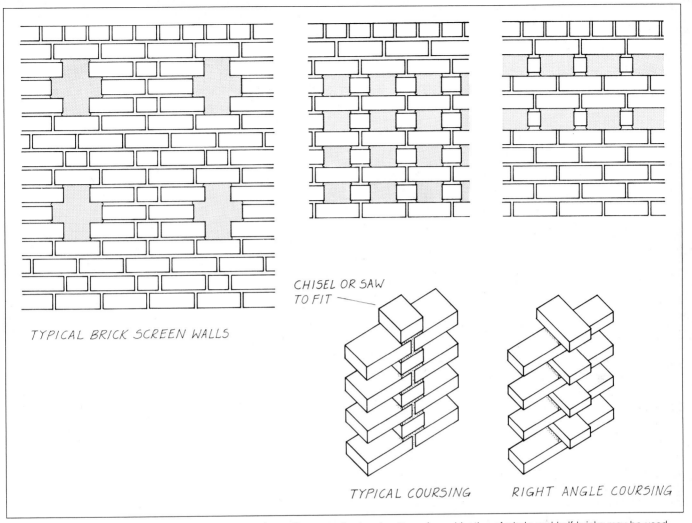

TYPICAL BRICK SCREEN WALLS

CHISEL OR SAW TO FIT

TYPICAL COURSING   RIGHT ANGLE COURSING

Brick screens may have a variety of opening patterns depending upon the bond pattern. A combination of whole and half bricks may be used.

to go. Refer to the illustration for a typical length within the serpentine wall, and sketch your wall in the same manner.

Constructing the wall. Once you have the wall centerline staked, build it using the basic instructions given above for other masonry walls.

BUILDING BRICK SCREENS
The brick screen wall or ''perforated'' wall is designed, laid out, and constructed similar to a concrete masonry screen wall and a solid masonry wall. In some designs it is easier to construct than a concrete masonry screen wall, since generally it requires less steel reinforcement. The pattern possibilities of the brick screen wall are ample, but they will all have a more squared-off quality than some of the free-form patterns available in concrete screen blocks.

Brick screen walls are commonly used as solar screens to cut off the direct rays of the sun without blocking the light completely. They are popular for setting apart activity areas. The screens help disguise air-conditioner condensing units and trash cans where you wish to enclose items but want to keep the air circulation.

Construction Methods
The brick-laying techniques for a brick perforated wall are the same as for a solid masonry wall. However, extra care must be taken to avoid putting any pressure on the screen before the mortar sets, since it has much less lateral strength than a solid masonry wall. You should also check with the building department. They sometimes have special requirements because of this lack of strength for screen walls of considerable height. Patterns are achieved by manipulating the position of brick within the courses and/or by leaving some of them out (voids or perforations). The wall may be flush, or selected bricks may be turned at right angles to the regular courses to form the voids or create deep shadows.

Creating the perforations. There are no hard rules for how much overlap (bearing surface) you need for the bricks that span perforations. However, the size of the bricks often tells you what the overlap should be. For example, if you are leaving out every other stretcher in alternate courses, and are supporting the stretcher courses with bricks turned at right angles and flat, then the stretchers should be centered over the headers—this would give you an overlap of half the width of a brick.

In general, let the brick indicate what the overlaps should be. You can use headers or rowlock headers as supports for your stretchers, but keep in mind that although perforations add pattern interest to walls, they also weaken it. The higher the wall, the more significant this weakening effect becomes. If you use patterns with more open space than the perforations shown, or that have less overlap, you should show your sketches to an architect or get an opinion from the building department before you start

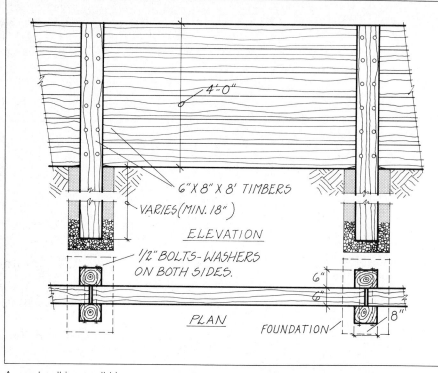

A wood wall is as solid in appearance as any masonry wall and may be as durable.

construction. Do not court problems by building unnecessarily weak walls.

POURED OR BROKEN-CONCRETE WALLS
Building with Broken Concrete

Broken-concrete walls can be beautiful. However, you may need to use more care in planning, laying out, and constructing the broken-concrete wall than if you were laying a wall in brick, block or other masonry. Broken concrete walls have a rustic look if they are laid with care—casual treatment of construction techniques will give a sloppy-looking wall. A poured concrete footing is best for all masonry walls, including a broken-concrete wall. Stake out the footing and wall using the same techniques discussed earlier for laying out masonry walls. Be especially careful in selecting the broken concrete pieces for the courses below ground. You need a good, level foundation; make frequent checks for level with a spirit level.

As you lay the wall, select pieces of broken concrete for each course before you lay it. Lay them out on the ground along the wall, as they will be when you lift them and mortar them in place on their course. Read the section on laying a stone wall later in this chapter. Broken stone walls and rubble walls share the same construction techniques.

Poured Concrete Walls

Poured concrete walls should result in a fluid, smooth look. Unfortunately, that is only achieved by first building what is almost a wall itself—the form. Actually, the form work will take much more time than pouring and letting the concrete set. The form work will be very similar to that for a footing and foundation, simply higher. Heavier reinforcement is required as the height increases. The reinforcement should be designed by a professional for your particular requirements.

BUILDING WALLS OF WOOD

A wood wall—as opposed to a fence—is as thick as a brick wall. It is constructed of heavy members such as railroad ties rather than of boards. Wood walls may be constructed similar to the brick pier wall described earlier. The posts serve as piers and the panel members, typically 4x4s, are coursed up like brick or block. The cost for the wood in a wall like the above is quite high, so it is suggested you use pressure-treated timber throughout for longevity.

Laying out the Wall

Note the route of the wall on the ground with stakes and string. Locate every post and use stakes to indicate the center of the posts. Find the positions of the posts for any gates or other openings.

Installing Posts and Panels

Set the posts. Techniques for this are discussed in the opening of Chapter 10. Next, install the base course of 4x4s by nailing the 4x4s to the posts with heavy nails (minimum of 3 each end) or by drilling holes and installing two ¼-inch diameter lag bolts at each end of the 4x4s. If the land is not level, you may have to step some of the courses down—again, this is about the same as stepping down fence panels; see the fence section in Chapter 10. As you nail the base course timbers in place, check them for level frequently with a spirit level.

BUILDING STONE WALLS

Rubble and ashlar stone encompass a wide range of stone types and methods of construction. In residential work it is best to keep the stone small enough so that none are too big for one man to handle. This size stone is probably in scale with most houses.

Rubble Walls

Rubble refers to stone just as it comes from the quarry or field. Masonry walls laid with these unshaped stones, without regularity of coursing, are called rough or ordinary rubble walls. Coursed rubble indicates stone masonry of roughly shaped stones that fit approximately on level beds and are well bonded. Rubble walls have mortar joints but, unlike ashlar walls, the joints are not consistently sized.

Ashlar Walls

In contrast to rubble walls, ashlar is hewn or squared stone. Within the term ashlar, there is a wide range of cuts and finishes, from rough-faced stone all the way to glossy marble. In general, ashlar masonry is bonded, having sawed, dressed, or squared beds with mortar joints.

Ashlar stones are precut and can be bought in thicknesses of 2 to 8 inches, heights of 1 to 48 inches, and lengths of 1 to 8 feet. In selecting stone for walls, choose the size and type appropriate to your needs.

Varieties of Stone

The stone most used in the United States are limestone, marble, granite, slate, and sandstone. In some areas a wide range of other stones is available.

Featherock, for example, is an espe-

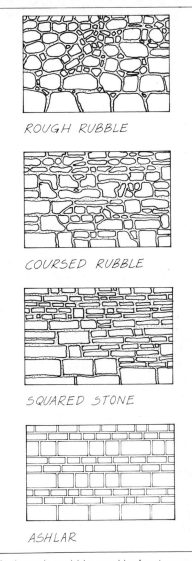

ROUGH RUBBLE

COURSED RUBBLE

SQUARED STONE

ASHLAR

Whether using rubble or ashlar for stone walls, base courses must be broad and firm.

cially interesting stone for many projects because of its light weight. It is quarried from the Mono Craters in the Sierra Nevada region of California. The stone is five times lighter than most stone. It permits great freedom of design. Because of its light weight, it is easy to ship, and can be found in garden centers far from California.

Mixing Mortar for Stone Walls

Absorbent stone should be moistened before laying, otherwise it will pull the water out of the mortar. Nonabsorbent stone does not have to be dampened. Your garden center can tell you which stone you have.

Because ordinary portland cement stains most stone, use nonstaining white portland cement in making mortar. Lime is usually stainless; portland cement-lime mortar may be acceptable. For ordinary

usage, mix 1 part masonry cement (ASTM Specification C91 Type II) with $2\frac{1}{4}$ or 3 parts mortar sand in a damp, loose consistency; or mix 1 part portland cement, $\frac{1}{2}$ to $1\frac{1}{4}$ parts hydrated lime, with $4\frac{1}{2}$ to 6 parts mortar sand in damp, loose consistency.

For more intense usage, such as in earthquake zones, areas of high wind, and areas subject to frost heave, mix your mortar from 1 part masonry cement (ASTM Specification C91 Type II) plus 1 part portland cement with $4\frac{1}{2}$ to 6 parts mortar sand in damp, loose consistency; or 1 part portland cement with 0 to $\frac{1}{4}$ part hydrated lime with $2\frac{1}{4}$ to 3 parts mortar sand in damp, loose consistency.

Laying A Stone Wall

Step one: creating the foundation. Lay out and construct a concrete footing as you would for a brick or block wall. A typical footing for a four foot stone wall that is 18 inches wide (the minimum width for a stone wall) would be no less than two feet wide and 8 inches deep. Two #4 steel reinforcing bars run continuously, should take care of the weight of the wall. This is for a simple dividing wall. If the stone wall is to serve as a retaining wall, see the section on retaining walls and/or consult a professional for design help. For a dividing wall the top of the footing should be below the frost line or protected against frost heave as required for the area. Check with your building department for specific code requirements.

If the footing is to be stone, stake out and dig the trench just as if you were building a concrete footing. A stone footing is *not* easier to build than a concrete footing. The stone footing is probably more difficult because it is harder to lay the stones level—and once you do, the stone foundation footing provides a less specific set of reference points from which to build than does the concrete footing. Lay larger stones as the base stones, placing them as level as possible. None of the stones should be shorter than the width of the wall. Choose stones that are flat underneath. You may have to use a stone mason's hammer and chisel to get them that way. Keep the joints as close to normal size as possible ($\frac{3}{8}$ inch to $\frac{1}{2}$ inch). The stones must be mortared for the wall to hold together.

Step two: choosing stones for the first

course. Lay out enough stone for a first course, regardless of whether the wall will be coursed or laid at random. A wall laid truly at random—that is, without regard to any of the stone characteristics—will not be satisfactory. Arrange the stone so that the size variations are distributed evenly along the first course. Select pieces suitable for bond stones: bond stones are stones the same width as the wall. When laid over smaller stones, bond stones serve to stabilize the wall by tying the stones together; mortar is a further help, of course. There should be a bond stone for every 6 to 10 square feet of wall, at a minimum.

Step three: mixing mortar. Mix mortar for about an hour of work (see the section on stone mortar). Do not mix more mortar because it begins to set after an hour.

Step four: laying the first course. When the concrete footing has set or the mortar in the stone footing has set, lay out the first course dry. In building a rubble wall, lay the larger stones nearer the base and work your way up in smaller sizes. This procedure usually gives a more stable, pleasing appearance to the wall, but there should not be a great variance in stone size from bottom to top. Each stone should be laid on its broadest face for stability and a more natural appearance. Avoid large spaces between stones in rubble walls. Where spaces are unavoidable, plug them with smaller stones carefully embedded in the mortar. If you do not, the mortar will have to be excessively thick to keep it from running out of the large gaps. The bed joints are mortared as for a brick or block wall, but the head (vertical) joints are heavily filled. A caulking trowel helps work the mortar into the crevices. Try to keep rubble joints between $\frac{1}{2}$ to 1 inch wide.

In ashlar walls the pattern you choose determines where the different size stones are placed. The joints should be about $\frac{1}{4}$ to $\frac{3}{4}$ inch. Build leads at each corner, just as you would for a brick or block wall, and fill in the intermediate area placing bond stones every 6 to 10 square feet. Work your way up with a story pole and line to aid you. Check your work frequently with a mason's level. All joints should be full of mortar, with no cavities in the wall.

Step five: topping rubble walls. Rubble walls do not need copings for functional reasons, nor do they seem to add much visually. This probably is because rubble walls, when laid properly, use smaller and smaller stones toward the top, which is finish enough. However, you can chisel stone so that it lays flat on the top of rubble walls, or you can chisel stones into more modular shapes for the top course. Mortar should be finished and excess removed. Where there is wide variance in joint size in rubble walls, some people color part of the mortar the same color as the stone, leaving what appears to be uniformly sized unstained mortar joints. For typical rubble walls, the joints are often raked out ¼ to ½ inch with a jointing tool, pointed trowel or caulking trowel, to fully accent the stone and play down the mortar joints. Ashlar joints should be consistent.

Solid wall top finishes. A special treatment for the top course of solid masonry walls does seem to make many walls look better, even if it is not necessarily functional. For example, a solid brick wall with running bond coursing has a more finished look with a header or

rowlock header course as the top course. Solid concrete block walls, such as 8 inch walls, can use either clay brick or concrete brick as a header or rowlock header course coping. You could use a 4x8x8 solid concrete block as a header or rowlock header coping. Adobe, ashlar, and slump concrete block are regularly sized, like brick and block and the same coping methods could be used on them as noted above for solid brick and block walls.

BUILDING RETAINING WALLS
Retaining walls require careful attention to structure, reinforcement, drainage, soil, and weather conditions. They often require a building permit and are expensive and difficult to build. If built incor-

rectly the wall will fail—collapse—causing considerable trouble and further expense. It is very important to have an engineer, or an architect or your building official check your plan against local codes and conditions. As with almost any home project, you can do the work yourself if you have a good plan and find the project economical. There are several different types of retaining walls. Before going far with your planning, determine which wall you need.

Gravity Retaining Wall
A gravity retaining wall is built of massive masonry and depends its weight and the positioning of the wall for stability. The wall is built with a slant toward the high grade side. The gravity retaining

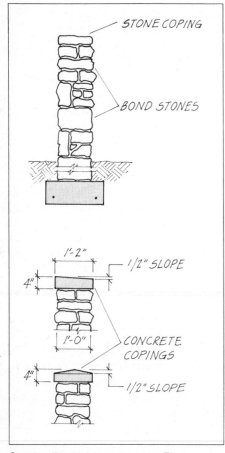

Stone walls require bond stones. These stones extend all the way through the wall, front to back, and are spaced every 6 to 10 square feet of wall surface.

The principles of construction for timber retaining walls resemble those of concrete and masonry, requiring foundations and footings for resistance to pressure from the soil.

wall shown in the illustration is of concrete block and is laid out and constructed like a concrete masonry wall, previously discussed. The difference is that the bottom, which you can see is larger, is slanted into the earth. This is solid masonry. The footing is concrete. The earth above presses down on the solid stepped block, helping to hold it in place. The great width of the concrete footing shown in the illustration (4 feet) resists the pressure from the earth behind the wall.

The gravity wall in the illustration requires no steel reinforcement, anywhere. But because so much material is required, gravity walls are expensive. The higher the wall, the more prohibitive the cost becomes. However, in areas where native stone is cheap and readily available, a gravity wall can be an economical solution. Stones must have a good fit for strength.

The depth of the footings in gravity retaining walls depends on the angle of the earth it retains, on the weather and soil conditions, the height of the wall itself, and the amount of reinforcement in the wall—if any. Check requirements with your building department.

Cantilever Retaining Wall

A cantilever retaining wall has a shape similar to an inverted T. The footing portion holds the stem in place and the whole structure is dependent on steel reinforcement. A reinforced concrete block cantilever-type retaining wall requires the following specifications:

(1) reinforcing bars should have standard deformations and a yield strength of 40,000 psi;
(2) alternate vertical reinforcing bars may be terminated at the mid-height of the wall. Every third bar may be terminated at the upper third point of the wall height;
(3) the wall should have horizontal joint reinforcement at every course or else a horizontal bond beam (a special concrete block) with two No. 4 bars every 16 inches;
(4) assume weight of solid backfill (granular soil with conspicuous clay content) is 100 psf and equivalent fluid pressure is 45 psf, that there is no surcharge and maximum solid bearing pressure is

1,500 psf. Surcharge refers to any additional loading the wall may experience due to a vehicle or other weight being near enough to the wall at the top to influence the thrust on the wall. All retaining walls discussed in this book assume no surcharge.

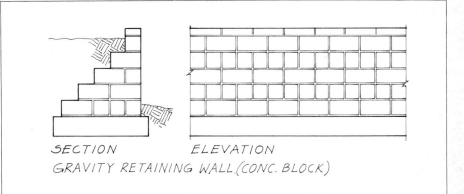

SECTION   ELEVATION
GRAVITY RETAINING WALL. (CONC. BLOCK)

Gravity retaining walls have widths ranging from ½ to ¾ of their height. Use concrete having a minimum 28-day compressive strength of 3,000 pounds/sq. ft.

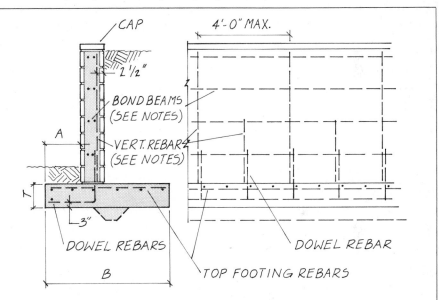

12" CONC. BLOCK CANTILEVER RETAINING WALL					
H	A	B	T	DOWEL AND VERT. REINF.	TOP FOOTING REINF.
3'-4"	12"	2'-8"	9"	NO.3 - 32"O.C.	NO.3 - 27"O.C.
4'-0"	12"	3'-0"	9"	NO.3 - 32"O.C.	NO.3 - 27"O.C.
4'-8"	12"	3'-3"	10"	NO.4 - 32"O.C.	NO.3 - 27"O.C.
5'-4"	14"	3'-8"	10"	NO.4 - 24"O.C.	NO.3 - 25"O.C.
6'-0"	15"	4'-2"	12"	NO.4 - 16"O.C.	NO.4 - 30"O.C.
6'-8"	16"	4'-6"	12"	NO.6 - 24"O.C.	NO.4 - 22"O.C.
7'-4"	18"	4'-10"	12"	NO.7 - 32"O.C.	NO.5 - 26"O.C.
8'-0"	20"	5'-4"	12"	NO.7 - 24"O.C.	NO.5 - 21"O.C.
8'-8"	22"	5'-10"	14"	NO.7 - 16"O.C.	NO.6 - 26"O.C.
9'-4"	24"	6'-4"	14"	NO.8 - 8"O.C.	NO.6 - 21"O.C.

A concrete-block cantilevered retaining wall requires considerable steel reinforcing in the footing, in the wall, and a series of bent dowel bars the provide strength to both.

If your wall will be subject to such a surcharge or is likely to be subject to extreme pressure during seasonal climatic conditions, this will have to be figured into the plan.

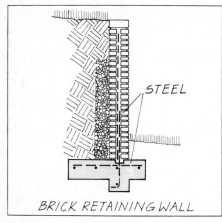

BRICK RETAINING WALL

A brick retaining wall and cavity must be reinforced with steel and filled with grout.

It should also be noted that drainage behind retaining walls is very important. Drainage can be accomplished by laying a bed of gravel behind the wall, for its full height, if possible. At the bottom of the wall, there may be a horizontal row of drain pipe to carry off the water; or there may be drain holes, called weepholes, through the wall at periodic intervals.

A Brick Retaining Wall

A brick cantilever retaining wall is built similarly to a brick cavity wall for the garden. Two parallel brick walls are laid the thickness of the length of one brick; a brick topping or trim can then be used. But the retaining wall contains heavier reinforcement than found in most garden walls (if they have any at all) and the retaining wall must be grouted full and tied to the T-shaped concrete footing.

Counterfort and Buttressed Retaining Walls

These retaining walls are similar to the timber retaining wall discussed next in that the spanning panels depend on vertical supports, posts, spaced periodically for their stability.

In a counterfort wall, the vertical supports are on the fill side of the panels, covered by the fill and not visible. In this arrangement the fill is pushing the panels and thus the vertical supports are in tension. The buttressed retaining wall is like the counterfort wall except the vertical supports for the panels are opposite the fill side and visible. This arrangement puts the vertical supports in compression. For residential use, this support arrangement can be unsightly and the space requirement may be prohibitive or impractical on small lots.

The retaining walls just discussed—gravity type, cantilever, brick, counterfort and buttressed—assume a height of 4 feet or greater and they all require professional guidance (especially detailed plans) from an architect or civil engineer. Otherwise, the building department may require that you remove it. It could fall, if not adequately designed and installed, possibly injuring someone. The depth of retaining wall footings below ground, the amount of reinforcing necessary—the whole structural design—include many variables that are frequently beyond the ability of even the advanced handyman. Seek professional help. However, for walls 3 feet 0 inches or less, where the grade is level at the wall top, retaining walls are much simpler and are within the capability of most homeowners.

A Timber Retaining Wall

For mild slopes that go to a level grade at the wall top, a timber retaining wall can be built easier than nearly any other retaining wall, even by one man. Labor is always a considerable expense—in cost if you contract labor and in time if you do it yourself. The timber wall described addresses both these items. And there are no forms to build as in a concrete wall. For mild slopes, no reinforcement is needed but for more difficult conditions the wall could be reinforced like a counterfort retaining wall. Shown is the wall with 6x8 posts at 8 feet on center. The posts measure 8 feet long and have been embedded 4 feet in the ground and surround-

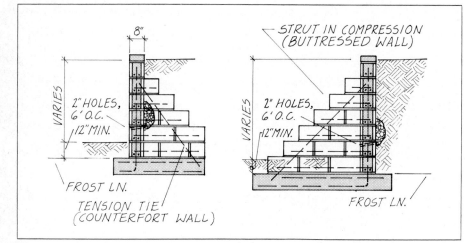

In the counterfort wall tension provides resistance to ground pressure. A buttressed wall uses compression strength against ground force. Drainage weep holes are needed in both.

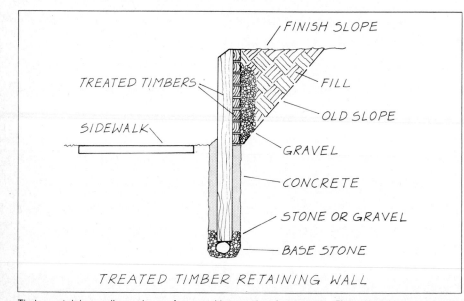

TREATED TIMBER RETAINING WALL

Timber retaining walls are heavy fences with very deeply set posts. Posts are given good base drainage and set in concrete so they will neither rot nor shift.

ed with concrete. The wall is really just a massive fence that retains soil. So see the section on fence layout because the layout procedure for the posts is the same—each post rests on a base stone, then gravel is shoveled in to several inches above the bottom of the post, then concrete poured up to grade and sloped up against the post.

The horizontal members are 4x6 timbers spaced approximately ⅜ inch apart. The spacing is maintained by simply leveling the first or bottom course of timbers, then laying a shim of ⅜ inch lath on each end of the member before laying the next one on top. Check each member for level using a spirit level and by frequent visual checks from a distance. The panel timbers are nailed to the posts from the fill side. In general, the horizontal members simply follow the line of a sidewalk or a lot line. Usable lawn area can be increased about 25% by a project like this while the actual work of maintaining the property will be significantly decreased by not having to mow the slope. The timbers should be ''Wolmanized''—a trade name for the pressure-treating process of the Koppers Company. Each timber absorbs .40 pounds per cubic foot of chromated copper arsenate.

The chemical will not leach out into the soil and the wood can be painted or stained, if desired.

Adding Weep Holes

It is necessary to reduce soil pressure against retaining walls by providing drainage (weep) holes, or by installing drain tile the length of the wall at the bottom of the backfill. Drain pipes through the wall are typically spaced 10 feet or less apart and approximately 8 feet above finish grade on the lowest side.

Filling with gravel. Add gravel the length of the wall; it should be deep enough to reach above the weep or drainage holes. You will have to dig away enough soil to give yourself space to work comfortably when you pour the footing for your retaining wall and then to build the wall itself. Before you add the fill to bring the grade up to the top of the wall, shovel in gravel the length of the wall until it is approximately a foot above the weep holes (the gravel should be approximately 4-6 inches thick). Where there is no serious frost heave, and drainage is the only problem, shovel gravel around all the weep or drainage holes. Add the gravel before you start filling soil against the wall when you have completed it.

Shovel the gravel in a few inches below the level of each weep hole and up above it a foot or so and let the gravel slide down around each side of the weep hole. Check to see that the weep hole is surrounded by gravel—at least 6 inches on each side and at the top and running several inches below the weep hole. Then shovel the soil in to the top of the wall.

Areas with frost heave. Where frost heave is a problem, install gravel 4 to 6 inches thick for the full height of the wall. Do this by using a 4x8 sheet of plywood as a temporary form for the gravel. Have someone hold the plywood about 6 inches from the inside face of the wall and shovel in gravel a foot or two deep. Then bring the soil up to the same level on the other side of the plywood. Lift the plywood almost to the top of the gravel and bring the gravel and soil up until the soil holds the gravel up against the wall. Finish the length of the wall in the same way. You will need only the one sheet of plywood and one helper.

For long walls of masonry, expansion joints should be designed and located by a professional to avoid cracking. The timber retaining wall drains particularly well due to the space between the timbers in the panels. Combined with liberal use of

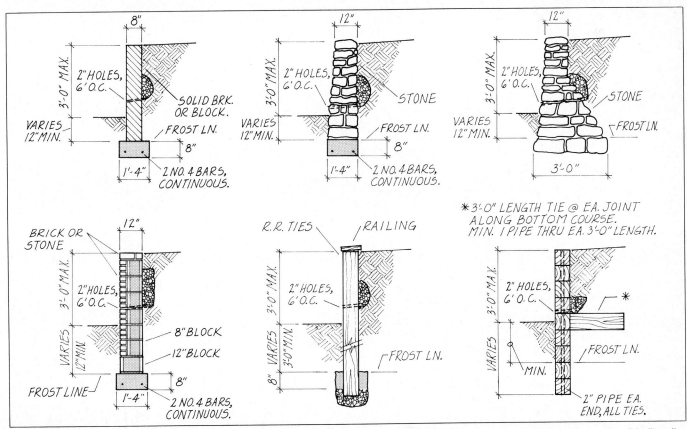

Retaining walls require good drainage to relieve water-pressure build-up. Water and frost heave pressure can crack even the most well-built walls.

gravel, this wall should never present a drainage problem.

Slanting the wall. All high retaining walls are likely to lean slightly when the fill is placed, Also, whether they really lean or not, high retaining walls may give the illusion of leaning, perhaps because of the difference in grade. To counteract this unsettling appearance, it is good practice to slant the wall slightly toward the fill. A slope inward of ½ inch per foot is typically used. For a wall 4 feet above grade, then, the difference in plumb at the top would be 2 inches. You can measure this distance by setting up a plumb bob with line and measuring the distance from the plumb line at the face of the wall to the point at which the wall slanted. For a timber wall, for example, set the posts in place so they are plumb. Then move the top in the appropriate distance from plumb. One way to do this would be to set a tripod of three 2x4s on which to set the plumb bob and line so that the line is flush with the face of the post. Then, simply push the post back the right distance and secure it in place like you would a fence post (Chapter 10) until you can pour the concrete around it. When all the posts are

like this, secure the panels.

Corbeling brick. If you want to slant a brick retaining wall inward (such as a wall 4 feet above grade), you can move each brick course in slightly as you go up. A 4-foot wall should slant in about 2 feet at the top. There are 18 courses of brick in 4 feet, so if you corbelled each course in ⅛ inch (starting with the first course above the base course), the wall would slant in 2⅛ inches at the top. It is suggested you not corbel any given course in more than ⅛ inch and do not slant the bricks like this except for the top 4 feet of the retaining wall. If the wall were 4 feet 8 inches, go up 8 inches with regular coursing, then start corbeling the courses.

Angling concrete block. Concrete block is not as easy to slant inward because the block coursing is taller and you would have to push the block courses back too far—you should not expose the block cells—to get the slant you need at the top. One solution for a 4 foot wall is to use larger blocks than you really need at the bottom and smaller ones as you go up. For example, use 12-inch wide blocks for the first two courses, then two courses

of 10-inch blocks, and the last two courses of 8-inch block. The blocks would be solid core and the fill side of the wall would be flush, so that the viewed side would "step" up, giving the desired slant effect.

Stone walls. It is harder to slant walls of brick and block than those of stone. The stones are solid, with no cells to consider and it is easy to make the bases a little larger and slope the wall inward as the courses are laid.

Walls Less than 3 Feet High
Retaining walls of 3 feet or less retain little soil and are not subjected to the forces of the higher walls. In areas of extreme cold, however, it is suggested you gravel all the way up the inside face of these walls and set all posts and/or footings on a minimum of 4 inches of gravel—check with your building department for code requirements. A variety of materials and configurations may be used. Depending on the design of your total landscape, you can choose the material that fits best: concrete block, concrete brick, clay brick, stone, brick veneer on concrete block, or railroad ties.

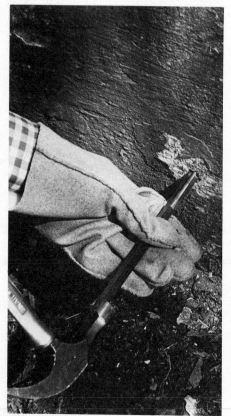

To add weep holes to retaining walls, drill the holes every two to three feet. Line the holes with short pieces of hose to help prevent water damage.

Excess water is released through the weep holes to prevent damage from moisture. The holes must be kept free of debris and dirt to permit good drainage.

A garden hose can serve as a hydraulic ram to penetrate dirt lodged in weep holes. Wiggle the hose as it is forced into the hole, before turning water on full.

A low rubble wall is used to define space in this setting. The higher rubble wall also defines space and creates a private lawn area.

The uneven surface of the rubble wall creates patterns of light and shadow. The stones are similar in size for a unified appearance.

10 WOOD FENCES

The first step in planning a fence is to check with the city building department about setback lines, height restrictions and any construction requirements that may exist. Your fence must conform to all restrictions, or you will find yourself having to take down the fence you just put up. Building departments sometimes publish data sheets answering usual questions about landscaping and other home improvements. They will mail a copy to you on request. If you use a landscape architect, he will be familiar with building department requirements and how to meet them.

Fences may serve several purposes. Solid fences provide security and privacy; light rail or picket fences merely deliniate a property line.

PLANNING THE FENCE

When you know the city restrictions, you can consider your design objectives: is the fence for privacy, security, wind control, decoration, or view or traffic control? Decide which objective (or combination) is most important to you. Keep the answers to these questions in mind as you begin your design process.

A fence is dramatically cheaper and easier to install than a masonry wall, and it offers just as much privacy, wind protection, and view control. It can be as decorative as a masonry wall but will not provide noise protection that a masonry wall will. However, most people will not find the degree of additional noise protection offered by a masonry wall worth the extra cost.

Most fence panels are in 6- or 8-foot lengths, although chain link fences may have 10-foot panels. The area you want to fence will probably not measure out to an even number of panels. Also, gates and other openings affect the spacing of posts. You have a choice in planning; either

Rough-sawn boards are effectively combined with heavy t-shaped mending plates to create a rustic fence. Filler boards are placed alternately on opposite sides of the stringers.

This tall fence provides considerable privacy and shade, but the staggered board pattern of the boards allows free air circulation.

adjust all the panel sizes to some dimension that equalizes all the panel lengths, or have one section run that is smaller than all the others. The odd-sized panel is usually located at the end of a fence run—at either end. When you locate the gates, you probably will want to treat them as "corners" and start your panel runs from each side, with the last panels smaller than the rest.

Choosing Materials

There will be several materials and designs that meet the objectives you have. Although wood is the most popular infill material, other alternatives (plastic panels for example) are available.

Wood for fences. Western red cedar or California redwood makes good fencing material and the natural beauty of the materials is unexcelled. Some experts recommend that you use only the heartwood for the posts. Heartwood is from the center of the tree and contains natural extractives that inhibit decay and discourage insects. Mountain cypress is another good fence wood. However, these woods are very expensive.

Fortunately, modern wood treating methods have made practical the use of cheaper woods that will last for years. There are quality differences in wood treatment, as there are quality differences in materials. The most effective treatment method is the one that gets the most of the right kind of preservative in the wood. For example, wood treated with creosote is good for many outdoor uses, but do not place it close to the house. Soaking wood in preservative—or brushing it on—is helpful, but not nearly as effective as pressure-treating the wood.

Concrete for fences. Although wood is the most commonly used material for fences, with other materials for infill panels another choice, it is possible to combine wood panels and concrete posts. Unless you have a project large enough to realize significant savings by mixing your own concrete, the convenience of dry-mix concrete will be worth the extra cost. Dry-mix comes in 45, 80, and 90 pound bags. If you mix your own concrete, use 1 part cement, 3 parts sand, and 5 parts gravel.

Estimating Material Quantities

When you have your fence designed, estimate the quantities of materials need-ed. Measure along the line to be fenced. Note the linear footage of the fence. Compute the number of posts, the amount of concrete you need for posts or post holes, and note any hardware and miscellaneous equipment you need, as indicated in the later detailed discussion of fence construction. After you know the material quantities you need, the suppliers can help you with cost estimates. This will aid your final choice of materials.

In figuring the concrete cost, for simplicity, figure the equivalent of one 80-pound bag of premix concrete per post. You can adjust up or down from that, depending on how you finally decide to prepare the concrete and how much you need. Other cost considerations are lumber type, quality and type of hardware and number, size, and quality of nails—galvanized, plain, or aluminum.

Finding Professional Help

In addition to fence contractors, lumberyards, building supply houses, building contractors, garden centers, nurseries, and others often build fences. Call several of them and give them your design requirements, number of gates, linear footage, and fence material and ask them for an estimate. They should not have to visit the site if you give them all the information they would normally come out for anyway, and you will avoid a sales talk. When they give you a price, ask them how much concrete they use in the post holes, and get a reading on the quantity and quality of materials within their estimate. Then you will know what you are paying for, and you can shop other contractors accordingly. When you have a price from a contractor for work and for materials that meet your quality requirements, subtract the cost of the materials from that price; the difference is what you will save by doing it yourself. It should be considerable.

Even if you do not have the time or skill to do the job yourself, the time spent in learning about your project will help you get the best contractor for the best price.

If you decide to build your own fence, it is likely to be wood. Wood fences are the most popular, the most versatile, and usually the easiest to build.

Although most commonly laid out in straight lines, fences can be built in short, modular sections and set in a series of angles to conform to any enclosure or topigraphical needs.

Tools for Digging Post Holes

The clamshell type post hole digger is probably the best all-around digger for most people. It is surprisingly fast, unless the soil is very hard or rocky. In that case, you may have to use a steel digging bar or pick, then shovel the soil out. In extreme cases, use a jackhammer with a spade tip. Another tool to consider is the manual auger. Two people can operate this tool fairly quickly.

Because of the typically short work times available for most home projects, the rented power digger is not always the most economical digging method. To be used most economically, all the holes should be dug at once so you can get the digger back as quickly as possible. However, when you dig all the holes at once, they may end up filled with water until you can get around to finishing the job. Take the weather into account in planning the use of equipment and the sequence of the project.

Regardless of which tools you use, keep your back straight when you dig postholes. Otherwise, your back muscles may be painfully and even seriously strained.

BUILDING THE BASIC FENCE

Typical fence posts are 4x4 or 4 inches in diameter. This size is good for most allowable fence heights with typical paneling. Stringers (the horizontal members to which fencing is attached) are at least 2x4s and perhaps 2x6s (or even larger) depending on the length of the stringers (distance between the posts), and the weight of the panel.

Setting Fence Posts

Posts may be set in earth, gravel and earth, concrete, or some combination of these materials. Depth is determined by the height of the fence and the climatic pressure that will be exerted on the fence. The most substantial method is to fill the hole with concrete. Masonry rubble may be used to extend the concrete. It is possible to set the posts in earth. The use of concrete to help stabilize posts is strongly recommended. All wood is very expensive; the concrete needed to ensure a straight, stable fence is well worth the relatively low cost.

Post hole depth. Generally speaking, the deeper the post, the better, but the depths will vary according to fence height. Also, standard lumber length and height restrictions influence the hole depths. Many cities, for example, have 6-foot-height limits, unless you gain an exception for some reason. A 6-foot fence will use 8-foot posts sunk 2 feet; a 4-foot fence will use 6-foot posts sunk 2 feet, and so forth. Even fences less than 4 feet high should have posts at least 18 inches deep. When you have to buy longer members than you actually need, you might as well put the extra length in the ground instead of cutting it away.

Creating post foundation. Keep post holes straight. They should be about 12 inches in diameter for a 4-inch post. Whatever the post setting method you use, always line the bottom of the hole with a base stone and/or gravel before you put the post in. This aids drainage and helps prevent decay. Gravel prevents concrete from getting under the post where it will seal off the bottom and hold in moisture, decaying the post. Gravel also helps hold the post steady in a vertical position while you tamp more gravel or earth around it, or while you pour concrete.

Fences may enclose all or part of a yard. They may be high or quite low, solid or only partially in-filled. Access gates may be placed anywhere to suit your requirements.

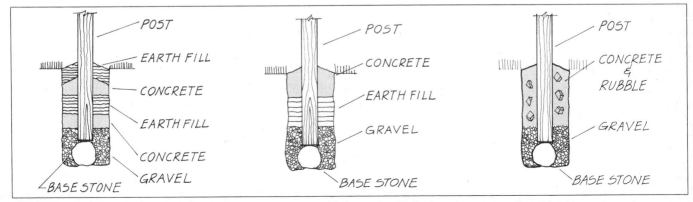

Posts must be secure in the ground and protected from ground water. Secure installation in most areas requires at least some concrete.

Setting corner posts and adding concrete. To align the posts, locate two corners along the run of fence you wish to work first. Set the corner posts in place. When placing earth or gravel around a post, put in a little at a time, then tamp it around the post so the water drains away from the post. If you are using a concrete

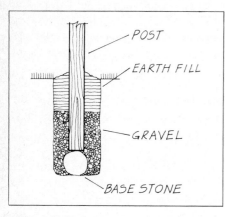

If your soil is firm and not given to extreme frost heave, you may position a fence post securely in gravel and earth fill.

collar, finish it so the concrete slopes down from the post so the water drains away. When using concrete, brace the posts to keep them steady while the concrete is setting. Several four-foot lengths of 2x4s, nailed to the post and staked at the ground, should hold the posts firmly. Before you pour the concrete, check the posts for plumb by using a spirit level on two adjacent sides. Pour the concrete to fill the hole. You may also fill the hole entirely with compactly tamped gravel. Let concrete cure several days before you add the stringers and panels to the posts. If you use masonry rubble to extend concrete, tamp the concrete with a 1x3 to eliminate air pockets around the rubble.

Aligning fence posts. Locate the center of each corner post at the top and drive in a nail. Leave enough nail exposed to attach a string to. Stretch a line tightly between the posts; do not work in runs so long that you cannot keep a string level by

tightening it. Locate the intermediate posts, gate posts, and any other interruption along the string. Mark the locations with tape. Transfer these points to the ground with a plumb bob and drive a stake to mark them. You may dig all the holes at once, or if your time is fragmented, you can do them as you as you find the time.

Fencing a slope. If you are fencing along a slope, you can either step the fence along the slope or follow the grade of the slope. In general, fences on short, steep slopes seem to look better when they are stepped; if the fence follows the slope, it appears to bulge or lean. Longer or gentler slopes can be followed. If you are in doubt, do a sketch of the slope to scale and draw the fence both stepped along the slope and with the fence following the slope.

Finding the slope. Put a stake in the ground at the top of the slope. Put another stake in level ground at the bottom of the slope (this stake has to be taller than the slope). Stretch a line between the stakes and level it with a line level. Measure the horizontal distance between stakes; this is the length of the run. Measure the distance from the string at the top of the long stake to the ground. That is the rise of your slope. Divide the rise by the run to find the slope. (See Chapter 3.)

Drawing the sketch. The sketch itself can be done at any convenient scale—⅛ inch=1 foot and ¼ inch=1 foot are typical. Sketch the profile of the slope accurately. Then lay tracing paper over the profile and draw different fence designs, stepping the fence down the slope or letting the fence follow the slope.

Setting intermediate posts. Stretch two lines on the outside face of the posts, one at the top and one at the bottom, close to the ground. Set the string out from the

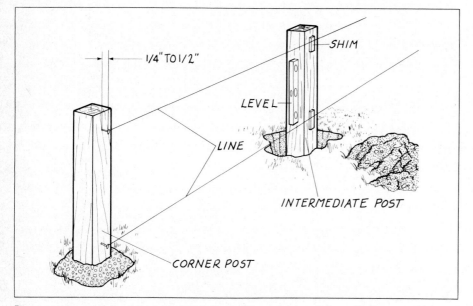

Posts must be carefully aligned, level and plumb. Shim on intermediate post is the same thickness as the distance between the face of the corner post and the string.

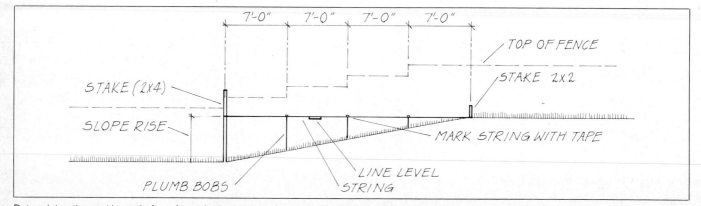

Determining the run/rise ratio for a fence is the same as for steps. The proportional relationship is determined by the section size.

posts about ¼ to ½ inch (the depth of some shim material you have on hand—¼ inch lath or ½ inch material). Install the intermediate posts, using the strings to keep the posts in the same plane and using a level to keep them plumb. Use a shim as described above as a handy check to keep the posts the proper distance from the string, and thus in the same plane.

Setting Stringers

Set the top stringer flush with the top of the posts and nail it where you want it—inside, outside, or within the frame. If within the frame, it is better to use a metal hanger for the stringer than to toenail it. Secure the middle and bottom stringers in the same way. For fences over level ground, and where the fence steps down a slope, use a spirit level to keep the stringers level. Where the fence follows the slope, secure the top stringer flush with the posts and locate the middle and bottom stringers by either measuring down from the top stringer when it is in place, or by running a string from post to post to help you locate the exact position of the stringers (secure the alignment string to the posts with nails).

It is fairly common to see 2x4 stringers laid with the wide side down. However, this should be avoided. Most designs can be achieved by laying the stringer with the 4-inch side vertical, which provides twice the strength as when laid on its side. In most cases it is convenient to let standard lumber lengths decide the length of fence panels; 8 feet is the most typical. Where 8-foot stringers are used, it is advisable to use three 2x4 stringers. This method will help keep the fence panels from warping or sagging in a few months. An alternate but less desirable method is to use two 2x6s. Board fence material should not stick up more than a few inches above the top stringer or below the bottom one; if it does, the unsupported

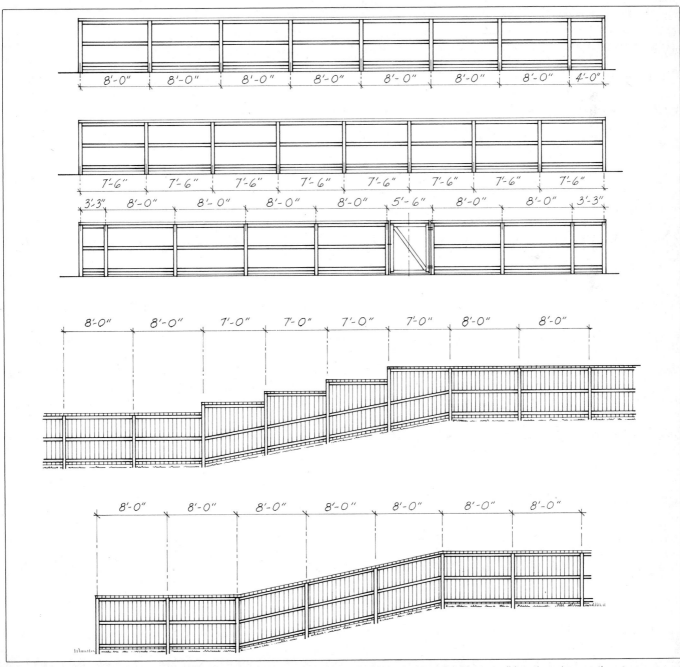

Fence sections should be no longer than 8 feet to ensure basic strength, divisions are determined by overall length and proportion.

boards will warp enough to cause a ragged-looking edge.

Nailing the Boards

The installation of the boards on the framework is the easiest part, so do not nail on the boards until the framework is as you want it. When you do nail the boards on, set the first board in place—at any end you wish to start from—and be sure it is vertical. Use a plumb bob and line to check. Butt the next board up against the first one, and so forth. After you nail up several boards, check with the plumb bob again to be sure you are keeping the boards plumb; the boards will not necessarily be perfectly straight, so you will have to adjust as you go along. This should be possible by shifting the adjusted board about an eighth of an inch, which will not be noticeable.

Nails and hardware. Use rustproof nails, screws, bolts, and gate hardware to avoid rust stains on the lumber and to ensure a longer-lasting fence.

Special Framing Conditions

There are times when a fence must be run above an object or dropped below its normal bottom to fill a void. And sometimes it must butt an object, such as a tree, and continue again on the other side. In these cases additional framing should be provided to prevent warping. Also, additional framing may be required on very steep slopes where you step the fence down so far that the distance between the bottom stringer and the ground is greater.

FENCE VARIATIONS AND STYLES
The Board Fence

The board fence is probably the most popular fence in use today. Since most urban landscapes and many suburban ones are a visual tangle, the simplicity of the simple board fence is often desirable.

Boards come in a range of widths, 4 inches, 6 inches, 8 inches, 10 inches, and 12 inches being typical. Six-foot lengths are common but you can buy them longer or shorter, however remember that many building codes set 6 feet as the maximum height for residential fences. The boards are usually 1 inch thick, but some companies now sell thinner versions. One-inch thickness is suggested with a stringer at the top and bottom of the board panels, and one stringer in the middle.

Decoration, where it is desirable, can be accomplished by simple top design and by manipulation of the framework as part of the fence design. The framework can be on the street side or the house side of the fence, or the board panels may be set within so that the frame is the same from either side.

Creating a shadow effect. For shadow effects, you may install the panels board on batten or batten on board. A batten is a small vertical member, such as a 1x3, to which you nail the boards. If you nail the boards over the batten (usually leaving a space of about 1 inch between the boards), it is called ''board on batten''. If you nail the batten over the vertical joints between the boards, it is called ''batten on board''.

Grapestake Design

Grapestakes were originally used for just what the name implies. They were split from the heart of redwood lumber for their decay and insect-resistant qualities. The stakes typically have a 2 inch diameter. The material weathers beautifully and lasts many years in its natural state. Nowadays, its cost is prohibitive, if you can find it at all. One obvious way to reduce the cost, is to cut the stake to 1x2 dimensions. This leaves one flat side, so you can install the stakes over a frame just as you would a board fence.

The slat fence—rough sawn in 1x2 pickets or slats—is a typical, less-expensive substitute for the grapestake fence. The smoother surface gives a more formal, finished appearance. Grapestakes or slats may be installed vertically or horizontally, inside or outside the framework.

Picket Fence

The traditional picket fence is about 3 or 4 feet high, with 3-inch pickets spaced 3 inches apart. There are a myriad of top designs, but it is unlikely you will find more than a couple of designs at the lumberyard. Perhaps this is because modern houses have much less custom mill-

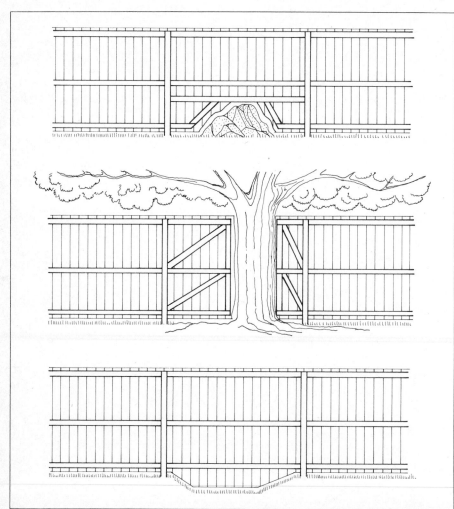

Fence sections may be adjusted to allow for natural obstructions that you cannot or do not wish to remove. Do not extend boards too far below bottom stringer or they will warp.

work than they did in the past, when fences were designed to harmonize with the houses. You may have to design your own picket and have the lumberyard cut it for you.

Picket fences define property lines and offer security and privacy—if you combine them with a planting. Most come in lengths of 3 and 4 feet; six-foot pickets are possible.

Stockade

The stockade fence is similar to the grapestake fence in appearance and texture. The units are often flat on one side and rounded on the other, saving material and making installation easier. The tops are pointed in a cone shape. Stockade fences are meant to give a rustic appearance; used in relatively short runs, they are handsome. There are fewer ways to alter the appearance of a stockade fence than other sytles. If overused, the stockade fence can be dull and monotonous. It works quite well for small areas where privacy is desired, and in combination with brick or stone walls.

Plywood Panels

Plywood panels offer the maximum in fence privacy. When the structure is built to accommodate standard plywood panels, plywood fences probably go up faster than any other fence. The framing is the same as previously discussed. Design questions include: will the paneling go over the framework? On which side will the panels fall? Should the panels be mounted between the posts?

Plywood panels come in 4x8 sheets; use only exterior grade plywood. Saw the sheets to the height you need and nail them up as you would any other material. If you use grooved plywood, keep the panels plumb with a plumb bob lined up on the grooves. If the grooves are installed horizontally, use a spirit level to keep the level. Plywood panels can be painted or stained; the panels make good backdrops for plant shelves or shrubbery. Plywood fence paneling is available in smooth or rough sawn finishes. A lap appearance is also available.

There are some drawbacks however. The panels shut out light; they offer the maximum resistance to wind and therefore must have the strongest framing structures; they may require extra bracing to prevent warping.

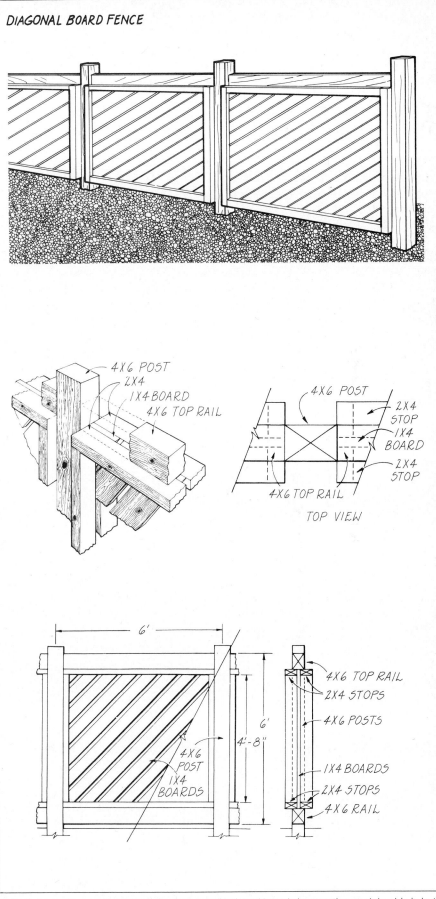

A sturdy board fence with infill panels of diagonally placed boards is attractive, and durable in both appearance and in fact. The diagonal pattern lightens the heavy look of the fence. Top and bottom rails are 4x6 used to support weight of heavy infill panels.

Lath Screens

The lath fence is light, airy, versatile, and beautiful. Lathwork was very popular during the Victorian period for garden structures, screens, and decorative work. It is still a valid, relatively inexpensive fencing method. However, it may be too delicate for use close to heavily trafficked urban streets. Children climbing can damage it, and its many surfaces pick up pollution as it passes into the fenced area. In more protected circumstances, such as backyards or areas where it will not be damaged, it is an excellent fence or screen. The spaces can be varied to determine the amount of privacy, or they may be closed entirely. This arrangement defeats its prime use, which is to offer privacy while allowing air to circulate freely and light to create shadow effects.

Shingle Fences

Shingle fences are valued for their decorative advantages. Otherwise, they have about the same advantages and drawbacks as a plywood fence. For small enclosed areas such as patios or balconies, they offer complete privacy and combine well with a variety of house materials. The major drawback is the amount of backing required in order to nail on the shingles.

Rail Fences

In urban and suburban use, the open rail fence is primarily decorative. It marks boundaries and offers protection for roses and other plantings. The long, low lines are attractive in both small and spacious yards.

WOOD PRESERVATIVE TREATMENTS

Preservatives make possible the use of woods that normally would not be suitable for direct contact with earth. This means that the less-expensive woods such as pine, cottonwood, and aspen can be made to last as long as or even longer than the naturally resistant woods such as redwood and cedar. Using the cheaper woods can sometimes save you as much as two-thirds on wood cost.

Wood preservatives are usually talked about in two catagories: oil-borne and water-borne. Three of the most popular oil-borne preservatives are creosote, pentachlorophenol, and copper naphthenate.

Types of Treatments

Creosote. Most of us remember creosote by its sharp, asphalt-like smell. In residential use, the smell and the stain preclude many uses. But in the country and for purely utilitarian use, creosote-treated members will last many years at low cost.

Pentachlorophenol. Pentachlorophenol has long been used as a preservative. It is composed primarily of carbolic acid and chlorine, diluted by solvents for sale as a concentrated solution. This solution can be diluted for use with oil or gas; the need for caution against fire should be obvious here. It is available as a ready-mix. The solution is more popular than creosote for residential use because it is almost odorless, "cleaner", and has only a slight petroleum smell, most of which disappears when the oils evaporate. Unlike creosote, "penta" can be painted.

Copper naphthenate. Copper naphthenate is usually more expensive than pentachlorpheonol, but it has the advantage of being safer around plants (penta-

This area is defined by the walls of the house, a privacy fence and a bench fence. The choice of material unifies the area.

chlorophenol solution is harmful or deadly to broadleaf plants). It is noncorrosive and odorless. It stains the wood a light green. Where this color does not interfere with the color scheme of nearby materials, the wood appears quite handsome. Copper naphthenate does not leach out into the soil.

Application Techniques

Cold bath method. Soaking wood directly in cold solution is the simplest and least expensive method. You can buy wood preserved in this manner or you can do your own. Use an oil drum or similar container, or make a temporary bath using several layers of polyethylene sheeting draped between cross ties to form a trough. The trough must be large enough to immerse the longest members without having to rotate them (as you would in a drum bath).

You can increase the depth of preservative penetration by piercing the wood with an incising tool (an ax with rows of teeth on the back of the head).

Pine takes about a day to absorb about 4 to 5 pounds of pentachlorophenol per cubic foot of wood. Other woods may require as long as a week to soak up the same amount.

Hot bath technique. The hot bath treatment increases the amount of preservative absorbed. The wood swells in the hot bath and when the preservative is cooled, the air spaces within the wood contract, trapping preservative in the fibers. As evaporation proceeds, the air spaces or tiny "pockets" within the wood are left coated with a film of preservative which protects the wood. The hot bath treatment should not be attempted by amateurs if the chemical contains flammable materials.

Brushing or spraying. The least effective and most laborious method of applying preservative is to brush or spray it on the wood. Even this method is better than no preservative at all. If you are patient and willing to apply several coats, the wood will eventually absorb enough preservative to protect it substantially.

Safety in preservative use. The solvents in some preservatives are flammable. If possible, it is best to avoid these types. If you must use them, take precautions against fire.

Some preservatives are highly irritating, and direct contact with the skin can be harmful. Wear goggles, rubber gloves and a respirator when working with preservatives. Take care that children and animals cannot get to the preservatives while the wood is being treated.

Pressure-treated Wood

Water-borne preservatives are most effective when applied under pressure. Commonly known water-born salt preservatives are Acid Copper Chromate (ACC), Ammoniacal Copper Arsenite (ACA), Chromated Copper Arsenate (CCA), Chromated Zinc Arsenate (CZA), and Fluor Chrome Phenol (FCAP). These preservatives are odorless and clean for residential use. Wood treated with them also can be painted.

Lumber to be pressure-treated is first air or kiln-dried until the moisture level is 25% or less. Then it is moved into a great "pressure cooker" cylinder, about 6 feet in diameter by 50 feet long (which explains how the lumber can be treated economically and why the process is out of reach of the do-it-yourselfer). As much as 1,000 board feet of lumber is treated at once.

The pressure in the cylinder is reduced, allowing the air pockets in the wood to expand. In this way, the process is similar to the hot bath process. The preservatives are introduced and the pressure increased, causing the wood to suck up the preservative as it can in no other process.

Maintenance Considerations

When wood not thoroughly saturated with preservative is cut, the ends should be soaked again or brushed thoroughly with preservatives. The ends are the likeliest places of moisture entry. Any cut or bored hole in the lumber should receive an extra treatment of preservative.

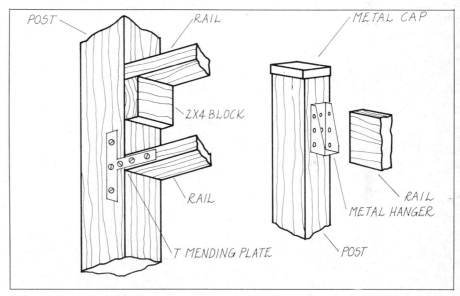

Stringers can be attached to posts in several ways. The most secure is with metal hangers. Stringers may also be attached with nailing blocks or T mending plates.

CONDITION OF SOUTHERN PINE STAKES (2x4 IN. NOMINAL x 18 IN.) FROM HARRISON EXPERIMENTAL FOREST, SAUCIER, MISSISSIPPI. STAKES PLACED IN TEST IN DECEMBER, 1949.

	Average Retention Lb./Cu. Ft.	No. in Test	Condition of stakes		Average Life Years
			Good	Termites and Decay	
CCA Preservative (Wolman Salts)	1.04	10	100%	0	*
	0.79	9	100%	0	*
	0.52	10	100%	0	*
	0.37	10	100%	0	*
Untreated Controls	——	10	0%	100%	2.8

*All stakes still in good condition
Source: A Comparison of Wood preservatives in Stake Tests published by Forest Products Laboratory, Forest Service, U.S. Department of Agriculture. Data courtesy of the Koppers Co., Inc.

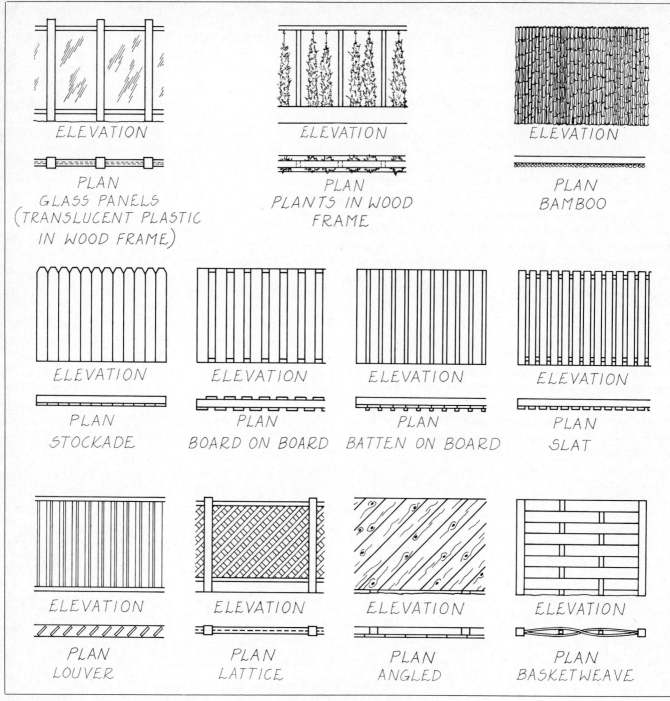

ELEVATION

PLAN
GLASS PANELS
(TRANSLUCENT PLASTIC
IN WOOD FRAME)

ELEVATION

PLAN
PLANTS IN WOOD
FRAME

ELEVATION

PLAN
BAMBOO

ELEVATION

PLAN
STOCKADE

ELEVATION

PLAN
BOARD ON BOARD

ELEVATION

PLAN
BATTEN ON BOARD

ELEVATION

PLAN
SLAT

ELEVATION

PLAN
LOUVER

ELEVATION

PLAN
LATTICE

ELEVATION

PLAN
ANGLED

ELEVATION

PLAN
BASKETWEAVE

Wood is adaptable to a variety of fence patterns and styles suitable for many settings.

Wood fences are relatively easy to install, and they solve a wide range of residential fencing and screening problems. They also are expensive and may do more than you really need. If this is the case, or if your needs are more basic, you should consider a wire fence.

BENEFITS OF CHAIN LINK FENCES

Wire fences may be used where a low budget solution is needed or where security and/or traffic control are the primary concerns. They may be functionally called for as well. For example, you might need to see through the fence—to watch children in a play area. Do not reject them for reasons of appearance—wire fences need not be ugly.

Several advantages of chain link fences are long life, relative ease of installation, and low maintenance. You can buy black, green or redwood-colored vinyl-coated chain link fencing that blends into the landscape—or add wood inserts. The fencing makes a good trellis for any clinging plant or vine, such as honeysuckle or ivy. Any of these plants will soften its appearance greatly or hide it eventually if you wish. Honeysuckle grows very rapidly. Hedge plantings can significantly cover the fence in a few seasons.

Choosing Chain Link Fencing

Wire fence contractors are very competitive, so you may want to get several bids before you do the project yourself. You may decide they can do it cheaper than you can. However, keep in mind that there is a wide range of quality in chain link fences. Be sure you get what you think you are paying for.

Chain link may be galvanized with zinc in a variety of weights per square foot (often .4 ounces of zinc per square foot) or it may be aluminum coated for an even longer-lasting fence. The vinyl coatings (polyvinyl chloride) also vary in thickness. The table below lists some data from one manufacturer.

Installing the Fence

Posts and post holes. Post holes should have a diameter three times the diameter of the post. Dig the hole 3 inches deeper than the post bottom, which should be 3 feet below ground surface and even deeper for particularly loose soils. Pour concrete the entire depth of the hole, working it in by tamping to avoid air pockets. As with all posts set in concrete, attach bracing (2x4s or any suitable material) to the post while the concrete sets. Before and after securing

the bracing to the ground, check the posts for plumb with a plumb bob and line. If the posts are square, check them for plumb, using a spirit level on two adjacent sides of the posts. Trowel the concrete up around the posts, sloping it for drainage.

Chain link and other components. The fences are usually bought in kits with all the necessary parts for assembly. Before you buy, be sure you talk with the supplier and know exactly what you are getting. The posts, for example, should be equipped with all necessary clamps for holding the chain link. The fence sections adjoining the gates should have a metal stringer and a truss rod. Any miscellaneous equipment particular to your job should be ordered.

A safety item to consider is the link top. Link is available with or without the "barbs" at the top. The barbs are good

A simple chain-link fence offers many advantages to a homeowner who needs security fencing. It will install quickly, is reasonably inexpensive and very durable.

SPECIFICATIONS: CHAIN-LINK WIRE

WIRE SIZE	OUTSIDE DIAMETER	MIN. BREAKING STRENGTH	PVC THICKNESS	STEEL THICKNESS
6 gauge	.192 in.	1,290 lbs.	.022 in.	.148 in.
9 gauge	.148 in.	850 lbs.	.015 in.	.118 in.
11 gauge	.120 in.	515 lbs.	.015	.090 in.

for security, but are bad for children, pets or neighbors.

Welded Wire Fences

Welded wire fencing material is so often misused and installed so poorly that it is seldom thought of as a material that, properly framed, can be aesthetically pleasing. There are several sizes of openings from which to choose—½-inch squares, 2x2½-inch, or 2x4 inch squares. These sizes are available with a galvanized coating. Some sizes are available with vinyl coatings—check at Sears or at a building supply house.

Welded wire makes an excellent trellis for plants and vines and aids in training, supporting, and keeping hedges straight.

Structure. The structure for a welded wire fence is its most important and visually dominant aspect. The structure should receive the same attention as if you were building a wood fence. And, like a wood fence, you can install the wire "panels" on either side of the frame or within the frame.

Assembly. It is probably easiest to assemble the fence by securing the wire to the side of the frame. Use staples of the same or heavier weight than the wire to secure it to the frame. For a more finished appearance, cover the wire edges at the frame with wood trim. The wire can be installed within the frame by using staples.

You may be able to install the wire over the frame by yourself, but it is better to have a helper. Stretch the wire as tightly over the frame as you can and be generous with the staples to avoid sags and bulges—and the appearance of being unstable.

OTHER POPULAR FENCES
Adding a Wrought Iron Fence

To many people, iron fences connote stability, security and formality. Consequently, they are still much used. More functional locations include around swimming pools and play areas, where they define areas without obstructing the view.

Iron is classified largely by its carbon content. Wrought iron has .04% carbon—cast iron has 2 to 6%. The fibrous structure of wrought iron allows it to be hammered on anvils and twisted into the nostalgic forms seen on and around buildings in Boston, Philadelphia, New Orleans, Washington, D.C., and a few other American cities. Most real wrought iron work that was done in the past has been lost. Obviously, there are not many blacksmiths to continue the tradition. For years, what most of us have called "wrought iron" fences actually are cast-iron designs, turned out like auto parts. But there are still a few craftsmen around who will design and construct, or construct your design.

Most iron fences are made from hollow metal tubing. The railings are typically 1 inch and the pickets ½ inch thick. Posts are usually sized by the manufacturer for the particular panels you buy. Wooden posts can be substituted for the metal ones if they suit your design better—consult the panel supplier for the post sizes needed to hold the panels. Wooden posts are always best set in concrete resting on a bed of gravel, as described in the wood fence section. Prefabricated and built-to-order fences also are available.

Installation. Installation of a cast-iron fence is very simple, assuming the panels are already fabricated for you. I suggest you purchase them in this form, unless you are prepared to weld the pickets to the top and bottom stringers. The panels are designed to support themselves, so the most important process is setting the posts, which are located and installed as if you were building a wood fence. The manufacturer, however, may have specific requirements. If so, you should follow them.

When the posts are set, drill holes through the end pickets (or the holes may already be provided), and secure the panels to the inside faces of the posts.

The panels should have been painted when you receive them. If not, you will have to paint them. Special metal paints are available at all building supply houses. If you do not keep the fence painted, it will rust—and welded pickets are obviously more difficult to replace than wood pickets. However, if properly painted, this type of fence will last for decades.

Canvas Fencing

Canvas serves as a good wind deflector and privacy screen. Bright colors make it a good choice for beach or vacation homes. You can also use the natural canvas or earth colors. Metal grommets all around allow you to "sew" the canvas inside wooden or metal (such as that used for chain link fences) frames.

Frame installation. The frame is like the frame for a wood fence; all the installation techniques discussed in the wood fence section (above) apply. The canvas is the "panel" that attaches to wood or metal posts, either at the sides or in the middle.

For the "sewing" installation method, a polyethylene or nylon rope is threaded through the grommets in the canvas and the canvas is stretched within the frame.

An alternate method of panel installation uses eye hooks (similar to screen door hooks). Hold the panel up to the frame, find and mark the location of the grommets on the frame. Then install the eye hooks and stretch the canvas over the hooks. As insurance against the canvas coming off, you can squeeze the hooks together with a large pair of pliers.

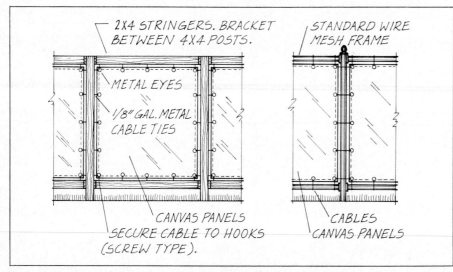

2X4 STRINGERS. BRACKET BETWEEN 4X4 POSTS.

STANDARD WIRE MESH FRAME

METAL EYES

1/8" GAL. METAL CABLE TIES

CANVAS PANELS SECURE CABLE TO HOOKS (SCREW TYPE).

CABLES CANVAS PANELS

If you need a privacy fence, but you do not want to build heavy infill panels, attach canvas to your posts and stringers. Canvas is durable and sections are easy to replace.

How to sew canvas. If heavier than 10-ounce duck, or if vinyl-coated, the canvas should be hemmed on the special equipment found at an awning shop. If hand-sewing 10-ounce canvas, use a No. 13 Sailmaker's Needle and Dacron thread. You can have the grommets installed by the awning shop, or you can put them in yourself. A lace-on panel will require grommets about every 8 inches, as well as one in each corner.

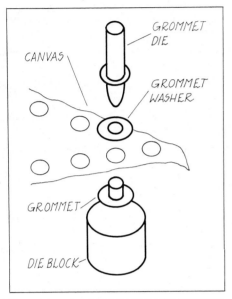

Canvas panels can be made by the homeowner with a sewing machine and grommet setting equipment. Punch holes and set grommets.

Fiberglass

Besides the typical translucent panels, other fiberglass treatments include flat, raised, recessed, and sculptured designs. Textures are available in smooth, matte, and sand. And it comes in a wide range of colors.

It is easy to associate fiberglass panels with junk yards, frozen milk stands, and drive-in movies. It has been grossly misused because it is a strong durable, relatively inexpensive material and people use it without proper framing. So, you see it hanging loosely on old sheds and neglected yards. Used with a good framework, fiberglass panels become good fences or wind screens that let in light and offer privacy.

Setting up the frame. Install the frame as you would a wood fence. You should decide whether you want the panels to overlap the side or fall within the frame. The panels seem to look best within the frame. If this is what you choose, mark a pencil line around the center of the inside of the frame to indicate where the fiberglass will fit. Then nail a 1x1 or similar trim piece close enough to the line so that when you secure the fiberglass to the 1x1, you can fit another 1x1 on the other side of the fiberglass. This creates a sandwich, with the panels in the center of the frame.

Placing the panels. Lap the panels by one ridge and secure them together with ¼-inch nuts and bolts. (The supplier should have any necessary washers or fittings.) The panels are secured around the edges at a maximum of 1 foot on center with ¼-inch screws. Drill all holes and do not attempt to put nails through the fiberglass. The 1x1s may be nailed in place. If you install the panels on the side of the frame, use wood trim over the edges to protect them and to give a finished appearance.

Precast Aggregate Panels

Precast aggregate panels can cover a fence framework—or a building. Finishes in a wide range of aggregate sizes are available, and the color range includes natural stone, quartz, and glass. The aggregates are fixed to the thermosetting resinous material. The recommended sheet thickness is ¾ inches.

Building methods for precast aggregate panels are not significantly different from plywood paneling or fiberglass paneling. You need a good frame, as if you were building a wood fence, and you may install the panels on either side or within the frame. Aggregate panels are only heavier than plywood by the amount of aggregate stuck to them, which is less than the thickness of the plywood itself. Secure the panels to the frame using ¼-inch screws at a maximum of 8 inches on center. Drill holes for all the screws before you place them. Do not drive nails through the aggregate. All edges should be protected with wood trim.

Prefabricated Fence Panels

Many fence styles can be bought preassembled and hung on your structure. Be sure you space the posts properly to accept the panels you want to use.

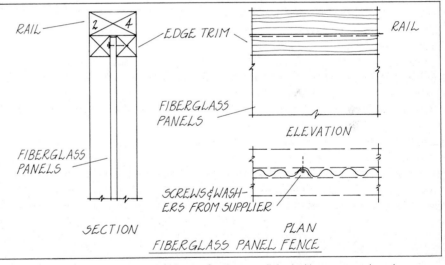

Fiberglass panels are held in a wood frame. Sections are linked with screws and washers.

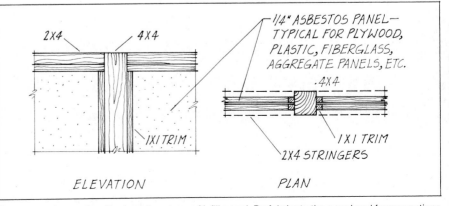

Fences can be made with almost any type of infill panel. Prefabricate the panel and frame sections and set them into posts. Section size will be dictated by infill material.

12 GATES AND OPENINGS

Gates and openings should be planned where traffic requires them for convenient access. If your yard should be closed—for security, or to protect children or animals—you need a gate. Otherwise, a simple opening will do.

GATE POSTS

Gate posts are installed like regular wood fence posts except that the concrete support reaches all the way to the top of the hole. You have more latitude in the use of concrete for regular fence posts than for gate posts.

Installing Extra Support

Sag rods (tension supports) are optional for the wood gate described here, but they are easy to install and add stability to the gate posts. They are rods (or cables) with bolts to secure them to the posts. The rods should be installed near the top of the gate post and run down to nearly the bottom of the closest fence post in the same panel. Use the turnbuckles in the rod to adjust the rod or cable tension to keep the gate post steady. The sag rod need only be installed on the hinge side of the gate. Sag rods can be bought in packaged form in most hardware stores and building supply stores.

Selecting Hinges

Hinges come in a wide variety of shapes and sizes. For most garden purposes any one of four basic types will suffice: the butt hinge, the T-hinge, the strap hinge, or the gate hinge. These hinges and their general application are discussed below. However, there is enough variation from manufacturer to manufacturer in mounting instructions that you should study the installation instructions for each hinge package you buy.

The butt hinge. This hinge is used on both interior and exterior doors. It is made up of two rectangular leaves with screw holes. The leaves are joined by a pin or metal rod. The doors in your house use this hinge. They are convenient when the doors need to be removed; tap out the rod and pull the door off. The hinges are recessed in the wood so that when the door closes, the leaves butt together with only the rod left showing.

The butt hinge is more difficult to install than the other gate hinges, and the use of screws instead of bolts produces a weaker gate than some of the other hinges. However, the butt hinge is a good solution when the hinge should be hidden.

The T-hinge. As the name implies, this hinge is shaped like the letter T. The T-hinge is mounted flush on the posts and gate with bolts. It can be bought in simple, utilitarian shapes, or it may be more ornate. It is easy to install.

The strap hinge. This commonly

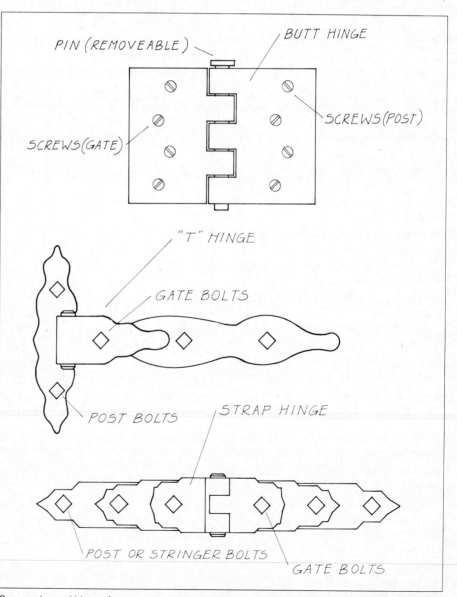

Commonly used hinges for gates are the butt, the T, and the strap hinges. The butt hinge is hidden and not as strong as the others that are held by bolts rather than by screws.

used hinge consists of two leaves that extend from a knuckle in the center. Strap hinges are available in many sizes and shapes; they are commonly used on storage boxes, garage doors, and gates. They are flush-mounted and may be screwed or bolted in place. Bolts are preferred for gate use.

The gate hinge. A gate hinge has two parts: an L-shaped lag screw or bolt secured to the fence post, and a leaf or strap that fits over the L of the first part. These hinges may be used with square or round posts, and the gate may be lifted off the L portion should you need to remove it.

Selecting Latches

There are several commonly used gate latches. Their purposes are identical, but they work in different ways.

Thumb latches. An ornamental thumb latch looks good with the gate hinge. There are also top mounted thumb latches. These latches may be more effective than other styles when you want to keep small children inside a yard.

Gate latch. The universal gate latch is another commonly used thumb latch. A string may be attached through the eyelet in the latch and run through a drilled hole in the gate in place of a handle outside.

Bolt locks. Bolt locks are often used as latches, but they actually are locks.

BUILDING A SIMPLE GATE
This example is for a simple board fence

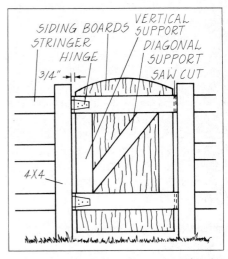

A gate can be built to fit your opening by following the instructions in the text.

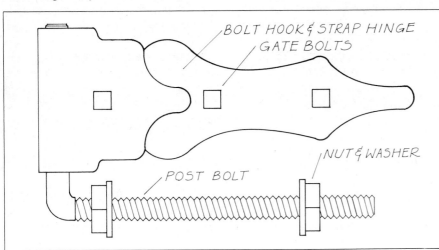

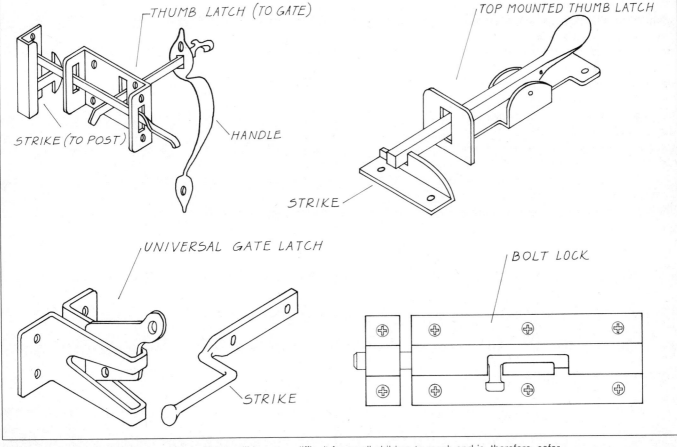

There are a variety of gates. A top-mounted latch will be more difficult for small children to reach and is, therefore, safer.

with 4x4 posts. The stringers are nailed to one side. For gate construction, follow these steps.

(1) Nail stringers across the top and bottom of the gate posts as you would across any other posts, but leave out the middle stringer.

(2) Attach the two vertical gate supports. Leave about ¾ inch between the supports and the fence posts.

(3) Attach the diagonal gate support. Note: the diagonal support slopes down from the top down toward the hinge side of the gate. It is important that the diagonal support be attached in this way.

(4) Cut 2x4s to fill in between the two vertical supports at the side and the diagonal gate support.

(5) Nail the siding boards across the gate posts as between any other fence posts.

(6) Select and install appropriate gate hinges and latch.

Installing the Hinges and Cutting the Gate

Saw down about a foot from the top, between the vertical gate support and the fence post—this will allow you to install the top hinge. Install the top hinge according to the manufacturer's instructions. Saw up about a foot from the bottom—this cut is between the vertical gate support and the fence post aligned with the first cut. This allows you to install the bottom hinge. You are letting the gate hold itself in place while you install the hinges. This method saves you a lot of measuring, since you will slice the gate out of the fence with the power saw.

To free the gate, saw between the vertical gate support and the post—opposite the hinge side. Open the gate; check the fit; sand and smooth raw edges; then make any minor trim cuts needed. Install the latch according to instructions. You may have to trim the gate again after the first rainfall (due to swelling), but this is a simple matter with a power saw.

SECURING GATES TO MASONRY

When hanging gates on masonry—especially heavy wrought iron gates—always provide adequate backing for the gate anchors you use, whether iron anchors, lead shields, or other fasteners.

If the gate attaches to the side of a brick cavity column, the column should be slushed full of concrete. Joint reinforcement appropriate to the weight of the gate should be used. An iron anchor may be built into the column and drilled to accommodate the hinges. The column also can be slushed full of concrete, allowed to cure, and drilled to receive a lead shield. The lead shield, available in a wide range of sizes, is inserted in the holes. When the bolt is screwed into the shield, it expands and holds the bolt in place.

If the gate is hung within an opening in a masonry wall, the wall should be slushed full of concrete a minimum of one foot from where the hinges are mounted. Increase the joint reinforcement in the wall for several feet back from the hinges. It is often possible to cast the receiving hardware in place when the wall or column is built. There are many variables that dictate the kind of gate hardware and anchors for the hardware that is set within the gate posts—the different widths and weights of the gate you choose, and the type of posts or columns you use. The design procedure remains the same.

Selecting the Hardware

First, select a gate appropriate to the fence you have. A massive iron gate will look out-of-scale with a board fence, unless you use a combination masonry wall with wood panels. Conversely, a light wood gate is likely to look flimsy in a masonry wall. In general, use wood gates for wood fences and iron or massive wood gates for masonry and iron fences (or walls).

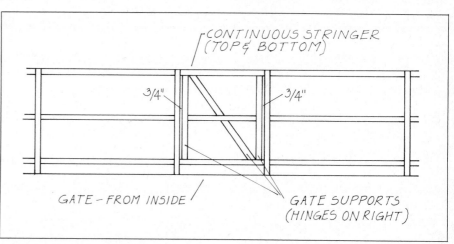

Another version of the continuous stringer fence and gate is shown here. This gate will fit exactly because the unit is built into the fence and sawn free.

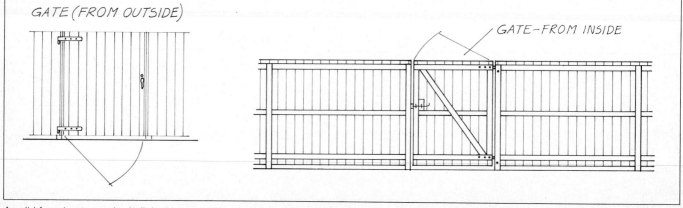

A solid-faced gate can be built in the same manner. The framework of the gate is covered to match the solid-faced fence.

Plan the gate posts or columns with your gate and hardware in mind. The gate installation, like many construction projects, is relatively simple, but the planning may require some design help from an architect or contractor—unless you are an advanced handyman.

When you have determined the proper location of the hardware, and while you are constructing the wall, insert the hardware in the mortar (before it sets) just as if it were a reinforcing bolt.

13 TOOLS AND EQUIPMENT

A small concrete project may be completed with concrete mixed by hand, but any project that requires more than a few cubic feet of concrete should be mixed in a power driven mixer.

In planning any project, it is important to consider the tools you need. Having adequate tools can spell the difference between success or failure of a project. Unfortunately, construction tools are expensive; unless you are sure you will use the tools for your projects with some frequency in the future, you should rent them. Most cities have several tool rental operations and the personnel there are helpful in instructing you in the proper use of the tools. Check with building supply houses; many rent tools—all of them sell tools.

The tools listed below are very basic to the concrete and masonry projects discussed in this book. They are by no means all the tools you may need, but they should give you an idea of what to have on hand. The most common woodworking tools for the projects in the book—saws, chain saws (for cutting cross ties and logs) or sledge hammers—have not been included because their uses are obvious or, if not obvious, information is readily available about them at any building supply store or hardware store.

Concrete mixing platform. A 10x12 mixing platform will handle most home projects. A platform that is 7x12 is the minimum for two people who will mix the concrete with shovels. To build a 7x12 platform, use three 2x6 stringers, each 12 feet long, spaced with two stringers along the edge and one down the middle. Cover the stringers with 1-inch tongue-and-groove boards. Nail the 2x4s tightly around the edge to keep the water from running off the platform. A galvanized sheet metal cover ensures a watertight platform and makes the platform last longer.

Shovels. You can buy concrete shovels, or create them by straightening out a garden hoe or spade. Your best course, unless you have considerable work to do, might be to rent one.

Measuring box. The measuring box is really just a frame—it has no bottom. The box is used to measure aggregate—sand and gravel and/or crushed stone—and for most home projects it should be 1 cubic foot in size. In case you need less than a cubic foot of aggregate, mark the inside of the box to show intermediate quantities.

Pails. You will need one or two graduated pails for measuring and carrying water.

Hose. A garden hose is satisfactory for home projects.

Tamper. Tampers are used for surface preparation of flat concrete work: slabs, walks, drives. To make one, build up a wooden weight about 8x8x12 inches and secure a 4-foot handle to it. Metal tampers are also available.

Wood float. You can build or buy a wood float cheaply. Floating is the second step in smoothing the concrete after it has been struck off or screeded.

Steel hand float or trowel. The trowel produces a very smooth concrete surface.

Edger. The edger rounds off the edges enough to keep them from chipping. It will also help free edges of newly laid concrete from the forms.

Groover. The groover is for finishing joints in walks and slabs.

Wheelbarrow. Rubber-tired metal wheelbarrows have a high body in the front to prevent spillage when the handles are lifted. Wheelbarrows may be expensive items and some are too heavy for most garden work. Unless you have a big job, use the ordinary garden wheelbarrow (if you already have one), or rent a concrete-handling wheelbarrow.

Claw hammer. You need a claw hammer for form work.

Levels. A line level is a short metal tube with a bubble tube that can be hung on taut lines to check for level. A mason's level comes in several sizes, typically 24 inches long with true edges. It has two or more bubble tubes; the mason's level is indispensible for concrete and masonry work.

Rulers. You will need a multiple folding rule for close work and a tape measure (50 feet should be long enough) for longer distances.

Chisels. Various mason's chisels are used to cut stone, concrete block, and brick. A builder's supply house should carry all the needed chisels and can tell you which ones you need for the job you are doing.

Planning. Planning has often been mentioned in this book. It is definitely an essential tool of construction. Most of us want to use the things we build as quickly as possible. We think of the physical construction of building the projects as the "real work". This is often an expensive attitude, because poorly planned projects usually do not work out as they were intended. Planning is another word for efficiency of effort, use of materials, and time spent.

A FINAL WORD

Because there are so many ways of doing landscaping plans, and because the locality in which you live influences construction techniques, professional consultation often has been suggested in this book. This book should help homeowners learn to use their building departments, HUD, and other government institutions. We all pay for them. Other professionals—such as architects, designers, contractors, or suppliers—are sometimes needed, although homeowners are reluctant to call on them. Professionals, on the other hand, routinely consult with each other. It is hoped that this book will help straighten out the maze of professional help available and guide the homeowner to appropriate and economical use of professionals.

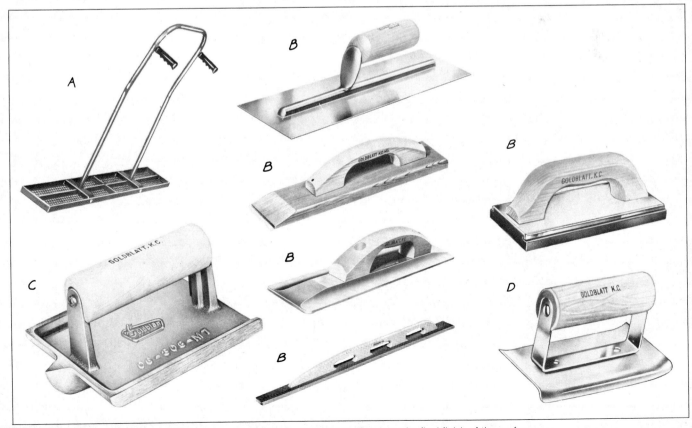

Concrete work requires: **A** tampers for preparation; **B**, floats; **C** groovers; **D** edgers for final finish of the surface.

Metric Conversion Charts

LUMBER

Sizes: Metric cross-sections are so close to their nearest Imperial sizes, as noted below, that for most purposes they may be considered equivalents.

Lengths: Metric lengths are based on a 300mm module which is slightly shorter in length than an Imperial foot. It will therefore be important to check your requirements accurately to the nearest inch and consult the table below to find the metric length required.

Areas: The metric area is a square metre. Use the following conversion factors when converting from Imperial data: 100 sq. feet = 9.290 sq. metres.

METRIC SIZES SHOWN BESIDE NEAREST IMPERIAL EQUIVALENT

mm	Inches	mm	Inches
16 x 75	⅝ x 3	44 x 150	1¾ x 6
16 x 100	⅝ x 4	44 x 175	1¾ x 7
16 x 125	⅝ x 5	44 x 200	1¾ x 8
16 x 150	⅝ x 6	44 x 225	1¾ x 9
19 x 75	¾ x 3	44 x 250	1¾ x 10
19 x 100	¾ x 4	44 x 300	1¾ x 12
19 x 125	¾ x 5	50 x 75	2 x 3
19 x 150	¾ x 6	50 x 100	2 x 4
22 x 75	⅞ x 3	50 x 125	2 x 5
22 x 100	⅞ x 4	50 x 150	2 x 6
22 x 125	⅞ x 5	50 x 175	2 x 7
22 x 150	⅞ x 6	50 x 200	2 x 8
25 x 75	1 x 3	50 x 225	2 x 9
25 x 100	1 x 4	50 x 250	2 x 10
25 x 125	1 x 5	50 x 300	2 x 12
25 x 150	1 x 6	63 x 100	2½ x 4
25 x 175	1 x 7	63 x 125	2½ x 5
25 x 200	1 x 8	63 x 150	2½ x 6
25 x 225	1 x 9	63 x 175	2½ x 7
25 x 250	1 x 10	63 x 200	2½ x 8
25 x 300	1 x 12	63 x 225	2½ x 9
32 x 75	1¼ x 3	75 x 100	3 x 4
32 x 100	1¼ x 4	75 x 125	3 x 5
32 x 125	1¼ x 5	75 x 150	3 x 6
32 x 150	1¼ x 6	75 x 175	3 x 7
32 x 175	1¼ x 7	75 x 200	3 x 8
32 x 200	1¼ x 8	75 x 225	3 x 9
32 x 225	1¼ x 9	75 x 250	3 x 10
32 x 250	1¼ x 10	75 x 300	3 x 12
32 x 300	1¼ x 12	100 x 100	4 x 4
38 x 75	1½ x 3	100 x 150	4 x 6
38 x 100	1½ x 4	100 x 200	4 x 8
38 x 125	1½ x 5	100 x 250	4 x 10
38 x 150	1½ x 6	100 x 300	4 x 12
38 x 175	1½ x 7	150 x 150	6 x 6
38 x 200	1½ x 8	150 x 200	6 x 8
38 x 225	1½ x 9	150 x 300	6 x 12
44 x 75	1¾ x 3	200 x 200	8 x 8
44 x 100	1¾ x 4	250 x 250	10 x 10
44 x 125	1¾ x 5	300 x 300	12 x 12

METRIC LENGTHS

Lengths Metres	Equiv. Ft. & Inches
1.8m	5' 10⅞"
2.1m	6' 10⅝"
2.4m	7' 10½"
2.7m	8' 10¼"
3.0m	9' 10⅛"
3.3m	10' 9⅞"
3.6m	11' 9¾"
3.9m	12' 9½"
4.2m	13' 9⅜"
4.5m	14' 9⅓"
4.8m	15' 9"
5.1m	16' 8¾"
5.4m	17' 8⅝"
5.7m	18' 8⅜"
6.0m	19' 8¼"
6.3m	20' 8"
6.6m	21' 7⅞"
6.9m	22' 7⅝"
7.2m	23' 7½"
7.5m	24' 7¼"
7.8m	25' 7⅛"

All the dimensions are based on 1 inch = 25 mm.

NOMINAL SIZE (This is what you order.)	ACTUAL SIZE (This is what you get.)
Inches	Inches
1 x 1	¾ x ¾
1 x 2	¾ x 1½
1 x 3	¾ x 2½
1 x 4	¾ x 3½
1 x 6	¾ x 5½
1 x 8	¾ x 7¼
1 x 10	¾ x 9¼
1 x 12	¾ x 11¼
2 x 2	1¾ x 1¾
2 x 3	1½ x 2½
2 x 4	1½ x 3½
2 x 6	1½ x 5½
2 x 8	1½ x 7¼
2 x 10	1½ x 9¼
2 x 12	1½ x 11¼

PIPE FITTINGS

Only fittings for use with copper pipe are affected by metrication: metric compression fittings are interchangeable with Imperial in some sizes, but require adaptors in others.

INTERCHANGEABLE SIZES		SIZES REQUIRING ADAPTORS	
mm	Inches	mm	Inches
12	3/8	22	3/4
15	1/2	35	1 1/4
28	1	42	1 1/2
54	2		

Metric capillary (soldered) fittings are not directly interchangeable with imperial sizes but adaptors are available. Pipe fittings which use screwed threads to make the joint remain unchanged. The British Standard Pipe (BSP) thread form has now been accepted internationally and its dimensions will not physically change. These screwed fittings are commonly used for joining iron or steel pipes, for connections on taps, basin and bath waste outlets and on boilers, radiators, pumps etc. Fittings for use with lead pipe are joined by soldering and for this purpose the metric and inch sizes are interchangeable.

(Information courtesy Metrication Board, Millbank Tower, Millbank, London SW1P 4QU)

WOOD SCREWS

SCREW GAUGE NO.	NOMINAL DIAMETER		LENGTH	
	Inch	mm	Inch	mm
0	0.060	1.52	3/16	4.8
1	0.070	1.78	1/4	6.4
2	0.082	2.08	5/16	7.9
3	0.094	2.39	3/8	9.5
4	0.0108	2.74	7/16	11.1
5	0.122	3.10	1/2	12.7
6	0.136	3.45	5/8	15.9
7	0.150	3.81	3/4	19.1
8	0.164	4.17	7/8	22.2
9	0.178	4.52	1	25.4
10	0.192	4.88	1 1/4	31.8
12	0.220	5.59	1 1/2	38.1
14	0.248	6.30	1 3/4	44.5
16	0.276	7.01	2	50.8
18	0.304	7.72	2 1/4	57.2
20	0.332	8.43	2 1/2	63.5
24	0.388	9.86	2 3/4	69.9
28	0.444	11.28	3	76.2
32	0.5	12.7	3 1/4	82.6
			3 1/2	88.9
			4	101.6
			4 1/2	114.3
			5	127.0
			6	152.4

Dimensions taken from BS1210; metric conversions are approximate.

BRICKS AND BLOCKS

Bricks

Standard metric brick measures 215 mm x 65 mm x 112.5. Metric brick can be used with older, standard brick by increasing the mortaring in the joints. The sizes are substantially the same, the metric brick being slightly smaller (3.6 mm less in length, 1.8 mm in width, and 1.2 mm in depth).

Concrete Block

Standard sizes

390 x 90 mm
390 x 190 mm
440 x 190 mm
440 x 215 mm
440 x 290 mm

Repair block for replacement of block in old installations is available in these sizes:
448 x 219 (including mortar joints)
397 x 194 (including mortar joints)

NAILS

NUMBER PER POUND OR KILO

Size	Weight Unit	Common	Casing	Box	Finishing
2d	Pound	876	1010	1010	1351
	Kilo	1927	2222	2222	2972
3d	Pound	586	635	635	807
	Kilo	1289	1397	1397	1775
4d	Pound	316	473	473	548
	Kilo	695	1041	1041	1206
5d	Pound	271	406	406	500
	Kilo	596	893	893	1100
6d	Pound	181	236	236	309
	Kilo	398	591	519	680
7d	Pound	161	210	210	238
	Kilo	354	462	462	524
8d	Pound	106	145	145	189
	Kilo	233	319	319	416
9d	Pound	96	132	132	172
	Kilo	211	290	290	398
10d	Pound	69	94	94	121
	Kilo	152	207	207	266
12d	Pound	64	88	88	113
	Kilo	141	194	194	249
16d	Pound	49	71	71	90
	Kilo	108	156	156	198
20d	Pound	31	52	52	62
	Kilo	68	114	114	136
30d	Pound	24	46	46	
	Kilo	53	101	101	
40d	Pound	18	35	35	
	Kilo	37	77	77	
50d	Pound	14			
	Kilo	31			
60d	Pound	11			
	Kilo	24			

LENGTH AND DIAMETER IN INCHES AND CENTIMETERS

Size	Inches	Length Centimeters	Inches	Diameter Centimeters*
2d	1	2.5	.068	.17
3d	1/2	3.2	.102	.26
4d	1/4	3.8	.102	.26
5d	1/6	4.4	.102	.26
6d	2	5.1	.115	.29
7d	2/2	5.7	.115	.29
8d	2/4	6.4	.131	.33
9d	2/6	7.0	.131	.33
10d	3	7.6	.148	.38
12d	3/2	8.3	.148	.38
16d	3/4	8.9	.148	.38
20d	4	10.2	.203	.51
30d	4/4	11.4	.220	.58
40d	5	12.7	.238	.60
50d	5/4	14.0	.257	.66
60d	6	15.2	.277	.70

*Exact conversion

APPENDIX

MATERIAL USAGE FOR REGIONAL WEATHER CONDITIONS

DEALING WITH LOW TEMPERATURES
Problems with Concrete

Many professionals prefer to wait for warm weather before pouring patio slabs, although there are ways to keep on working in low temperatures.

Many U.S. builders, especially in the north central states, believe it is economical to pour in winter. They use various forms of insulation, movable shelters and even liquid sealers to cure the concrete. Liquid sealers prevent the evaporation of moisture if they are applied immediately after the concrete surface has been finished. They cannot be applied, however, when there is water on the surface because they will be absorbed into the surface of the concrete and a continuous membrane will not be formed. Matt Starck and Sons in suburban Milwaukee use a sealer when pouring in late winter and early spring. "The spray sealer helps the concrete cure," says Starck. "It seals in some heat and the moisture."

Marvin Anderson Company in Minneapolis pours concrete steps, porches and patios all winter long using temporary box shelters. They cure their concrete work with a temporary propane or oil-fired heater. Concrete experts recommend that a fuel-burning heater not be placed directly on a fresh concrete slab because direct heating may over-dry local areas, particularly corners and edges. The experts also recommend cooling an area gradually after heating to prevent cracking and surface deterioration. This can be accomplished by leaving the shelter or cover in place and simply shutting off the heaters and allowing the enclosed warm air to cool down naturally to the outside temperature.

Bob Schmitt in Strongsville, Ohio, pours concrete during the winter as long as temperatures are above 20°F. His concrete crew looks for a two- or three-day break in the weather, pours and insulates the concrete with straw and plastic sheeting or one-inch-thick Styrofoam slabs. The plastic sheeting holds the Styrofoam in place and keeps the straw dry. Using these insulators, the concrete will cure in about one week.

Avoiding Frost Damage

The result of frost damage is not always recognizable, but some of it is. Surface scaling is perhaps the most easily recognized result of frost damage. It is more severe if de-icing salts have been used. Scaling of an inch or more in depth can occur and is progressive. Pattern cracking or "map-cracking" is caused by differential dimensional movement between concrete near the surface and concrete at greater depths. Its alligator-like appearance may be seen on such structures as platforms and piers. Frost action also can produce "D-line cracking", in which cracks run parallel to and near the edges and corners of such elements as sidewalks and pavement slabs. "Crumbling" or "powdering" is evidence of advanced destruction from frost action. It is often seen where concrete was frozen in the plastic or "green" state or in poor quality concrete.

Concrete that is allowed to freeze soon after placement gains very little strength and some permanent damage is certain to occur. Concrete that has been frozen just once at an early age may be restored to nearly normal strength by providing favorable curing conditions. Such concrete, however, is not as resistant to weathering nor is it as watertight as concrete that has never been frozen. The critical period after which concrete is not seriously damaged by one or two freezing cycles is dependent upon concrete ingredients and conditions of mixing, placing, curing, and subsequent drying. For example, air-entrained concrete is less susceptible to damage by early freezing than concrete without entrained air. Also, all concrete should be allowed to undergo some drying before exposure to freezing temperatures because new concrete in a saturated condition is most vulnerable to freezing.

Freezing of the plastic concrete before it has begun to set does no ultimate damage provided subsequent curing conditions are favorable. A certain "prehardening" time is required, however, before the green concrete can be subjected to below freezing temperatures without damage. This period ranges from 24 to 72 hours under normal conditions according to various investigations, and is influenced by proportioning, cement type accelerators, and entrained air.

Heating water, mortar, masonry. When the temperature falls below 40°F, masonry materials such as water, sand, brick, and block need to be heated. Warm mortar ensures a sufficient delay before the temperature drops to the freezing point to permit the brick to absorb enough water from the mortar to allow it to cure properly. Heating the mixing water is one of the easiest methods of raising the temperature of the mortar. But, according to Portland Cement Association, it shouldn't be heated above 160 degrees F because of the danger of flash set when it comes in contact with the cement. Portland Cement Association recommends that the temperature of the mortar mix does not exceed 120 degrees F or be less than 70 degrees when placed. They say that mortar temperatures in excess of 120 degrees F can cause excessively fast hardening with a resulting loss of compressive strength and bond strength. The water can easily be heated in oil drums with a fire underneath, or the drum can be placed on top of a cut-down, coke-burning, salamander. Sometimes drums with water coils around the inside are used. When steam is available, rapid heating is accomplished by injecting steam into the water.

Heating sand. In weather below 32 degrees F, the sand is also heated. Sand must be free of snow and ice and its temperature must be above freezing. It can be heated by piling it around or over a large-diameter, horizontal pipe where a slow-burning fire is built. Two or three oil drums laid end-to-end with tops and bottoms removed can be substituted for the pipe. It is important that the sand isn't scorched. Builders in the north central states pile sand around a 36 in. pipe and heat it with a Silent-Glow oil-burning unit. Another method of heating sand is to pile it over a 14- or 18-in. piece of culvert pipe, then build a fire in the pipe. Setting the water barrel at one end of the pipe will heat water at the same time the sand is being heated. If steam is available, steam coil pipes or steam jets can be run under the sand to heat it. In Copenhagen, the sand is warmed with steam lances. The sand doesn't need to be heated above 45 or 50 degrees.

Builders in Canada usually heat both water and sand. Some of them keep a fire under the mortar pan while laying bricks or blocks. U.S. builders in the northeastern U.S. will also heat sand and water when they work. Dwayne Ford in suburban Minneapolis says that his masonry subcontractors always heat the water and sand but only use standard mortar in the mix. Bob Wallner in Duluth says that his masonry subcontractors also heat the water and sand and use only Type N mortar in the mix.

Heating mortar. When boiling water is used to heat the mortar, the Masonry Contractors Association recommends that part of the sand be added to the mixer before adding the water to prevent a flash set in the cement. Although this precaution is generally included in mortar specifications, actual field tests conducted with boiling water added directly to the cement failed to produce any sign of flash set. This was partly due to the temperature of the water dropping during the time the boiling water was conveyed from its container to the mixer and to it being further cooled as it hits the cold mixer. Some masonry contractors recommend adding sand to boiling or near boiling water before adding the mortar mix.

The National Concrete Masonry Association recommends that mortar for cold-weather construction be mixed in smaller quantities than usual to avoid excessive cooling before being placed. Metal mortar boards with built-in electrical heaters may be used, but care must be taken to avoid overheating or drying the mortar. When work is stopped for any length of time, the top of the wall is protected to prevent rain and snow from wetting the concrete masonry blocks. When doing large tract developments, the Canadians often use three-sided temporary frame and polyethylene shelters to mix the mortar. The shelter has a roof and a protective tarp that is used to cover the open side in strong winds. In Scandanavian countries, mortar materials are placed in insulated bins. The mortar is mixed and stored in electrically heated bins. When needed, the mortar is put into wheelbarrows and buggies.

Masonry Protection

There are two aspects to the problem of protection of masonry work from the elements. One is during the construction itself, when both the mason and the masonry must be considered, and the other is after the masonry is completed

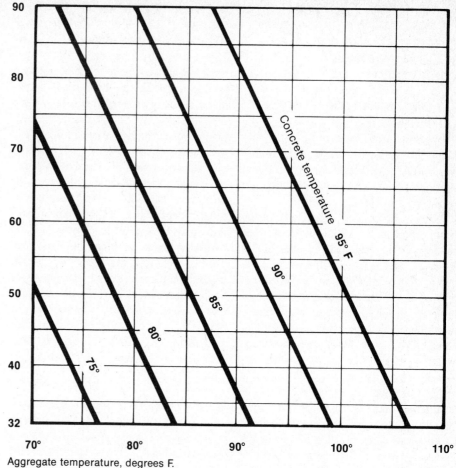

Chart based on the following mix proportions: aggregate, 3,000 lb.; moisture in aggregate, 60 lb.; added mixing water, 240 lb.; cement, at 150°F., 564 lb.

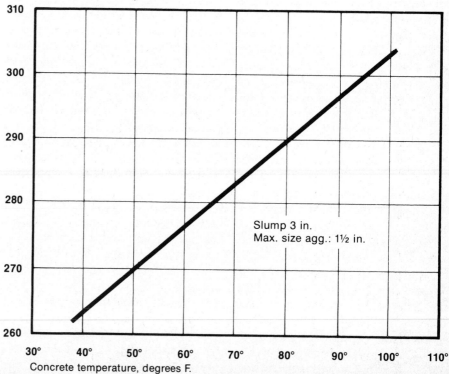

but not yet cured. Temporary enclosures for concrete masonry construction range from simple tarps to elaborate shelters containing entire buildings. Materials used for temporary enclosures include canvas, reinforced polyethylene sheeting and corrugated reusable fiberglass panels. The use of clear plastic enables light to enter the construction area and permits solar radiation to warm the enclosed space. Enclosures made of 2x4s and plastic sheeting can be moved from place to place during a series of repeated building operations. Scaffolds can be enclosed with polyethylene or canvas tarps, or panels prefabricated with plastic coverings may be attached to the scaffolding.

Comments from the Portland Cement Association

Builders in the northeastern and north central U.S. cover the bricks if they know that snow or rain is coming, but many of them don't bother to cover concrete block. Ray Estes of Estes Real Estate Builders in Flint, Michigan, says that his masons follow Portland Cement Association recommendations. He covers both brick and block with a tarp and heats them with an oil-fired gun blower before using them. Matt Starck and Sons in suburban Milwaukee store brick and concrete block inside a covered building or garage. ''This way, the material is always dry and we don't have to heat.''

Surface preparation. According to Brick Institute of America, brick should not be laid on a base covered with snow or ice. They recommend that the tops of unfinished walls be covered at the end of the day's work to keep the masonry dry and to keep it free from ice and snow. Portland Cement Association warns that concrete blocks should not be laid on ice or snow because there will be no bond between the mortar and the surface. If they are laid on ice and snow, the blocks can also move when the ice or snow melts. Brick Institute of America recommends that masons use a portable flame thrower or ''roofer's torch'' to clean the ice and snow from the surface.

Mortar mix. The function of lime in masonry mortars is to improve water retention and workability. As colder weather approaches, it is advisable to replace some of the lime with cement to obtain a high-early-strength mix to resist

the forces that can develop if freezing occurs. Many masons, who use Type O mortar (1 part cement to 2 parts lime) in the summer, will switch to Type N (1 part cement to 1 part lime) in the winter. According to DBR, the excellent results that can be obtained with the use of Type N mortar can make additives unnecessary. U.S. Army Corps of Engineers' Cold Regions Research and Engineering Laboratory states that British builders recommend a winter mix that is rich in cement. They use 1 part cement, 1 part lime and 6 parts sand, or 1 part cement and 6 parts sand with an air-entrained plasticiser.

Heating brick and block. Brick Insti-

tute of America recommends thawing wet, frozen masonry units, and heating dry units that are colder than 20 degrees F. If masonry units are wet and frozen when used, not only is it difficult to obtain a bond, but also it is difficult to build a wall that is straight and level because the units tend to slide in the mortar. If the cold masonry unit is wet or frozen, its absorption may decrease due to ice blockages in the pores of the unit. Masonry units that are dry, but excessively cold, will rapidly withdraw heat from the mortar and increase the likelihood of freezing.

Portland Cement Association says that when air temperature is below 20 degrees

Mixing water temperature, degrees F.

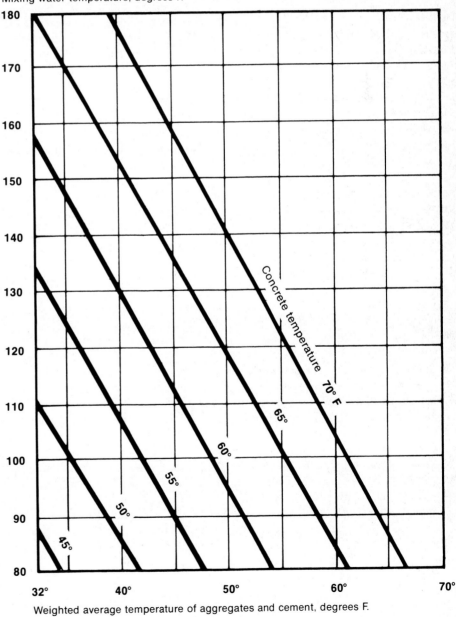

Weighted average temperature of aggregates and cement, degrees F.

Chart based on the following mix proportions: aggregate, 3,000 lb.; moisture in aggregate, 60 lb.; added mixing water, 240 lb.; cement 564 lb.

F, the concrete or brick masonry units should be heated to at least 50 degrees F to prevent sudden cooling of the heated mortar as it comes in contact with the cold block. Portland Cement Association recommends heating the units by stacking them in front of the heater with the cores set horizontally to permit hot air to be blown through them. Portland Cement Association says that a simple way to let heat circulate around large stacks of materials is to separate the courses with 1x2 furring strips, then blow hot air in and around each unit. A large stack can be heated with one blower discharging heat under one end of a tarp or cover. According to Portland Cement Association job-site tests, the most efficient dimension for heating blocks are 4 units wide, 6 units high and 16 ft. long. Block courses are separated vertically with 1x2 in. wood strips spaced horizontally to aid free circulation of hot air around each unit.

Masons in Minneapolis and St. Paul prefer using fully cured concrete block that is thoroughly dry with a maximum moisture content of 25 to 30 percent of total absorption potential and preferably only about 20 percent. The fully cured blocks help mortar set faster to avoid danger of frost damage. Masons in Milwaukee like to use only thoroughly cured blocks with a moisture content of about 20 percent of total absorption potential. They warm the blocks when temperatures dip below 18 degrees F. Robert Schmidt in suburban Milwaukee says that his masons warm concrete blocks and bricks when the temperature gets down to around 20 degrees F. Ray Estes in Flint, Michigan, says that his masons regularly heat bricks when the temperature gets down around 20 degrees F. "They usually cover the brick with a canvas tarp, then heat it with an oil-fired blower," says Estes.

Canadian builders solve many of their material heating problems with tight delivery schedules. They schedule brick deliveries so they aren't sitting on the site very long and don't have a chance to get damaged.

Using additives. According to both Brick Institute of America and National Concrete Masonry Association, most of the commercially available "antifreeze" mixtures for mortar are misnamed. They are accelerators rather than mortar freezing-point depressants. If used in quantities, they will significantly lower the freezing point of mortar, but they will also lower the compressive and bond strengths of the masonry. Consequently, neither Brick Institute of America, National Concrete Masonry Association nor other masonry organizations recommend their use as an antifreeze.

The primary purpose of an accelerator is to hasten the hydration of the portland cement in the mortar. The compounds commonly used as accelerators are calcium chloride, soluble carbonates, aluminous cements, calcium aluminate and some organic compounds. Calcium chloride is the most commonly used accelerator, but it may produce undesirable side effects such as corrosion failures of joint reinforcement, door bucks, metal ties and anchors in masonry. Its use can contribute to efflorescence and may cause spalling of the masonry. According to the International Masonry Industry All-Weather Council, its use is not recommended with masonry containing metal ties, anchors and reinforcement. Nor do they recommend its use in amounts that exceed two percent of portland cement or one percent of masonry cement by weight.

An excellent method of accelerating the set of mortar rather than adding calcium chloride is to add an additional quantity of portland cement if masonry cement mortar is being used. According to the Mason Contractors Association of America, one bag of portland cement to one bag of masonry cement produces a mortar that has sufficient early set to make it equivalent to a conventional mortar mix with an accelerator added.

Most builders in the northern U.S. and Canada use one or two percent calcium chloride in their mortar mix, along with heating the masonry material. But some builders say that their masonry subcontractors do not use calcium chloride in the mix. "Our masonry subcontractor uses standard mortar mix and no additives," says Fred Lince of Pineglen Construction Company Ltd., Ottawa. "He heats the sand and water, and even keeps a fire under the mortar pan, but doesn't use any additives." Harold Posnick of Builtwell Homes in suburban Minneapolis says his masonry subcontractors don't use additives either. "They use standard Type 1 mortar cement and heat the materials, but don't include accelerators or antifreezes in the mortar."

Masonry subcontractors in Duluth, Minnesota, and many other cities in the north central U.S. do not use calcium chloride in the mortar mix. "My block mason puts a two-pound coffee can full of calcium chloride flakes in a ¾ barrel of water, then adds a cupful of flakes in the mud as it's being mixed," says Bob Wallner in Duluth. "But none of the masons up here use any special kind of mortar, just standard Type 1 mortar mix, and they heat the sand and water." Robert Schmidt in suburban Milwaukee says that his masonry subcontractors use calcium chloride in the mortar, but it can cause problems. "My masons heat sand, water and brick, then add one or two percent calcium chloride. But this creates a problem sometimes because calcium chloride bleeds in the spring."

Air entrainment. According to the MCAA, masonry cements that contain air-entraining agents produce a mortar that is much more durable during freeze-thaw cycles than conventional mortar mix. To obtain full air-entrainment, Mason Contractors Association of America recommends mixing the mortar in a mechanical mixer for a full five-minutes after the last shovelful is added to entrain the air. National Concrete Masonry Association says, however, that excessive air-entrainment in mortar will result in lower bond strength in the masonry. They do not recommend air-entrainment for use in cold weather construction. Masons in the northern U.S. and Canada use standard mortar mixes without air-entrainment.

Antifreeze compounds. According to a report by the Army Engineers Waterways Experiment station, alcohol is the only organic compound that has been used successfully in mortar for cold weather masonry. Tests made by the Army Engineers indicated that mortar made with water and methanol alone or water and methanol plus accelerators such as triethanolamine and calcium chloride ($CaCl^2$) is not satisfactory at low temperatures because of excessive setting time or very slow strength gain. But some masonry subcontractors in the U.S. successfully use alcohol in their mortar mix. Gordon Poulas in suburban Boston says that his masonry subcontractor puts alcohol in the mortar mix to keep it from freezing. "He works in temperatures a few degrees below freezing," says Poulas, "and his work has been good over the years." He adds that his masonry subcontractor is one of the few that will work during cold weather in the Boston area. Joe Starck in suburban Milwaukee says that his masons will work in temperatures down to about 10 degrees F. "They use 'ANTI-HYDRO' in the mix," says Starck, "which keeps the mortar plastic and helps the masonry to set-up before freezing." "ANTI-HYDRO" is a solution containing calcium chloride. United Masonry, a large volume masonry subcontractor in Alexandria, Virginia, is successfully using "EUCO", a Euclid Chemical Company product that contains both calcium chloride and a rust inhibitor. Doug Hottle of United Masonry says that during the past winter season there has been no problem with "EUCO." He says that the manufacturer claims that their additive will not corrode metal ties, cause efflorescence, nor affect the strength of the mortar bond. Hottle says that their men work in temperatures of 26 degrees F and rising. "They always heat the sand and water," he says, "and then add EUCO."

Heating devices. On small jobs, simple oil-burning or propane salamanders are generally used within the enclosures. Portable hot air heaters are used to heat larger areas. These heaters are usually the oil-burning or propane portables that can be moved easily to provide protection where needed. Duct attachments enable several areas to be heated at once. Infrared lamps have been successfully employed in heating walls and don't require attention during the period of use.

Enclosures. Large tents or inflatable lightweight plastic enclosures are also used to enclose sites for masonry work. Some areas have been enclosed with plastic sheets and tarps or insulated sheeting. Another technique is the one of temporary shelters built with prefabricated panels covered with polyethylene sheets. These sheets are often made of reinforced polyethylene to increase the lie of the panel.

Masonry organizations make various recommendations for laying brick and block in winter. When the air temperature drops to between 20 and 25 degrees F, BIA recommends using supplemental heat. But when the air temperature drops below 20 degrees F, they recommend heated enclosures. They recommend windbreaks if the wind velocity exceeds 15 mph, and they recommend covering unfinished masonry with tarps, insulated batts or straw. Portland Cement Association recommends that walls be enclosed and artificial heat be provided when the temperature is below freezing. They recommend that heat be permitted to flow on both sides of the wall for 24 to 48 hours, otherwise one side may freeze. Protection that is supplied at 4 p.m., says Portland Cement Association, might prove insufficient at 4 a.m. Length of time of protection is in accordance with "American Standard Building Code Requirements for Masonry." Other masonry organizations say that masonry walls should be kept above freezing for at least 48 hours after they are laid up. They say that tarps are usually sufficient for this purpose for temperatures down to 25 degrees F. At lower temperatures, they say that artificial heat inside temporary enclosures are required. They also say that both sides of the wall should be heated.

GROUT

Construction grout is similar to cement in appearance; but denser, to provide resistance to shock, vibration, water, or chemical wear. Also, and this is important in many applications, grout does not shrink nearly as much as concrete products. So grout is often used as joint filler for clay, ceramic, and mosaic tiles, where a precision joint is required. And grout is used to provide a durable, strong base under heavy equipment, machinery, columns—any heavy load.

Before using grout, all surfaces should be cleaned and dampened with drinkable water. Any loose material, dust, grease, oil, paint should be removed. If the surface to which the grout is added is very smooth, as in trowel-finished concrete, use an acid etch to prepare the surface for grout. The above are general instructions; you should follow the manufacturer's instructions for preparation, which are similar to mortar, discussed elsewhere. Another precaution: do not mix more grout than you can use in thirty minutes, and do not attempt to use grout that has stiffened up on your mixing platform. Do not attempt to apply grout in temperatures below 40 degrees F.

COPING WITH HOT WEATHER
Wood

Builders in hot, dry areas build with masonry block, frame-stucco and use wood. But wood is actually one of the more difficult materials to use in the desert. Kiln-dried studs warp and twist in some cases if they are not used within 24 hours. "Even with kiln-dried lumber, stud loss amounts to about five percent," says Bert Harper of Mt. Helix Construction in El Centro, California. "Center-heart grain will twist and warp in two days." Harper says studs are wrapped with three sets of metal bands when delivered but will begin to warp as soon as the bands are broken. Most builders advise that stud packages should not be broken until all studs are ready for use.

Framing. Besides the uncomfortably high temperatures that cause productivity loss in central and southeastern California, Arizona and Nevada, wood stud loss caused from warpage due to low humidity and direct sun is a problem during the summer. Builders and framing subcontractors estimate that stud loss amounts to between 1 and 5 percent during the months of June, July and August. "Even using kiln-dried lumber, stud loss amounts to about 5 percent," says Bert Harper in El Centro. He says studs must be used as soon as the bands around the stud package are broken, then wrapped immediately with paper-backed wire mesh stucco backing to shield them from the sun's direct rays. "The paper will stop the warp, but without it the studs look like wooden pretzels in two days."

Harvey Weltmer of Hallcraft Homes in Phoenix says they can count on a one or two percent loss from warping and twisting. "We try to get kiln-dried lumber because anything with a higher moisture content will warp and twist excessively." He adds that framers put the lumber loss factor in their bid. Yale Epstein in Tucson says his framers never break the band on a stud package unless they are going to use the whole thing. "We use only kiln-dried lumber. It costs 5 cents more per board foot, but it's worth it."

Sand and dust seepage is another framing problem to which builders in hot, dry climates give special attention. Desert wind storms will drive sand and powdered dust through any unsealed crack or crevice. "We design and construct for sand seepage," says Gib Egan in Palm Springs. "We always caulk the sill plate, install weatherstripping and caulk the entire house."

Framing productivity drops during the hot summer months in the desert regions, and in some cases, it drops drastically. Egan says framers will lose up to 40 percent efficiency.

Masonry Block

Both stucco and masonry block are commonly used in desert areas. "We use stucco and masonry block," says Heyward Anderson in Phoenix, "but masonry block is our main material." He says that stucco tends to get hairline cracks. Masonry block with a mortar wash finish, on the other hand, is virtually maintenance free.

Some masonry subcontractors in desert areas wet down masonry units before laying them, but most of them just use more water in the mortar mix. On hot days, they sometimes place tarps over the top of the wall to keep it from the direct sun. But more often, they will wet the wall with a sprinkler after the block has been laid.

According to Robert W. Shuldes, speaker at a recent Mason Contractors of America All-Weather Conference, mortar tubs, mixers and wheelbarrows should be cooled off by dousing them with water on hot, dry days. "A mixer, mortar tub or wheelbarrow that is sitting out in the hot sun is too hot to be touched with bare hands," says Shuldes. "Yet, many times a mason will drop fresh mortar right on the hot surface, which is like dropping an egg in a frying pan." Shuldes says that a rapid increase in temperature drives off some of the mixing water, reduces plasticity in the mortar and makes for a very poor bond.

Shuldes also recommends that mortar should be mixed only when needed. "Mixing it in advance in hot, dry areas just lets the mortar heat up and dry out," says Shuldes. He also recommends using cool or cold water in hot weather and adding a little extra water to the mix. "The rapid rate of evaporation will remove the excess water," he says. "Water, with its high specific heat (high capacity to absorb heat), is the most efficient means of reducing the mortar temperature."

One practice that many masonry subs follow in hot, dry climates is to lay out shorter bed joints. In moderate temperatures, long bed joints are all right, but in hot, dry weather, the mortar in a long bed joint can stiffen before the units are placed, and consequently, the bond will be affected.

Masonry

The heat of the sun, especially in hot, dry areas, quickly dries out mortar and masonry block. The lack of moisture in the block and in the mortar reduces the quality of the bond, according to the Brick Institute of America. Some masonry subs periodically wet down their masonry blocks and bricks with cool water to keep them from drying. Old-time masons kept their bricks under water.

Concrete

High temperatures accelerate the setting of concrete and more mixing water is generally required to get the same consistency. In very hot weather, fresh concrete may be plastic for only an hour or less before it sets. Ninety degrees F is a reasonable limit for placing concrete; but the combination of hot, dry winds and high temperatures increases the rate of concrete setting and shortens the time that the concrete can be handled and finished. In hot, dry weather, concrete cracks tend to form both before and after it sets. Air-entrainment is also affected in hot weather. At high concrete temperatures, the amount of air-entrainment must be increased.

Stucco. The large area of stucco exposed to outside air allows rapid loss of moisture by evaporation. In hot, dry areas, loss of moisture is especially acute. If moisture is not maintained, the chemical curing action in the stucco will not continue. Evaporation is increased with increased air circulation and higher temperatures. Consequently, frequent spraying is required in hot, windy weather. Both the first and second coat is sprayed at least twice a day to keep the stucco surface from drying. Subcontractors in parts of southeastern California and Arizona apply stucco early in the morning before the temperature goes over 100 degrees F.

Paint. Paint surfaces may blister if paint is applied in direct sunlight in high temperatures, paint manufacturers say. They warn that solvents in paint dry out quickly in hot weather, making the paint more difficult to apply. If the building surface is hot, manufacturers warn that the paint may set-up too fast and cause lap marks. Painting experts say hot metal can't be painted because the flow will be uneven and flash-off will occur.

PROCEDURES
Tools and Equipment

Both heavy equipment and hand tools need to be regularly checked in hot, dry weather. Heavy grades of oil and greases are used in heavy equipment. Proper weight oil must be installed in hydraulic systems. In dusty areas, the oil filter has to be cleaned often. For lightweight hand tools, heavier grades of oil are used in the gear case. Workmen are careful not to overheat hand tools and to check them to be sure air vents aren't clogged. Metal hand tools have to be stored in the shade because they are too hot to handle if left in the sun.

Excavation problems. Caliche and adobe clay cause the most excavation problems in hot and dry climates. Both are rock-hard clay that usually require special equipment to excavate. Caliche contains encrusted carbonates that form on soils in dry areas. "Caliche is the big problem for our excavators," says Heyward Anderson in Phoenix. "Some of them have to use jackhammers to break up the earth before it can be excavated. For tough soil conditions, we use a special excavator with a ram-hoe to break up caliche and rock." Ernie Lopez of Royalbilt Homes in El Centro says adobe clay is just like brick. "You hit it with a pick, and it will bounce back at you. You need a jackhammer or special equipment to break up the earth before you can excavate." Lopez says that stretches of adobe clay can crop up anywhere. "You can't tell for sure where you'll find it. There's a lot of adobe in Holtville, outside of El Centro, but a few blocks away, you might get the nicest sandy silt you can find."

Concrete cautions. In hot weather, concrete operations must go quickly. The setting rate of concrete increases rapidly as the temperature goes up. Concrete that is easy to handle at 70 degrees F may not be recognizable as the same material at 90 degrees or more. Ninety degrees F, however, is a reasonable and practical upper limit for placing concrete in hot weather.

The combination of hot, dry weather and high winds is always a problem when placing large, exposed slabs. High temperatures increase the rate of concrete setting and shorten the time that the concrete can be finished. According to the Portland Cement Association, the concrete should remain plastic long enough so each layer can be placed without development of cold joints or discontinuities in the concrete. In hot weather, cracks tend to form both before and after setting. If cracks develop before hardening, they can be healed by immediately reworking the concrete.

Preparing the concrete mix. The most practical method of maintaining low concrete temperatures is to control the temperature of the concrete materials, and cool water is one of the most effective ingredients to do this. Crushed or flaked ice is even more effective than water in reducing concrete temperature. "We always use ice in the summer to cool the concrete below 90 degrees F," says Don Briscoe of Massey Sand and Rock Company in Indio, California. "We also use rainbird sprinklers to cool the aggregates." Briscoe says at the end of a one-half hour trip, the concrete will be between 80 and 90 degrees F, even though it was cooled before leaving the plant.

Aggregates have an important effect on the temperatures of fresh concrete because they represent 60 to 80 percent of its total weight. Suppliers often shade aggregate stockpiles or keep them moist by sprinkling. "We wet the rock with spray and that brings the temperature of the concrete down 2 to 5 degrees," says Dave Holiday of Massey Sand and Rock Company in El Centro.

Concrete foundations. Most single-family and townhouse construction in central and southeastern California, Arizona and Nevada is slab-on-grade. There are few problems in preparing the footing and slab bed in these areas except when the builder is working in caliche or adobe soils. In sandy clay and desert soil, preparation for the footing and slab bed involves thoroughly wetting the foundation area and rolling the soil until the needed compaction is achieved.

When working in caliche soil, builders often dig through its 12- to 24-in. depth and fill the excavated area with sand. Then the sand is wetted before pouring

the slab. "The sand provides a more stable base for the slab than caliche," says Yale Epstein in Tucson. "Caliche swells and shrinks and can crack a slab."

Adobe clay runs deeper than caliche and builders usually don't try to dig through it. Bert Harper of Mt. Heliz Construction Company in El Centro says he reinforces all concrete with steel mesh to stabilize the expansion and contraction caused by the adobe clay. "I use two rolls of steel mesh and saturate the earth with water before pouring the slab."

Transporting the concrete. Concrete must be transported as quickly as possible during hot weather. Delays contribute to loss of slump and increase the concrete temperature. Crews should be large enough to handle and place the concrete immediately upon delivery. The time between the mixing plant and the placing point should not be much more than one-half hour. It is not the quantity of water or slump that is important but the time required for the initial set of the concrete. If the slump drops more than 4 in. in a batch, the concrete probably should be discarded and should not be retempered by adding water.

Ground preparation. The wooden forms, reinforcing steel and all inserts are liberally sprinkled with cool water before placing the concrete. The entire subgrade is saturated with water so it will not absorb water from the mix. Wetting down the area outside the form also cools the air and increases the humidity. "You have to wet the sand real well before the pour," says the project supervisor for one builder in El Centro. "Most of the subs will run a sprinkler all day and maybe all night. That wets the sand all the way through and compacts it. Then they hose down the surface right before the pour." Gib Egan of Wessman Construction Company in Palm Springs, California, says that the slab bed is wet down for three or four days with rainbird sprinklers before the pour. "Then it is thoroughly wetted once more right before the pour," he says. Frank Canul in Las Vegas, Nevada, only wets the 2 in. of sand on top of the pea gravel (and polyethylene film) before pouring the slab. "As long as the sand isn't absorbing water, that's all you need," he says.

Placing the concrete. Concrete placement in hot, dry climates should be scheduled in the cool morning hours between 5 and 9, but can sometimes be poured in the late morning or early afternoon, depending on the temperatures. "My men pour concrete at 5 a.m.," says Gib Egan in Palm Springs. "And they work fast so the concrete won't set before they get it tamped and finished." Bob Cannon of Cannon and McMorris in El Centro, where the temperature goes as high as 130 degrees F, says his subcontractors rarely pour anything after 9 a.m. "If we do pour in the afternoon, we use a retardant," he says.

Bert Harper in El Centro says his subcontractors start before daylight and work hard for four or five hours, then quit. "They don't try to pour in the afternoon," he says. "It's just not worth it." But Harvey Weltmer in Phoenix, where 115 degrees F is not uncommon during the summer, says that his concrete subcontractors try to make two pours per day during the summer months. "One is in early morning and the other is in late morning," he says. "The second pour is always driveways, patios, and sidewalks. They don't schedule pours for afternoon."

Pouring the concrete. Concrete experts recommend not pouring concrete when temperatures are over 90 degrees. But in hot, dry, desert regions, where temperatures during the day soar to 120 or more, this is not possible unless the concrete is poured early in the morning or late in the evening. Don Briscoe in Indio says that the California codes allow home builders to pour concrete up to 95 degrees F. "By 10 a.m., the temperature is sometimes over 100 degrees," he says. "If it's poured after this, it sets too quickly and is too hard to work." Another problem that suppliers warn about is the possibility of "cold joints", where the surface of the previously poured batch has become excessively dry or where partial set has taken place.

Finishing the concrete. Finishing concrete in hot, dry regions requires extra care. According to Portland Cement Association, finishing should be done promptly after the water sheen disappears or after the concrete can support the weight of a man. The rapid drying of the concrete at the surface may cause plastic shrinkage cracking and "cold joints" in slabs. Temporary sunshades and windbreaks help to minimize cold joints. Portland Cement Association recom-

mends that forms should be loosened as soon as possible without damage to the concrete. They also recommend that water should be applied at the top of the exposed concrete surfaces and allowed to run down inside the forms. Wood forms should be sprayed with water while they are still in place. Otherwise, they may absorb part of the mixing water. It is also important, says Portland Cement Association, that the water applied to the surface not be excessively cooler than the concrete. This helps to reduce cracking caused by stresses due to temperature change.

Curing the concrete. Curing protection in hot weather should begin as soon as surfaces are hard enough to resist marring. Curing compounds can be applied immediately after final finishing. Curing with water works best and helps keep the slab cool in very hot weather. Twenty-four hours of water curing before applying a curing compound is highly effective. Portland Cement Association recommends curing by fogging with a fine mist of water. This operation requires proper fog nozzles, not garden nozzles that cause excessive washing action.

According to Portland Cement Association, the need for adequate moist curing is greatest during the first few hours after finishing. If moist curing is not continued beyond 24 hours, the concrete surfaces should be protected from air drying with plastic sheeting or sealants. Concrete subs in desert regions of California, Arizona and Nevada use oil-base sealants to keep moisture in the finished concrete. A common sealant is "Hunt's process", a petroleum-base compound that is sprayed directly on the finished concrete while it is still wet. "We always use a light-film sealant to keep the moisture in after the concrete has set," says Gib Egan in Palm Springs. Bob Vernam in Phoenix says that Knoell Homes doesn't use any special precautions during the summer months, they just pour the concrete wetter. "But we do use Hunt's process to keep the moisture in," he adds. Yale Epstein in Tucson says his subcontractors don't use ice or any other special ingredient in the mix, but they do use Hunt's process to keep the moisture in the finished concrete. A number of other sealants for concrete are also used satisfactorily throughout the country. Although sealants are commonly used for

residential slabs, many concrete subcontractors cure with water only. Don Briscoe in Indio says that Massey Company cures with about one-fourth to one-half inch of water on the slab, retained by slightly projecting edge forms. "We use Hunt's process only for curbs and gutters," he says. Concrete subs also use plastic sheeting to cover the finished slab to prevent moisture loss. "My subs put polyethylene sheeting over the finished concrete," says Bert Harper in El Centro, "and it does about the same job as a sealant."

Adding retardants. Admixtures that tend to retard the setting time of concrete are sometimes used by desert concrete subcontractors. It is often said that retardants tend to increase plastic shrinkage cracking, and so their use in hot, dry weather may be questionable. In some cases, however, they offer the only practical solution to the problems of handling the concrete. Dave Holiday of Massey Sand and Rock Company in El Centro says builders order Pozzilith in slab pours. "In this kind of heat, you need something to slow down the set," he says. But Don Briscoe of Massey Company says the average residential builder in Indio won't use Pozzilith. "It depends on the local conditions and the individual subcontractor," he says.

Air-Entrainment. The concrete subs pouring residential slabs usually don't order air-entrainment in the mix. At high temperatures, the amount of the air-entraining agent must be increased to produce the same amount of air content that is produced in moderate temperatures. Hot weather can also make air-entrained concrete especially hard to finish because of the small amount of bleed water produced. The concrete surface may develop a rubber-like feel before it has hardened, making it difficult to finish it without leaving ripples or ridges. A small reduction in air content or the use of a magnesium float rather than a wood float may help.

Additional cost. The average extra cost of concrete in the summer time usually amounts to $2 or $3 per cubic yard. Using ice in the mix costs about $1 more per yard and Pozzilith or retardants cost between 50 cents and $2 per cubic yard. "Ice costs about two and one-half cents per pound and adds at least $2 per cubic yard to the cost," says Don Briscoe in Indio. Dave Holiday in El Centro says the standard three ounces per cubic yard to Pozzilith will add an extra $2 to the cost of concrete.

WET WEATHER

Using Concrete. Wet weather can both help and hinder concreting. Although a light rain can be beneficial in curing concrete in hot weather, heavy rains can cause erosion of the fresh concrete, muddy conditions and work stoppage. Concrete pouring can be satisfactorily performed during periods of light rain. But builders usually cancel ready-mix deliveries when even light rain is falling to avoid the consequences of heavier rain if it occurs.

Concrete scheduling is highly dependent on current weather conditions. Concrete is most susceptible to rain damage in the first four hours after pouring. One heavy shower has more damage potential on fresh concrete than a full day of continuous light rain. Protecting slabs and decks from heavy rain can be more difficult. They can be covered with portable panels and possibly heavy gauge plastic sheeting. Rain falling after the slab has set has no ill effects; in fact, it is even beneficial for curing. In wet weather, where speed of set is essential, and it looks as though time is limited before another rain, concrete subcontractors have used high early strength concrete to speed the set time.

Roger Medors of U.S. Homes in Houston says that his company usually pours concrete even if rain threatens. "Otherwise, we would never get it scheduled," he says. Medors adds that some grinding is necessary due to rain erosion of soft concrete. "We have to grind two or three slabs out of the 80 or 90 that we place each month," says Medors.

Builders say that concrete pours in Florida and the Gulf Coast States are scheduled for early morning during the summer months. There is little pouring done in the afternoon. "The crews start an hour earlier in the summer, usually by 6:30 or 7:00 a.m.," says Jack Dwyer of La Monte-Chimberg in Tampa. "They don't like to pour after 12 noon." He says the early pours are not only necessary because of the heat and humidity but because there are rains every afternoon between 3 and 4 p.m. during the months of June and July. Dwyer says that slab work is covered with plastic sheeting as soon as it is finished to prevent heavy afternoon rains from eroding the surface.

During the rainy summer months, Bob Lee of Lee Associates in Tampa says that his concrete subs cover all flat work immediately after it has been poured for at least the remainder of the first day to prevent rain damage to the soft concrete. After the first day, however, Lee says that the rain is helpful in curing the slab. "A continuous light rain supplies the surface water that the slab needs to cure properly," he says. Some builders in the south and Gulf Coast States sprinkle or "fog" their concrete slabs for the first few days to help them cure properly.

Besides rain, wet weather building brings the additional problem of mud and surface water. Especially in areas where there are clay soils and heavy rainfall, surface water and mud become serious problems. Clay soils do not readily absorb surface water so that extra drainage and pumping are necessary. Concrete subcontractors in the Houston area, where heavy gumbo clay is common, carry water pumps as a standard part of their equipment. They often need to pump water from the footing trenches and foundation area before pouring the concrete. Heavy mud in all wet weather areas perhaps presents the most difficult problem. Gumbo soil sites in the Houston area get so bad that builders pump the concrete because the ready-mix trucks can't get in. Builders try to beat the mud by dumping loads of crushed rock or gravel on access roads and driveways and using heavy planks and timbers as tracks for delivery trucks to travel on.

Working with Masonry

Steady or heavy rain will stop masonry work unless shelter is provided. Light rain, however, will not affect a masonry wall if mortar has set up enough so it doesn't smear. If a wall has not set up, it must be covered during rain. Canvas tarps, plastic sheeting or even a partial or complete enclosure will serve to keep a masonry wall dry.

Masonry subcontractors in the south, Gulf Coast States and in the northeastern states usually place a cover over a masonry wall at the end of the day in wet weather to protect the fresh mortar. Bob Hay of Joseph M. Ripley, Inc., a concrete and masonry products supplier in Jacksonville, says that masonry subs in his area cover all brick at the end of the day in rainy weather to keep the fresh mortar from washing out. He says the masonry subcontractors turn scaffold boards on edge at night in rainy weather to prevent splashing from the scaffold onto the masonry. You can also keep the ground at the base of the masonry work covered with straw, sand, sawdust or plastic sheeting to prevent rain from splashing dirt stains on the masonry.

Mortar in all wet weather areas should be stored in a dry place. If it cannot be stored inside, it should be stored off the ground on skids and covered with canvas or plastic tarps. Masonry block and brick in wet weather areas should also be stored under tarps so the block or brick units are not saturated when they are laid. To continue masonry work during moderate or heavy rain, it is necessary to have a partial or complete shelter. This is about the only way that masonry work can continue successfully in rainy weather.

Putting up Framing

According to wood and timber experts, framing lumber used in wet weather should be covered immediately after it is delivered to the building site so it will not weather. The constant wetting of the surface of the wood by rain, followed by rapid drying when the sun comes out, results in checking and deterioration of the wood surface. This increases the hazard of infection by decaying agents. One builder in Mobile, Alabama, says to store lumber under protective waterproof coverings, using cross sticks for ventilation.

THE EFFECTS OF REGIONAL WEATHER ON BUILDING TIME AND COSTS

Average Percent Increases in Time by Type of Building Activity for Worst Three Weather Months vs. Best Three Weather Months

TYPE OF BUILDING ACTIVITY	NORTH	MID SOUTH	DEEP SOUTH	Mountain	Desert	WEST North coast	South coast
Survey	4	4	3	4	5	8	3
Lot layout	5	4	3	10	2	7	3
Clearing lot	10	7	8	7		15	6
Stake basement	9	5	5	7		5	3
Dig basement	14	10	10	15		16	1
Insulate basement	2	2	3	5		2	1
Form footings	8	8	8	9		15	8
Cast footings	8	7	7	10		12	8
Insulate footings	4	1	1	15		3	
Form foundation walls	9	9	8	15	3	15	9
Cast foundation walls	7	10	7	10		17	8
Strip foundation walls	4	3	2	12	3	6	4
Lay block foundation wall	15	9	15	16	2	15	2
Drain tile and sump	10	8	10	12		15	3
Waterproofing foundation wall	8	10	10	3		8	4
Backfill	11	10	6	7		16	6
Gas service	15	4	5	12	2	4	1
Electric service	8	6	4	8	2	4	3
Water service	12	5	4	7	2	12	3
Cast basement floor slab	10	10	10	12		12	3
Decking	6	8	12	5	2	6	4
Rough framing	8	8	10	9	3	5	9
Chimney and fireplace	10	8	12	12	2	12	4
Finish grade and clean-up	22	12	14	15	2	25	9
Landscape and sodding	20	16	16	22	2	20	10
Rough plumbing (DWV)	3	4	5	8	2	7	4
Rough plumbing (water piping)	3	3	5	4	2	6	4
Rough heating	2	2	4	6	3	4	4
Rough electric	1	2	4	1	3	1	4
Roofing	8	10	10	10	2	16	6
Install windows and doors	4	2	4	6	2	5	5
Furnace hookup gas or oil	3		2	3	2	1	
Brick veneer	15	16	12	15		12	3
Exterior siding	10	8	6	10	2	10	8
Hang drywall	3	3	4	6	2	5	6
Finish drywall	5	8	12	12		9	10
Exterior prime	11	8	11	10	2	10	10
Exterior finish	14	10	12	8	2	14	10
Interior paint	2	4	5	5			8
Electric finish					2		1
Plumbing finish					2		1
Heating finish		1			2		1
Cast garage floor slab	11	7	10	10	2	12	4
Cast sidewalks and porches	18	10	13	16	2	16	6
Cast apron and driveway	19	9	13	16	2	16	6

Average Percent Increase in Time by Type of Building Activity (Continued)

TYPE OF BUILDING ACTIVITY	NORTH	MID SOUTH	DEEP SOUTH	Mountain	Desert	WEST North coast	South coast
Excavation	16	15	10	15	3	18	16
Foundation	7	7	10	18	ND	15	15
Floors	7	8	5	20	ND	5	11
Rough framing	6	6	5	13	2	8	10
Electrical	0.5			1	7	ND	2
Plumbing	1	1	2	2	ND	2	3
Interior finish	4	8	1	10	ND	4	8
Finish carpentry	1	7		5	ND	3	6
Roof	7	5	3	7	ND	8	4
Siding	6	7	1	8	ND	8	8
Exterior painting	5	8	2	3	ND	8	6

(Source: HUD's 1975 Survey of Home Builders' All-Weather Building Practices by NAHB Research Foundation)

Glossary

Aggregates Crushed stone, gravel or other material used with cement and water to form concrete.

Ashlar Masonry composed of rectangular units of burned clay or shale, or stone, generally larger in size than brick and requiring proper bonding; having sawed, dressed or squared beds, and joints laid in mortar. The units may vary in size and produce a random pattern. Stone is cut square and is usable for walls or patio wearing surfaces.

Backfilling A process whereby earth is removed from an area to permit construction; and is then used as support for the construction; to return earth to an area from whence it was removed.

Bond(s) In brick, refers to: (1) the methods of interlocking or tying together individual units so that the whole construction is stable, or (2) the pattern made by a series of bricks and mortar joints, or (3) structural adhesion of the mortar, brick and reinforcing material.

Broom finishing Texturing of a concrete surface by stroking with a stiff broom while the concrete surface is still fresh.

Butter The process of applying mortar to brick or to other masonry units.

Capping The process of finishing the top of a masonry wall. The capping gives a visual finish as well as structural solidity. Usually placed over flashing to keep rainfall from entering the lower wall, the capping unites the two sides of a wall. The capping pattern is usually different from the pattern of the wall.

Chalkline A string coated in chalkdust which when pulled taut against a surface and released will leave a straight line mark on a surface. This chalkline is used to mark a guideline for masonry construction.

Collar joint The large vertical and longitudinal joint which lies between the wythes of a two (or more) wythe wall.

Concrete A basic building material used for footings, poured foundations, walks, drives and streets, as well as for patio wearing surfaces. Concrete consists of a mixture of cement, sand, aggregate and water. Concrete continues to harden over a long period of time and becomes harder and stronger with age, although it is subject to cracking under the pressure of heat, cold, and water.

Control joints The lines cut into a concrete surface to ensure that when the slab cracks under normal water, frost, or heat pressures, it will crack only along these control joint lines. These are cut to a depth of ¼ to ⅕ the thickness of the slab, and placed every 4 to 10 ft. in each direction. Failure to use control joints will cause uneven fracturing of the slab surface.

Course In masonry work a course represents one layer (horizontal row) of brick or block in a wall.

Darbying A smoothing of the surface of a concrete slab after initial leveling. Darbying is done with a darby tool or a long, smooth piece of lumber or steel.

Deformed billet A reinforcing rod used to increase stability and unity of a vertical masonry construction. Deformed indicates that the rod has a twisted shank which allows the mortar to grip the rod securely for maximum stability to the wall.

Expansion joint   A planned break in the continuous surface of a patio or wall into which a compressible material has been placed to absorb pressure when the surface expands when heated. This joint prevents buckling or crumbling of the surface or structure. Commonly used materials for expansion joints are wood, oakum or asphalt. Expansion joints are required wherever dissimilar materials adjoin since they will expand and contract at different rates.

Exposed aggregate   A decorative surface treatment of concrete created when the smooth wearing surface of the concrete slab is washed away before the concrete has fully hardened to reveal a layer of coarse stone aggregate which has been embedded just below the surface.

Face   In masonry, a layer of brick or block which covers interior construction. It also refers to the wearing or exposed surface of a masonry unit.

Floating   A finishing process in laying a concrete slab. After the surface has been leveled, a smooth piece of wood or steel is drawn across the surface of the wet concrete. Once the concrete has set to the point where there is no moisture apparent on the surface, a second floating is done to ensure that the final surface is level, smooth, and unmarred.

Footing   The portion of a foundation which directly transmits the structural load to the ground. For decks, footings are usually placed only where the posts will be located. Footings also are required for support columns for overhead cover and for some fence posts.

Headers   In brick masonry, headers are brick set in a course so that the small face or end of the brick is visible on the wall surface. In a two-wythe wall, the header lies across both wythes to tie them together in a structural bond.

Lead   The section of a wall built up and stepped back on successive courses. A line is attached to the leads as a guide for constructing a wall between them.

Lintel   A beam, used to support masonry, placed over an opening in a wall.

Masonry   Brick, tile, stone, block, or other material, usually small enough to be handled by one man, that bonds together with mortar to form a permanent structure.

Mortar   An elastic mixture of cement, sand and water which is used to bond units of masonry together.

Parge (or parget)   A coat of cement mortar on the face of a masonry wall, similar to a smooth stucco; also the process of applying such a coat.

Perforated walls   A one-wythe masonry wall in which the pattern of the units is staggered and hole spaces have been left.

Pier   An isolated column of masonry, usually a support for a section of wall or other separate stuctural unit. When such a unit is integrated into a wall of the same type of material, it is a pilaster.

Pitch (grade)   The angle or slope of a basically horizontal surface. In construction, usually built into a roof or exterior floor or slab for purposes of drainage.

Plumb   On a straight vertical line. A wall which is plumb is straight up and down with no lean. When constructing a wall or deck or roof, plumb must be checked regularly to ensure vertical stability.

Portland cement   A type of cement (not a brand name), this combination of many elements is largely lime and silica and is basic to the making of concrete and mortar.

Retaining walls   A wall built with the specific intent of holding back or securing a slope of ground, especially where the slope has been cut back to give a larger, even area at a lower level. The retaining wall, must be designed to withstand enormous pressure and requires a substantial footing to redistribute the pressure to the ground. Most retaining walls require the drilling of weep holes to relieve the buildup of ground water pressure.

Risers   In stairs, the board which supports the front edge of a tread. A cleat-supported tread can exist without a riser in a flight of open stairs.

Rowlock   A brick laid on its face edge so that the normal bedding area is visible in the wall face (sometimes spelled *rolok*). This placement of brick is often used as a capping course on top of a wall.

Slump   A test for the consistency of concrete conducted by filling a conical tube with concrete and measuring the subsequent difference in height after the concrete has settled and the tube has been removed.

Story pole   A marked pole for measuring masonry courses during construction.

Stretcher   A brick which has been laid in a course with the long, narrow face outward; the most common placement of a brick.

Stringers   Wood or metal supports for a flight of stairs, running at an angle from the lower to the upper level. Stringers may be cut out and the treads attached to the cuts, or cleats may be attached to the inside of the stringers so the tread attaches to the cleats.

Struck joint   A mortar joint which has been finished off, smoothed and evened after the brick, block or stone has been put into place.

Wall tie   Any of a variety of prefabricated metal reinforcing pieces designed to conform to the requirements of different types of masonry construction.

Weep hole   A hole drilled in a retaining wall to allow water to seep through and thus relieve pressure against the wall. The holes should be lined with pipe or hose so that the wall will not be weakened.

Wythe   In brick masonry, each continuous vertical section of masonry one unit wide. A masonry facing is usually one wythe deep. A free-standing wall may be two or more wythes deep.

LOCATIONS OF CLIMATOLOGICAL STATIONS

How to Benefit From These Stations

Services vary from company to company, but as an example one private weather service for contractors and builders offers two scheduled forecasts each day, as well as updated information when it appears that the weather will change significantly. The weather information comes as a telephone call to the builder, first at 6 a.m., then at 4 p.m. The second call serves as a planning guide for the next day. The next day's 6 a.m. forecast either confirms the previous day's 4 p.m. call, or adjusts the report so the builder knows what changes have taken place.

Daily forecasts will give detailed weather information on expected weather over the next 48 hours. These are broken down into three-hour segments along with summaries of the outlooks for the following three days. The service tailors each forecast according to the actual building site, so that forecasts differ measurably for areas 15 to 20 miles apart. Forecasts are provided for all seven days of the week, with full-time 24-hour-a-day follow-up on weather changes.

Costs for this type of weather service are based upon how many locations have been requested by the builder or contractor. A service that offers two forecasts each day, with follow-up calls that inform the builder of interim changes, can range between $600 and $1,000 per month. This high cost can be spread out among several builders in an area; the group rates are less. A builder may subscribe for one month at a time, or for a couple of weeks.

Climatological Source List

1. "Rainfall Frequency Atlas of the United States" (U.S. Weather Bureau Technical Paper No. 40) provides detailed information about ice lines and precipitation amounts from 30 minutes to 24 hours for return periods from 1 to 100 years. The Atlas is available for $15.25 from the National Climatic Center (NCC), Federal Building, Ashville, N.C. 28801.

2. "Design Snowloads for the Contiguous United States" gives snowloads in pounds per square foot on the ground in recurrance intervals of 2, 10, 25, 50 and 100 years. It is available for $5 from NCC, Federal Building, Ashville, N.C. 28801.

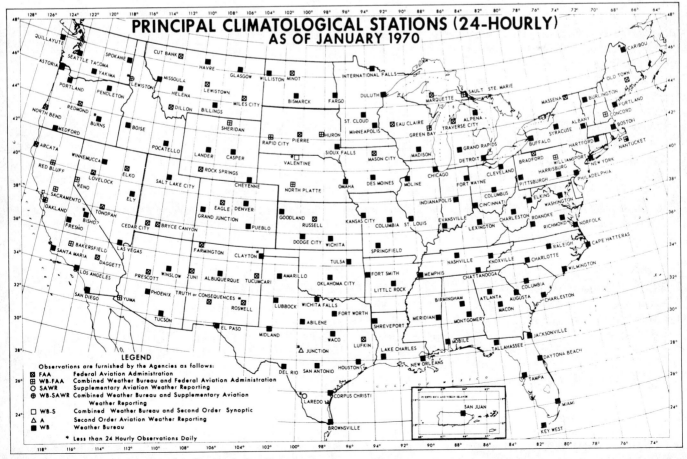

Source: National Climatic Center, Ashville, North Carolina

3. "Local Climatological Data" (LCD) is a monthly and annual periodical published for each one of 291 NWS weather stations. The annual contains a weather summary for the past year along with general summaries that date back as far as 1935. One summary table in the annual is titled "Normals, Means and Extremes". It includes historical weather data on temperatures, wind velocity, precipitation and sky conditions by dates. The annual LCDs also contain tables for average temperature, precipitation, heating degree days, cooling degree days, and snowfall. Each table gives monthly data from as far back as 1935 to date. Annual subscription rates for each of the 291 LCDs are $2.55 per year.

4. NCC also publishes summaries of each of the 2,000 or more NWS weather substations. These summaries include most but not all of the information contained in the annual LCD. The substation summaries cost 25 cents and are available from NCC, Federal Building, Ashville, N.C. 28801.

5. "Average Monthly Weather Outlook", published by the National Meteorological Center in Washington D.C., provides generalized information about each of the 50 states in the U.S. It gives a general 2-week forecast for each of the 50 states. It is published 24 times per year and the annual subscription rate is $7.50. It is available from the Superintendent of Documents, Government Printing Office, Washington, D.C. 20402.

6. "Monthly Normals of Temperature, Precipitation, and Heating and Cooling Degree Days" is published every 10 years by NCC and contains monthly historical data for each state. The latest available issue is for 1941 thru 1970. The cost is 25 cents per state, and it is available through NCC in Ashville.

7. "Climatic Atlas of, the United States", published by the Environmental Data Service, contains various 7-day forecasts of weather for planning of production, equipment maintenance and operations involving perishable materials. The service also includes weather warnings, revisions and modifications, when necessary, at least two hours in advance of the changes. The weather information is related directly to the building site or sites where construction is taking place.

SOUTHERN PINE GRADE DESCRIPTIONS FOR DIMENSIONS AND FRAMING LUMBER

American Softwood Lumber Standards
PS 20-70 Classifications

PRODUCT	GRADE(S)	CHARACTER OF GRADE AND TYPICAL USES
Dimension		
Structural Light Framing, 2 in. to 4 in. thick, 2 in. to 4 in. wide	Select Structural, Dense Select, Structural	This high quality wood is comparatively free of characteristics that can reduce strength or stiffness. It is recommended wherever high strength and stiffness, and good appearance, are necessary.
	No. 1, No. 1 Dense	These provide high strength, and are recommended for any type of general utility and construction; the grades offer good appearance.
	No. 2, No. 2 Dense	Although the grades are less restricted than is No. 1, they are still suitable for use in all types of wood construction; they have tight knots.
	No. 3, No. 3 Dense	These two assigned design values meet a broad range of design specification requirements. They are recommended for general construction, particularly if appearance is not a determining factor. There are many pieces that would be considered No. 2 but for a single characteristic that makes them unacceptable. It is recommended for low-cost, high-quality construction.
Studs		
2 in. to 4 in. thick, 2 in. to 6 in. wide, 10 ft. and shorter	Stud	This category has stringent requirements for straightness, stiffness and strength. It can be chosen for all stud uses, even load-bearing walls. The crook is restricted in 2 in. x 4 in. up to 8 ft. to ¼ in.; the wane is restricted to ⅓ of lumber thickness.
Structural Joists & Planks, 2 in. to 4 in. thick, 5 in. and wider	Select Structural, Dense Select, Structural	The advantages are: high quality, with few characteristics that will reduce strength or stiffness. These are recommended if high strength and stiffness are required and good appearance is desired.
	No. 1, No. 1 Dense	For high-strength situations, these are recommended. They have general utility for construction purposes, and offer good appearance.
	No. 2, No. 2 Dense	Less restricted than No. 1, these are still suitable for the same types of construction, and have tight knots.
	No. 3, No. 3 Dense	The assigned stress values in these categories meet a broad range of design needs. These are recommended for any general construction provided that appearance will not be a determining criterion. There are many pieces that would qualify as No. 2, if not for a single characteristic that makes them unacceptable. Use for high-quality, but low-cost, construction.
Light framing, 2 in. to 4 in. thick, 2 in. to 4 in. wide	Construction	This can be used for general framing purposes, since it has both good appearance and strength.
	Standard	This has the same potential usage as Construction grade, but will have larger defects.
	Utility	This provides combination of strength and economy, and is suitable for blocking, bracing, and plates.
	Economy	Various lengths are usable for bracing, blocking, bulkheading, as well as for other purposes where looks and strength are not the determining factors.
Appearance Framing 2 in. to 4 in. thick, 2 in. and wider	Appearance	This is designed for exposure cases. It combines the strength characteristics found in No. 1 with a high-quality appearance.

CONCRETE SPECIFICATIONS
PREVENTING SURFACE DEFECTS ON CONCRETE

Scalling: Concrete slab breaks into scales about 3/16″ thick.

Cause: The freeze/thaw cycle starts before concrete is cured.

Prevention: Keep the temperature of the newly poured concrete above 50 degrees using things such as blankets for at least one week.

Cause: Salt & other de-icing chemicals eat into surface.

Prevention: Use linseed oil mixture on surface or use air entrained concrete when pouring new outdoor slab.

Cause: Not waiting long enough for the finishing steps of screeding, floating and trowelling. Doing these steps before concrete has hardened properly and while surface water still stands on surface top.

Prevention: Don't finish concrete while surface water is still on top. Either remove the water or wait for it to evaporate.

Crazing: Entire surface of the slab has fine cracks because the slab has shrunk.

Cause: The concrete slab dried too fast because of heat, sun or high drying winds.

Prevention: Keep the surface of the concrete covered immediately after screeding and before finishing.

Cause: The second floating was done too soon. There was too much moisture on the surface bringing too many fine particles to the surface.

Prevention: Start second floating only after all excess moisture has disappeared and concrete has started to set up.

Dusting: Surface of a newly hardened slab seems to have a powdery coating.

Cause: The concrete mixture was off; with too much silt or clay.

Prevention: Use a fine aggregate only.

Cause: The second floating was done too soon with too much surface water on the slab.

Prevention: Wait for the second floating until all surface water has disappeared and concrete begins to harden.

Cause: The concrete slab is curing improperly producing a weak structure and dusting.

Prevention: Make sure that curing time is long enough and controlled by moisture content and temperature.

INDEX

CONTRIBUTORS ADDRESSES PICTURE CREDITS

We wish to extend our thanks to the individuals, associations, and manufacturers who graciously provided information and photographs for this book.

American Olean Tile   2583 Cannon Avenue, Lansdale, Pennsylvania 19446 54 lower left

Michael Bliss, Landscape Architect   222 Sunset Drive, Encinita, California 92024 17, 25

Brick Institute of America   1750 Old Meadow Road, McLean, Virginia 22101 34 lower right, 77, 93 right center

Monte Burch   Humansville, Missouri 65674 45 center, 47 right center and lower left, 71, 103, 122

California Redwood Association   One Lombard Street, San Francisco, California 94111 57 lower right, 59, 105, 111

Rick Clark, Photographer   10843 North 45th Lane, Glendale, Arizona 85304 36 lower left, 37 lower, 40, 41 upper left, 43, 44 upper left, 56 lower, 60, 68, 98

Georgia Pacific Corporation   900 SW 5th Street, Portland, Oregon 97204 24

Dennis Getto   Milwaukee, Wisconsin 53221 33, 51 center, lower and right

Goldblatt Tool Co.   511 Osage, Kansas City, Kansas, 66110 123

Herb Hughes   3033 Willow Lane, Montgomery, Alabama 36109 78

Koppers Co., Inc.   Koppers Building, Pittsburgh, Pennsylvania 15219 16, 42 upper right, 57 upper and center right, 65, 106

Lied's Green Valley Gardens   N63 W22039 Highway 74, Sussex, Wisconsin 53089 15, 24, 25

William Manly, Interior Designs   6062 North Port Washington Road, Milwaukee, Wisconsin 53217 5

National Concrete Masonry Association   P.O. Box 781, Herndon, Virginia 22070 55, 77, 87 right center and lower right, 89, center right, lower right, lower left

Richard V. Nunn, Media Mark Productions   Falls Church Inn, 6633 Arlington Boulevard, Falls Church, Virginia 22045 30 center left, 34 lower left, 45 lower center, 49 lower right, 50, 102

Portland Cement Association   5420 Old Orchard Road, Skokie, Illinois 60077 36 lower right, 37 upper right, 39 lower left, 44 lower center and lower left, 45 right center, 46 lower center, lower left, 48, 64, 69, 80, 81, 83, 84, 85, 86 right center

Sears, Roebuck and Co.   Sears Tower, Chicago, Illinois 60601 115

Tile Council c/o Lis King   Box 503, Mahwah, New Jersey 07430 53

Wausau Tile   P.O. Box 1520, Wausau, Wisconsin 54401 34 upper right, 49 upper right

Western Wood Products Association   Yeon Building, Portland, Oregon 97204 56 upper